B. U. F.

B. U. F.
Oswald Mosley and British Fascism

BY
JAMES DRENNAN

Antelope Hill Publishing

The content of this work is in the public domain.
Slight alterations have been made to the text for readability suited to the modern reader, and annotations have been added.

Originally published in 1934, London.
Republished 2020 by Antelope Hill Publishing.
Printed in the United States of America.

Cover art by sswifty.

The publisher can be contacted at
Antelopehillpublishing.com

To
C. M.
WHO WANTED THIS BOOK WRITTEN

—Contents—

Quotations ix

Introduction 1

  I. The Background of the Bourgeois Mind 9

  II. British Capitalism in Retreat 23

  III. The Character of Labour-Socialism 39

  IV. Mosley Emerges 51

  V. Mosley in the Second Labour Government 71

  VI. The New Party: Attempt at Social Compromise 97

  VII. Fascism and the Crisis of the West 121

  VIII. The Nature of Fascism 143

  IX. Mosley and British Fascism 169

—Quotations—

"We still hold the same purpose; we still proclaim the same vow. Before we leave the mortal scene we will do something to lift the burdens of those who suffer. Before we go we will do something great for England. Through and beyond the failures of men and parties, we of the war generation are marching on, and we shall march on until our end is achieved and our sacrifice atoned. To-day we march with a calm but mighty confidence, for marching beside us in irresistible power is the soul of England."

OSWALD MOSLEY

"Mosley has been here. A man of courage and intelligence."

MUSSOLINI

"Sir Oswald Mosley—a very interesting man to read just now: one of the few people who are writing and thinking about real things, and not about figments and phrases. You will hear something more of Sir Oswald Mosley before you are through with him. I know you dislike him, because he looks like a man who has some physical courage and is going to do something; and that is a terrible thing. You instinctively hate him, because you do not know where he will land you; and he evidently means to uproot some of you. Instead of talking round and round political subjects and obscuring them with bunk verbiage without ever touching them, and without understanding them, all the time assuming states of things which ceased to exist from twenty to six hundred and fifty years ago, he keeps hard down on the actual facts of the situation. When you pose him with the American question: 'What's the big idea?' he replies at once: 'Fascism'; for he sees that Fascism is a big idea, and that it is the only visible practical alternative to Communism—if it really is an alternative and not a half-way house. The moment things begin seriously to break up and something has to be done, quite a number of men like Mosley will come to the front who are at present ridiculed as Impossibles. Let me remind you that Mussolini began as a man with about twenty-five votes. It did not take him very many years to become the Dictator of Italy. I do not say that Sir Oswald Mosley is going to become the Dictator of this country, though more improbable things have happened."

BERNARD SHAW—*In Praise of Guy Fawkes*

—Introduction—

A study of Oswald Mosley needs no apology. Those who dislike his personality—they are not few, those who disparage his abilities—they are fewer, and those who fear his policies—they are many, have either to admit that he is the most startling, the most objectionable, or the most stimulating among the men who have created or disturbed the politics of post-war Britain.

At thirty-seven, Oswald Mosley is already an experienced parliamentarian. None of his generation, and not many of his contemporaries, can claim the same continuity of experience throughout the history of the two post-war decades. His changes of political allegiance which have aroused the hostility of the older parties seem rather to represent the unsatisfied search for a valid creed by which so many other men of his years have in their own minds been troubled. During the Coalition Parliament, Mosley first emerged as the associate of Lord Robert Cecil, Colonel Aubrey Herbert and Lord Henry Cavendish-Bentinck, in a forlorn effort to represent something of a new Tory ideal in that ill-assorted and heterogeneous assembly. Again, with others of his generation, he suffered disillusion in the ranks of the Labour Party, and emerged—at the sacrifice of an orthodox political career—to attempt a leadership of his own. As an orator even his most caustic critics will admit that he is outstanding. As an administrator he proved his abilities in a field where his opportunities were restricted both by circumstances and by colleagues. His failures as a tactician in politics may yet prove to have laid the basis of his success in the strategy of statesmanship.

But it is not as a younger parliamentarian that Oswald Mosley attracts the interest of his fellows, and arouses the fury or enthusiasm of the crowd. A great glamour has gathered round his figure—so strange, so provocative, in the dun ranks of English politicians. He is very English—as it were, a composite ghost of English history—yet his enemies complain that he is so "un-English." Perhaps they mean that he lacks that "bourgeois" stamp which has moulded to its flaccid type the generations of English politicians who have grown up since the Industrial Revolution. There is something of the Elizabethan in his gallant, rather arrogant, air. He is the Englishman of the Carolean tennis-court; of the dueling-ground rather than of the Pall Mall Club. Then again, with his wrestling, boxing and fencing, he has walked in the tradition of the Regency "buck," in a time when people have got into the habit of expecting younger politicians to have horn-rimmed spectacles and soft, white hands, and to spend their holidays at Geneva.

He is a big man of blood and bone, of strong tones, no feeble creature of grey shadings. He is a personality, with all his individual qualities and faults, no self-complacent bladder of conventions. It is, of course, important in a leader, this question of distinctive personality, and it is no doubt a symptom of the determinism of history that each period, each new phase, throws up its peculiar individuals, who respond in an observable degree to contemporary currents of opinion, taste and underlying aspirations. The suave and placid Walpole; the morose, dynamic Pitt; his pedantic, determined son; the cynical, ineffectual Fox, were each in their day the expression of passing moods and attitudes to life in the governing class. So, in the nineteenth century, Disraeli, the supreme type of the company promoter, showed the way to Empire, and Gladstone stood for millions of whiskered, frock-coated Dissenting investors, who took their profits, disapproved, and explained to their white consciences the intrinsic virtue of all profit. Again, in the post-war period, when the British middle class contemplates the incredible fact that the capitalist system is fallible and passing, and that all the standards of the Victorian age are crumbling into the abyss, they produce the cautious Stanley Baldwin, with his limpet philosophy, his refusal to believe the unbelievable, his pipe-poor symbol of a lost tranquility. He would be pathetic, were his pathos not so dangerous; and MacDonald, too, the quack doctor of the boarding-house advertisement readers, who assuages alarm by his confession that, after all, the family practitioner was right.

Mosley is of another world to these—of the world that is coming into being. An omen and a portent to some; to the majority, according to their opinion, a class-traitor and a revolutionary, or "an unscrupulous adventurer," who "might have done great things in one party or the other."

Mosley is, at the least, an interesting phenomenon in modern English politics; and in his greatest potentiality he stands for new and revolutionary conceptions in politics, in economics, and in life itself. He may emerge with his young men from the small faction-fights in the mean halls of mean streets to the leadership of modern England. Or he may fail and be forgotten more than Dilke, and pitied less than Randolph Churchill. If England slips into another long Walpolean lassitude, as it did after the Marlborough wars, and if some form of continuing "National Government"—a revivified Whigdom—proves to be the measured expression of the English mind through a period of quiescence or decay, then Mosley will have achieved the greatest personal tragedy in English history since Bolingbroke.

But the interest of Mosley transcends the biographical subject. He has identified himself with a movement—as yet in England embryonic— which has its parallels in the already mature Fascism of Italy, and in the recently insurgent Nazi movement in Germany. Fascism—National Socialism—whatever we like to call it, is essentially a European movement—a political and spiritual transformation, having its roots and taking its expression from the oldest seats of European culture. This movement—varying in character according to local and national conditions—may be regarded historically as in the nature of "a renascence of the Europeans," which represents at once an economic revolt against the obsolete capitalist system, and a spiritual reaction against the materialist and internationalist concepts of Marxism. Philosophically it has been regarded by some as the last orgasm of an overmature and already senescent European civilization. No prophet has received such immediate justification as Oswald Spengler, whose *Untergang des Abendlandes*, appearing in 1918, foresaw the present phenomenon of the rallying of the "formless masses" of the great cities to the emotional appeal of individual "Caesarian" leaders. It is indeed characteristic of this phenomenon of the last two decades that we find it difficult to give any names—other than those of the respective leaders— to the various manifestations of the new insurgence. But Fascism is the conscious revolt of a generation determined to escape its overhanging doom in the building of a new destiny. Fascist thought, even to the extent that it accepts the Spenglerian analysis as a relatively incontrovertible interpretation of past history, repudiates the pessimism of the great

German's conclusions. Fascism holds that our present European civilization, as the master of great scientific resources which were not available to the men of previous "world-civilizations," can overcome the diseases inherent in its hitherto uncontrolled development. Modern man is at least within reach of knowing himself—as Spengler himself witnesses in the magnificent monument to modern thought of which he is the creator. The great problem of the twentieth century is a problem of *integration*. And the first and most immediately important aspect of that problem is a political one—*the integration of the State*. Only when the control of the State has passed into the hands of those of its citizens who are prepared through discipline to submit themselves and to sacrifice their own individual interests utterly to the service of the nation, only then can these masters of the State turn to the more formidable problem of the mastery of the machine—and the process of mastering the machine implies of course the complete subordination of capital, which is, in fact, the machine, in so far as the machine is conscious, functioning and alive. The technical problems implicit in the effort to secure and to hold the mastery of the State demand the concentration into a group or "fasces"— we might almost here use the English word "fist"—of the minority, who in the early stages of the movement towards national integration are prepared to submit themselves to the strict discipline and the tireless effort necessary to carry through such a revolution in the life of the country. This active minority accepts, and indeed demands, personal leadership, by contrast to the confused head-counting and lobbying intrigues of the orthodox "democratic" parties. It also upholds the authoritarian principle, as a necessary foundation to the policy of dynamic action, which it is the object of this new revolutionary movement to carry into effect. Fascism differs from the "Caesarism" of Spenglerian thought, or from the "Bonapartism" which is a phenomenon of the earlier democratic phases, in that it consciously demands authoritarianism as an essential part of its approach to modern problems. Fascism represents a permanent, conscious movement, whereas "Caesarism" and "Bonapartism" were merely involuntary and adventitious reactions to calamitous circumstances. Fascism is essentially an entirely new manifestation of the modern political mind, and its equivalent cannot be found in any previous historic phase. Spengler is only right to the extent that the mass appeal of "Caesarism" undoubtedly remains potent, and to this extent the Fascist doctrine touches the imagination of those politically subconscious masses who find themselves exhausted and exasperated by the incapacity of the democratic system to evolve any solution of modern political and economic problems.

The possibilities of the development of a revolutionary momentum in Britain on lines similar, and in some degrees parallel, to the contemporary successful movements on the continent of Europe, are by no means so obscure as the complacent class of parliamentary politicians is pleased to believe. It is here that Mosley, as the first political leader of Fascist capacity to appear in England, possesses a significance which clearly surpasses the artist's interest in the man. And any study of Mosley as a modern political leader, admittedly of some significance, must imply an accompanying consideration of the development of the Fascist conception in Europe, and, further, an examination of the degree to which British history can justify the assumption that Fascism is a growth which is potentially no more foreign to British soil than was Norman feudalism, pan-European Catholicism, Bohemian Protestantism, Dutch Parliamentarism, French Social Democracy, or German Marxism. We have, in fact, to consider whether all political movements which have developed within the framework of European culture, have not in fact become common to the European world.

Oswald Mosley, two years ago, was generally admitted by judges of political "form," to have an important political future. His isolation, more recently, from all orthodox political associations and from all parliamentary activities, has not been without significance. This young and undeniably powerful political mind stands or falls by the success or failure of the Fascist conception in Britain. He has built up an organization which has, from the beginning, been given little publicity, but which is now upon a national basis, and which is gathering impetus from month to month. His earlier failures, and the ridicule which has been heaped upon his movement by the owners of a Press who quite naturally dread its success, has tended to lull the orthodox parties into a sense of ignorant security. The present writer remembers a similar sense of security in Berlin, less than five years ago, when a prominent individual, now closely identified with the Nazi Government, referred to Hitler as a man of fantastic ideas, representative of no coherent body of opinion within the Reich.

Oswald Mosley, in his book, *Greater Britain*, and in more recent speeches and writing, which have taken his ideas still further, proclaims the need for a disciplined corporate con-sciousness which must prelude the drastic reorganization of the political and economic structure of Great Britain on lines compatible with the needs of the twentieth century. His policy requires the comprehensive readjustment of the capitalist system, and while modest ownership in property would not only be preserved, but expanded so that it had a broader basis within the community, it cannot be disguised that the private ownership of great accumulations of wealth, and its use in directions which cannot be considered to be in the interests of Great Britain regarded as an economic unit, would be rigorously curtailed. The whole parliamentary system, which has been so developed in the interests of powerful sectional groups as to make continuity of national policy impossible, and the authority of the executive abortive, would be liquidated. It would be replaced by a system based on the representation of the productive forces of the country—agriculture and industry—and such a body might be entrusted to enforce a policy which would ruthlessly ignore all interests which could not be shown to operate to the direct benefit of the inhabitants of Great Britain. The application of Fascist principles, rather than the present democratic theories, to certain problems of empire, would of course completely transform the present situation, in which our parliamentary leaders are awaiting the results of a process of disintegration in a spirit of placid and impotent optimism.

But the political and economic implications of Fascism are not so fundamental as the sequence of moral and spiritual reactions which derive inevitably from the Fascist faith. Through the stale and weary streets which modern Capitalism has permitted to its industrial millions, from the emptying, blighted fields that fed Britain to her greatness, men are called to revolution. But it will be a national revolution, carried in the cold anger of a disciplined intent to integrate the race.

As Mosley in his resignation speech from the Labour Government, when his mind was already feeling its way subconsciously towards Fascism:

> What I fear—what I fear much more than a sudden crisis is a long, slow crumbling through the years until we sink to the level of a Spain, a gradual paralysis beneath which all the vigour and energy of this country will succumb. This is a far more dangerous thing, and far more likely to happen unless some effort is made. If the effort is made, how relatively easily can disaster be averted... What a fantastic assumption it is that a

nation which within the lifetime of everyone has put forth efforts of energy and vigour unequalled in the history of the world should succumb before an economic crisis such as the present.

At this later juncture, when the tempo of crisis is tending to arouse the awareness of all elements of the people, Fascism appeals alike to those elements among the younger-minded middle class who are conservative by temperament and strongly nationalist in spirit, and to those rarer and more dynamic individuals who, naturally revolutionary in their outlook, have been disappointed and exasperated by the failure of all leadership from the Left to approach any fulfilment of their aspirations. Such are the classic social elements who have in other European countries germinated Fascist revolution. The British character—in the passivity of which the democratic parties repose an exaggerated degree of confidence—will not fail, in the event, to respond to the proper stimulus.

Chapter I

—The Background of the Bourgeois Mind—

In the "Khaki" Election of 1918 the people of Harrow returned in the Conservative interest a young Air Force officer, who at that time was just twenty-two years of age. Oswald Mosley arrived at Westminster with a reputation for arrogance among his contemporaries at Winchester and Sandhurst, a pronounced taste for fox-hunting and a precocious interest in political philosophy. He had few of the orthodox advantages which generally appertain to the aristocratic sprig who prefers to occupy his time in the House of Commons rather than in other equally agreeable directions. An old-established but slightly eccentric Staffordshire family could offer him an ancestor who had fallen at Naseby and a grandfather who had been the physical original for the Victorian figure of John Bull. But the surety of Cabinet rank which crowns a connection, through blood or hymen, with one of the great oligarchic families of the Tory heaven was in no way his. Moreover, he quickly showed that he possessed an intellect—which if it be not haloed, as it rarely is, by one of the very stateliest of coronets—is to Tories almost more deplorable than criminal propensities. "Tom" Mosley, in a word, was never popular with the Tory rank and file, as no one is who may, quite possibly, be laughing at them. And he had about him that blending of good looks, real charm and an almost Gallic wit—which is not appreciated by an aggregation of middle-aged men, singularly deficient in those qualities.

The Parliament in which Mosley found himself was wealthier than any Tory Parliament had ever been before, and less distinguished by merit of either birth or intellect than any Labour Parliament was destined to be after it. It used to be called, without any degree of physiognomic inaccuracy, "the hard-faced Parliament," and the popularity of one of its members, Horatio Bottomley, earned for it the description of "Bottomley's Pit," in deference to the average of the intellectual standard found therein. Into it were gathered several hundreds of men, who, by virtue of great and sudden accretions of wealth during the preceding four years, had earned the respect of those Conservative Selection Committees who are more concerned with the capacity of the candidate to subscribe than either to act or to think. Men who had recently found patriotism so profitable were anxious to pursue those careers of diligent service to the nation, which might now carry them forward to the remote and icy social peaks, towering so far above the low ranges of buying and selling which they had already scaled.

It is not suggested that the "parvenu" composition of this Parliament was not all that a party machine can desire. It is the most that the Conservative Party machine desires, and it is what it generally contrives to have. There is always a strain of anarchic irresponsibility towards his "class obligations" in the blood of that almost extinct bird—the English (or Scots or Irish) aristocrat. Without going back into the remoter past of Parliamentary history—to Edward Fitzgerald, to George Gordon or to Byron, we can remember Charles Dilke and Cunninghame Graham, Auberon Herbert and Aubrey Herbert, and—more mildly—Henry Cavendish-Bentinck, Robert Cecil, and various Russells. The powers that rule the political world remember them all quite well. Hence, while they do not altogether object to enlightened young men who "sow their wild oats" in advertising the great, palpitating soul of the Tory Party before they are forty, on the whole they prefer either numbskulls from the 'shires or men who are "pleased to meet you."

The physiology of Toryism is peculiar, and should be studied by anyone who is considering English politics. The modern Tory Party—in spite of its intrinsically "bourgeois" constitution, is still ruled by the great oligarchic families—the Cecils, the Stanleys, the Cavendishes and—newcomers who have not yet attained to the usage of their family name—the Londonderrys. These great oligarchs personally supervise neither their own properties nor that great property which is common to them all—the Tory Party. They prefer, both on their estates and in politics, to make use of agents. These

The Background of the Bourgeois Mind | 11

agents are sometimes younger sons and sons-in-law—if they can be found competent enough; otherwise they have recourse to that janissary corps of the capitalist class—the legal profession. The number of lawyers with double-barreled names (they seem to be born with them like Harley Street specialists with surnames for Christian names) who have sat on Conservative Front Benches during the last century is really remarkable. The mind, then, which succeeds in the Tory Party is the mind of the deferential junior dependent of the "great house," or of the competent "undertaker"—to use an Elizabethan term. The men of the "near-families," if they have ability, are suspect, and if they have independent spirit, mutiny. Their efforts are aborted, or they find their way to the Radical benches, where they may be observed in any Parliament—particularly those who come from the "Celtic fringe." Disraeli is the only "outsider" who has succeeded in "putting himself across" the Tory Party, and his success was the success of the company promoter, who appeals always to the imagination of those avid "great bourgeois" families who have kept rich with the British Empire.

Here we must define the term "bourgeois" in the sense in which it will be used not infrequently in this book. "Bourgeois" has long served to imply a state of mind rather than a class. It is the state of mind which arises as a result of living in the capitalist state of society. In a capitalist country there is no such category as an aristocracy. The upper strata of society, some of whom have inherited names which were once associated with aristocracy, are, in the French sense— *haute bourgeoisie*. Whole sections of the so-called working class— workers by hand—have, ever since the Industrial Revolution, been in process of becoming more and more "bourgeois." The "bourgeois" state of mind began to develop at the end of the Middle Ages, when the feudal system showed clear traits of dissolution, and when the hitherto unimportant trading class began to emerge from their political obscurity. As the system of capitalist economics gradually became the *system of life* of the countries which had formed part of feudal Christendom, both the institutions and the social outlook of the people of the different countries involved in this transformation assumed new forms. So, with capitalist economics, there developed bourgeois-capitalist institutions, a bourgeois-capitalist phil-osophy and history—above all a bourgeois morality. The aristocrat, of course, survived, here and there, as a biological type, just as the peasant survived as a type, and still remains the dominant type in those countries like Ireland, Spain and Poland, which are round the fringe of the industrial core of Western Europe. Like all other biological types, the aristocrat does not maintain his characteristics under conditions which are unfavourable to survival. Least of all is the type found among the families of the "great *bourgeoisie*" of England. These families are, in fact, the supreme—and at the same time the most refined—expression of the bourgeois mind. For some have all the dim delicacy of Cambridge "dons," and others have evolved as a family trait that natural good-fellow-ship which is found in golf-club secretaries. They have for so long developed bourgeois characteristics as a form of defensive colouring that they have become in themselves almost perfect specimens of the bourgeois animal. And ultimately the pattern of the Englishman has become stamped upon the modern bourgeois type, so that to this day Hungarian and Polish noblemen who wish to attend shoots in Scotland or the great annual bourgeois *festas* at Le Touquet or Cannes have their suits made by Bond Street tailors.

How different was the aristocrat—the great leader and artist of the medieval world, who—as was natural—achieved his finest manifestations during the Renaissance, when his own background of the feudal world was, in fact, already within the shadows. The Plantagenet princes, the Mortimers, the Percys, the Bigods and the Courtenays, were dim Shakespearian memories when the last of the English aristocrats strode to their predestined scaffolds. They had neither the charm nor the flair nor the grace of those superb expressions of their type—the princes of the great Italian cities, Sforza and Medici and Visconti, Colonna and Orsini. Robert Devereux, Earl of Essex, was a poor English copy of the diamond-cut Italians, but he had the instinct—though not the competence—for leadership; the anarchic aestheticism and the grand conception of personal life and death, which had once characterized the brilliant aristocrats of medieval England. It was a trick of fate that he should have played and lost against the last lingering mammoth of yet another world—the world of Gaelic tribalism. It was the insignificant epilogue of a story long since told, when the last Irish king raised his hosting against the last Norman lord—when Hugh O'Neill harassed the Earl of Essex through the wet Ulster woods. He was loved of the people, was Robert Devereux—as he rode through the London crowd with his gay gentlemen, scattering gold pieces right and left. He ended his life upon the scaffold, as it was right he should, with that graceful gesture of contempt for the realities of an unreal world with which the gallant man can leave it.

The aristocrat died out at long last in Scotland. There was, of course, Montrose—and the Young Pretender, who lives more vividly in the heart of the North than their whole gallery of kings. Fate again showed a piquant cynicism when it brought the Highland clans, with their half-Polish prince out of the mists, through the streets of Glasgow and Manchester on the eve of the Industrial Revolution. The '45 illustrated well the mind of bourgeois England, and the mind of its great bourgeois houses, when poor Highlanders and Irish sailors and small country lairds came out for the bonnie Prince, while the great English lords sat tight and waited to see which side was going to win.

The aristocrat lived and died magnificently. He gave always of himself. He gave a fine spectacle to the people, in his death as in his life. It was good that now and again "one man should die for the people," and on the scaffold the aristocrats perpetuated the popularity of their order. So soon as the aristocrats ceased to be romantic they ceased to have significance—they became merely the colourless owners of great properties. And a duke in a motor-hearse is a poor substitute for Montrose strolling to the block.

It is not that the aristocratic type could have survived in any modern world—although their meaner characteristics of sheer anarchic piracy are now being reproduced by such unattractive modern barons as the Press-lord and the gangster. The aristocratic order had seen its fate sealed as early as the Battle of Bosworth. They were destined to become obsolete, as the patricians of the old Roman Republic passed to extinction with the emergence of the cosmopolitan and un-Roman Empire, when the relationship of the great bourgeois families to the older houses was even more doubtful than that of the Smithsons to the medieval Percies is to-day. Had the Tudor policy of the Nation-State and of a controlled capitalism succeeded, it is likely that we might have had to-day a classless nation, distinguished only in social grades by the existence of numerous functional categories, who would not have been alienated from each other by vast differences of economic status. As it was, the bourgeois class-dictatorship, and not the functional State, emerged from the chaos of the Parliamentary Wars, which saw the overthrow of the Tudor Nation-State conception.

The old Parliamentarians expressed the reality of their class-power with a directness which their more subtle successors have long since learnt to avoid. Thus Cromwell and Ireton justified the refusal to grant a universal—as opposed to a property—franchise in the following memorable declaration:

> If one man hath an equal right to the choosing of him that shall govern him—by the same right of nature he hath an equal right to any goods that he sees: meate, drink, cloathes to take and use them for his sustenance. If the master and servant shall be equal electors then clearly those who have no interest in the kingdome will make it their interest to choose those that have noe interest. It may happen that the majority may, by law, not in a confusion, destroy properties; there may be a law enacted, that there shall be an equality of goods and estate. (*The Clarke Papers*, Camden Society, Vol. I.)

The new type of political chieftain, who proceeded to mingle with, and ultimately to dominate and absorb the remnants of the old aristocratic order, were typical expressions of the bourgeois mind of their generation, and natural leaders under the new dispensation. The fact that these men aped the manners and way of life, and acquired the territorial honorifics of an older order, does not alter the fact that they were essentially an upper *bourgeoisie* rather than an aristocracy deriving from feudal overlordships and from State-service. A perusal of any work devoted to the peerage will reveal how the majority of the great families of the English oligarchy have founded their fortunes either in the practice of the Law or in commerce. And the British Constitution growing out of the Parliamentary Wars and the Glorious Revolution of 1688 was founded on the essentially bourgeois interests of property, security and the conception of class-permanence. The Parliamentary Wars had been fought to overthrow the nascent authoritarian state of the Tudors and the Cecils, which was at once curbing the power of the new bourgeois class, and crippling their methods of making themselves rich. The political tradition of "liberty," and the whole technique of democracy, derive from the bourgeois revolutions of the seventeenth and eighteenth centuries, when in the newly industrialized countries of Western Europe—in Holland, England and France—the small but rising groups of commercial capitalists were impelled to advocate the subversion of State authority in order to establish their "liberty" to get and keep rich. Mr.

The Background of the Bourgeois Mind | 15

Stirling Taylor, in his admirable *Modern History of England*, has adequately developed this theme. In the great days of the Tudors and their competent and ruthless ministers were laid the foundations of a national State and of a seriously planned economy. In those brilliant days of English history, the control and regulation of capital was a definite aim of State policy. The economic freedom of the individual—freedom, that is, from starvation—was assured by a system of control of the conditions of labour, and assistance for the destitute, which was without parallel in the Europe of those days. Had the Elizabethan system been maintained, the coming of the Industrial Revolution and of the Age of Mechanics might have been a slower process, but it must undoubtedly have been steadier and more ordered.

Against the weaker hand of the Stuarts—who were very poor Machiavellians—the rising bourgeois class rose in greedy wrath. Mr. Stirling Taylor shows, in a few memorable pages, how it was the reforms of Strafford, and particularly his enlightened measures for the relief of poverty in the North, which brought down upon his head the vengeance of Parliament. Our history has been written for us for so long by Whig historians, that we can hardly discern now that the struggle for the political freedom of the Englishman in the Parliamentary Wars was, in great degree, a rather sordid struggle for the "freedom of the market." The City of London financed the Parliamentary armies who overthrew the national monarchy and set up, in effect, a system of group-dictatorship—through the corridors of the House of Commons—of the new bourgeois capitalist power. The Old Lady of Threadneedle Street, in her flapperdom, made quite a passable Joan of Arc.

From the scaffold of King Charles the victorious Whigs marched in triumph into the nineteenth century. John Somers, the ablest contemporary apologist of the Revolution of 1688, underlines—with that unconscious hypocrisy which is the most superb achievement in the manners of the bourgeois type—the three virtues of liberty, property and patriotism upon which the theoretical justification for the dominance of his class was destined to repose:

> Our representatives, to secure us from the encroachments of this and all succeeding ages, have thought fit to declare and establish the rights of the people so fully, and upon such sure foundations, that England is now the securest and happiest nation of the world, *if the nation can but be sensible of their*

own happiness... Nothing could be more terrible to the English, *who are so much in love with liberty and property*, than to see themselves be dragooned out of both with the help of so powerful an ally as Louis XIV.

It is only necessary to substitute the name "Stalin" for that of Louis XIV, to make these words entirely modern, and in every respect suitable for delivery either by Mr. Baldwin or Mr. MacDonald.

Mr. Wingfield Stratford, in his monumental *History of British Civilization* refuses to allow that the Whigs inherited the open cynicism of Cromwell and Ireton:

> When, therefore, we say that the Revolution established an oligarchy in power, it must not be in oblivion of the fact that to no one of that age, so far as we can ascertain, was this perfectly apparent. To the Whigs, who stood most whole-heartedly for the new order of things, it was a triumph of law, of justice and of liberty. Moreover, this is substantially the verdict of Macaulay, of Hallam, and of Burke. And yet it is a fact not to be seriously disputed, that during the century and a half that followed the Revolution, power became gradually concentrated in the hands of a small minority, who used it to repress the common people to a state of impotence and degradation scarcely precedented since "the devils and wicked men" of King Stephen's days.

A sublime unconsciousness of moral error is a very definite characteristic of the bourgeois mind, which has become associated by tradition with the English character, because the whole texture of English thought is now saturated with the bourgeois outlook. The avoidance of evil, the ignoring of misery, the hatred of all violence, the quacking for personal liberty within the stockaded shelter of the police-protected bourgeois State, are all indicative of the pathology of the shop-keeper, who rejoiced at the passing of the armed bands of the Middle Ages, and saw only a world in which all who had the ability might now continue to traffic in peace. With the ideal of liberty—which meant primarily liberty from interference by superior authority—was developed the ideal of property—a conception which in the Middle Ages was by no means clearly formulated. The ideal of property was closely interwoven with

The Background of the Bourgeois Mind | 17

that of liberty, for liberty implied, in fact, liberty to enjoy property. In discussing John Locke, the father of English Liberalism, Wingfield Stratford says:

> Not the least characteristic feature is the importance Locke attaches to property. There are cases, he points out, where it would be justifiable to kill a man, but a crime to take his purse. It was during the eighteenth century that brutal assault went comparatively free, while to steal a sheep was a hanging matter.

We have only to proceed across Mr. Wingfield Stratford's span of a century and a half to arrive at the ultimate expression of John Locke's conception of the importance of the property idea in the bourgeois State. When Lord Byron addressed the House of Lords, in 1812, on the second reading of the Framework Bill (which punished by death the destruction of a frame-knitting machine or of the lace it wove), he summed up, not only the evils of the Industrial Revolution, but the evils of that bourgeois society, which could fail even to recognize the existence of the crimes which it was perpetrating. Byron, referring to the rioters who had been destroying machinery:

> You call these men a mob, desperate, dangerous and ignorant... Are we aware of our obligations to a mob? It is the mob that labour in your fields and serve in your houses, that man your navy, and recruit your army, that have enabled you to defy all the world; and can also defy you when neglect and calamity have driven them to despair... The rejected workmen in the blindness of their ignorance, instead of rejoicing at these improvements in arts so beneficial to mankind, conceived themselves to be sacrificed to improvements in mechanism. In the foolishness of their hearts they imagined that the maintenance and well-doing of the industrious poor were objects of greater consequence than the enrichment of a few individuals by improvements in the implements of trade, which threw the workmen out of employment, and rendered the labourer unworthy of his hire. (Parl. Debates, XXI, 966 *et seq.*)

During the first half of the nineteenth century, the final destruction of the precarious balance between industry and agriculture occasioned the

Chapter I

political extinction of the old Tory land interest. The Tory Party, and the land-owning interest—with all their faults—were of their very nature national. They were concerned with the land of England. Commercial Capitalism is, on the other hand, essentially internationalist. "Free Trade," which became the cry of the Whig democrats, implies in its essence "Freedom of the Market"—"Freedom for Capital." If one flies in an aeroplane to-day over the wide lands of the Kingdom of Great Britain and Northern Ireland, it is not difficult to see that those who cared so greatly for the "Freedom of the Market" cared not at all for the well-being of their own country. The Highlands of Scotland have been depopulated as if by plague. The farming lands of England are being deserted, as if from invasion. Ireland has been thrown away as not worth the holding. The same political and economic policy of *laissez-faire* which sacrificed the land to international trade was led, when circumstances required, to sacrifice industry too. The replacement of "paternal industry" by the joint-stock company has achieved the final emancipation of capital. The capitalist who takes the trouble to pick up his telephone, can switch his capital, literally, "from China to Peru." Capital, in the present phase, remains within the authority of no national government—it is supremely international.

It would be quite unscientific to pretend that the complicated historical process, through which the present stage of bourgeois-capitalist power has been evolved, is altogether the result of a policy which has been consciously followed by the succeeding generations of the governing class, either in Britain or in other of the bourgeois-capitalist countries. A revolution, such as the English bourgeois revolution of the seventeenth century and its economic sequel—the so-called Industrial Revolution—not only creates its own theoretical background, its series of interpretations, but a whole miswritten history of its own. And many generations of men, some single-minded patriots in their own consciousness, others seeking the perpetuation of their own class predominance with the cunning of instinct, have worked to the blind end that the International of Wealth shall rise above the desert fields of England. The bases of bourgeois democracy lay in the subversion of the developing authoritarian states of the seventeenth and eighteenth centuries, and when a system, which finds its original justification in a subversive philosophy, is forced to formulate a methodology of power, that methodology can only find expression in terms of surrender. The Whigs, themselves representing ill-disciplined factions in the possession of irresponsible power, were impelled by inevitable tendencies to develop a political machine, which extended to the wider and more incoherent sections of the people vast and vague powers of intervention which they had neither the capacity nor the intelligence to use. With the formal surrender of their sectional prerogatives, the governing class—practiced at least in politics—were impelled to develop the ingenious technique of government by electoral corruption, by mass-suggestion, and, most important, by elaborate deception, for it is only by deception that the implications of surrender may be avoided. As, under the influence of the Industrial Revolution, an increasing proportion of the population became detached from the land and from interest in the ownership of small properties, an animosity against private property developed among the masses of the people who had been deprived of all association with direct ownership. The development of mass-production tended to restrict the opportunities for real economic independence among each new generation of individuals, and as men became less independent in their private lives, they were fobbed off by the concession of a greater degree of political "liberty"— at once useless to themselves, and ultimately dangerous to the State. It was thus that the Whigs first canalized the dangerous social effervescence which followed the Napoleonic Wars and resulted from the economic dislocations of the Industrial Revolution. The Whigs rallied the mob to carry the Reform Act, which crowned the final victory of the commercial *bourgeoisie* as the dominant class within the nation. Scarcely was this new edition of "the Glorious Revolution" complete, when the new industrialists tightened up the economic net in the Poor Law "Reform" of 1834. As Wingfield Stratford says:

> All the resources of scientific ingenuity were devoted to securing that the lot of those who were dependent on the tender mercies of the State should be worse in every way than that of the poorest starveling outside—no light undertaking when we remember that the spectacle of one of the latter starved to death under a hedge was not unknown.
>
> The middle-class legislators were going to take no chances. The aged and infirm who were no longer capable of providing for themselves were doubtless assumed to be suffering from their lack of providence, it was better at any rate that their lives should be allowed to waste away under conditions that

combined the minimum of expense with the maximum of affliction. Little children whose parents were imprudent enough to bring them within the clutches of the State would have the sins of those parents visited—with a vengeance—on their heads. The workhouse test was applied with the utmost strictness. With comparatively few exceptions he or she who wanted relief must go for it to the workhouse, a place which the poor, paying it an altogether unmerited compliment, called a Bastille, and which was really a house of slow torture by every indignity that arbitrary tyranny could devise for the helpless and friendless, torture by the tearing of parents from children, and of husband from wife in their declining days... This Poor Law of 1834 was regarded as a triumph of reforming legislation by the class which the Reform Bill had elevated to power. It had many advantages; it certainly had the effect of enormously reducing the number of paupers, when it was no worse to die outright than to be kept alive by charity. It was likely to provide a cheaper supply of labour, when the alternative to accepting the employer's conditions might be to enjoy those of the Bastilles... The workers took these things in far from good part, and especially in the industrial districts of the North and Midlands, were infuriated at the shabby return they considered the middle class to have made them for their help in securing the new franchise. (Stratford, pp. 971-2)

Joseph Stephens, a Methodist preacher of High Tory principles, who regarded the middle class as the real enemy and the Reform Bill as a national disaster, voiced the impotent resentment of the workers in old Covenanting terms, which must have shocked the God-fearing manufacturers who had promoted their excellent Bill:

Those who are to go to Hell hereafter are not the Antinomians, not the Unitarians, not the Mahometans, the Pagans, the Catholics, or the Protestant Churchmen... there is not a word about creeds or articles of belief; there is not a word about any particular professions; there is not a word about any rites or ceremonies or institutions... but those who go away into everlasting death, they are men of all lands, tongues, trades and politics, that have refused to clothe the naked, and that have not visited and sympathized with the sick. Christ says so.

It is not without significance, both in regard to the general trend of political power in this country and to the relative economic state of the workers in the present day as compared with a hundred years ago, that the ultimate extension of the franchise by a Conservative Government should have been received with complete lack of enthusiasm by its beneficiaries, and should have been followed by the controversies which have thundered round the "Not Genuinely Seeking Work Clause," the Anomalies Bill, and the Means Test. The workers have at long last learnt that in the "bourgeois" State votes are in no way synonymous either with political power or with economic security.

The characteristic qualities of bourgeois political idealism are to be discovered in the conceptions of liberty and property. The idea of liberty is rather a spiritualized plea for property, and implies liberty of enjoyment. Order is the necessary pre-requisite to the liberty to enjoy property, and hence we arrive at that superb motto of capitalist society—"Law and Order." But with the necessity for "Law and Order'" goes a rooted objection to interference by the State with the rights and prerogatives of property. The objection to Socialism is therefore as fundamental to the bourgeois mind as was the objection to the autocratic state of the Stuarts. The State is a necessary evil in any form of ordered society, but it must be so regulated to serve, rather than to hinder or to check, the interests of the bourgeois class. Hence has been gradually evolved the elaborate system of Parliamentary Government, which is a system of maintaining the minimum necessary State machinery, and at the same time of subordinating that machinery, in the name of civil liberties, to the control of one or other of the groups into which the bourgeois class—owing to its varying economic interests—is divided.

The bourgeois mind is also subconsciously influenced by the pathological dread of the bourgeois type for violence. While bourgeois society suffers the extremes of misery and degradation to destroy the texture of whole sections of the community, the mere suspicion of physical violence—political or personal—will arouse an almost religious horror. The tragedy of a world war, which is after all an orthodox political method hallowed by practice, shocked the British political mind far less than the near terror of armed revolt in Ireland—to which they capitulated with remarkable expedition. It is not only alien to the old game of surrender and a devious recovery on the roundabouts which they understand so well, but it introduces dangers which are quite strange to the whole technique of bourgeois democracy. That is why the Fascist movement, in Italy and Germany, has provoked in bourgeois political circles an anger and a dread which was scarcely manifested, even in an earlier stage, against a Communism which they find no great reason to dread.

Out of the night of history old shadows are appearing which menace their complacency. The disciplined movements of devoted minorities are more fearful than the incoherent waves of mass resentment which they have learnt well how to circumvent with squads of their own bourgeois special constables. Growing groups of unknown men out of the streets are laughing the unbeliever's hollow laugh at all those things the democrat has taught the people to hold dear. Worst of all, a figure appears that they had thought was gone forever over the grey scaffolds of the Reformation. Sir Herbert Samuel, a Liberal of singular perspicacity, believes that Europe is returning to the conditions of the twelfth century. Professor Laski wails against these new men, who have "no inhibitions." The oligarchs and the democrats dread this classic figure more than anarchy—for it is the figure of the Leader, the natural aristocrat, whom they had thought long dead and buried in the obloquy of Whig history. It showed in the heavy frame of Rhodes, and may have stirred in Edward Carson, but those men were born too early. Now it comes out into the stark day—in the grim serenity of Mussolini, in the harsh force of Hitler. And behind them stride the eternal *condottieri*—the gallant, vivid Balbo, the ruthless Goering. The figure has not yet been recognized in England, but these men move the people—as no democrats can ever do—to rise up from the dreary life of the machine. They still feel secure, the democrats in England, because they are incapable of thinking, except in terms of the bourgeois mind, and they have no sense of the perspectives of the age in which they live.

Chapter II

—British Capitalism in Retreat—

Oswald Mosley has been actively concerned in British politics during the whole period of fifteen years which have passed since the end of the German War. The development of his mind during all this time may be said to have passed through three phases. First he entered the 1918 Parliament—as was natural for a young man without any earlier political experience—on the wave of national enthusiasm which placed the Coalition Government in power for nearly four years. He was thereby involved in the first post-war phase of the struggle of the capitalist class in Britain to confront the political and economic crisis which threatened to overwhelm the whole system upon which their ascendancy was based. Mosley's development during the five years in the House of Commons before he threw in his lot with the Labour Party shows itself in his speeches and writing of that date. He appears to have been constantly questing and uncertain, and his mind was governed rather more by vaguely generous sentiments than by a deliberately formulated attitude towards the questions of the day. His emotional initiative is understandable enough in a young man in the early twenties—for all that generation had been disturbed and changed by the experiences of the recent war. They came into the life of post-war England with few illusions and many doubts, and they found the control of all branches of the national life in the grip of men who were utterly strangers to them, in experience, outlook and intent. There was something symbolical of his generation in the dark, restless figure of Oswald Mosley, as he limped forlornly about the corridors of the "hard-faced" Parliament. He concerned himself, in those days, very much with the Irish question, and together with other Tories of the calibre of Aubrey Herbert and Henry

Cavendish-Bentinck, he slashed the Government of the day on the indiscriminate reprisals—which they were not only permitting, but organizing—against the civil population of the South of Ireland. His attitude on the Irish question was, however, significantly realistic, as he wrote to his constituents at Harrow:

> In the summer of 1920, before cowardly outrages on a large scale had occurred in Ireland, or had been advocated by leaders of the Sinn Fein Party, I urged the negotiation of peace on a Dominion basis with the elected representatives of the Irish. The Government then rejected that policy with contumely and embarked on a policy of special coercion and reprisal. This policy failed because it was inefficient and misdirected by the political control to which it was subjected. It was criminally inefficient in that it exposed our men to unnecessary dangers which resulted in terrible losses. It was misdirected because our retaliatory measures fell only upon the innocent and failed entirely to deal with the guilty. The measures of the Government were only a danger to those whom they should have protected... After the loss of 600 killed and a proportionate number of wounded, and the spending of a very large sum of money, the Government decided, at the moment successful crime had attained a zenith of violence, to accept the policy which they had rejected when crime was relatively non-existent... My part in the matter, however, was entirely consistent, for I had been willing to concede to reason what the Government only yielded to violence, and accordingly supported them in their belated peace policy. This support, however, did not extend to one most disgraceful episode. The Government, in the precipitate reversal of their policy, abandoned the Southern loyalists to their fate. I had always insisted that this small minority should be given the option of evacuation with compensation prior to the withdrawal of the English troops. Many terrible outrages have occurred as the result of denying them this opportunity. (Address to the Electors of Harrow, October, 1922.)

Mosley was failing to reconcile himself with the trend—or rather the stagnation—of thought in the Conservative Party, but at the same time he had not yet found himself able to define his attitude to the extent of identifying himself with one of the other two major parties. He was very frank in his doubts, and he laid them clearly before his constituents, who in the General Election of November, 1922, gave him a majority of more than 7,000 over his official Tory opponent—no mean tribute from a middle-class constituency and one of the strongholds of the Conservative Party. Just before the election, Mosley wrote:

> Periods of temporary confusion such as the present, are recurrent in English history, and invariably follow any great upheaval which obliterates old issues and creates new problems. On this occasion the magnitude of the upheaval is reflected in exceptional confusion. Some people imagine that it is possible to pass through an earthquake and still to find the old familiar landmarks standing. But it is mere blindness to reality to ignore the basic fact that the world of politics, for better or for worse, is new. The war destroyed the old party issues, and with them the old parties. The Unionist Party long preserved a semblance of unity in its support of the late Government, but it has now split into fragments, and thus has completed the dissolution of the old Party alignments. Some of the fragments may possibly be pieced together, but it is evident that they will contain elements as discordant as those which composed the late Coalition, for the new Government embraces men who differ fundamentally in every great issue of the immediate future.
>
> *The Party system must, of course, return in the very near future, but it will be a new Party system.* The great new issues will shortly create new Party alignments, which will truly divide the lines of men and determine their permanent associations. Then, and not before, I am prepared to form my Party allegiance. In present conditions it appears to be unnecessary and inadvisable for a politician who is not bound to existing Party machines and personalities, to adopt a label which, in the mind of the electorate, must be associated with past controversies with which he was not concerned. This consideration is especially true in the case of a young man who is necessarily concerned not with the past, but with the present, and still more with the future. My intention not to wear a label

which, at present, may be confused with past controversies, *does not mean that I adopt the empty independence of men who can agree with no one*, or who refuse to co-operate with others who are animated by the same beliefs. It is unpatriotic to maintain an impotent aloofness when pressing problems demand the co-operation of like-minded men. I am not a free-lance incapable of such co-operation, and *am prepared to work immediately with men who hold similar opinions* in face of the great new issues of our day. I claim, however, that in the present transitional condition of politics it is unfair to ask men who come fresh to post-war problems to form party ties and allegiances before the alignments of the future are clear. (Harrow, October, 1922.)[1]

The policy which Mosley was then adumbrating as an Independent candidate is worth noting, because in it he combines, with the traditional Tory conception of the nation, a sense of disciplined radicalism which was at that time new in English politics, and which he was destined to develop ten years later in more advanced and effective forms. He wrote:

Under present circumstances, it is the duty of the Government to fix a definite sum which experts consider to be within the taxable capacity of the country, and to ration the Departments well within the limit of that figure. The sum available should then be allocated to the Departments in accordance with their relative importance. It is evident that great economies can be effected *by cutting adrift from all extraneous adventures and commitments, and withdrawing to the normal bounds of Empire.*

This was hardly a policy which was likely to recommend itself to the modern Conservative Party, which—bound fast by the international interests of the City of London—had already seen the country committed to an elaborate and futile debt-collecting policy on the Continent of Europe, and which had allowed itself to become involved in the erection and subsequent protection of pseudo-democratic card-houses throughout the Middle East. But Mosley drives his point home, and brings down

---

[1] The italics are in the original document.

upon himself the vindictive anger of the Tory Central Office:

> There must be no entangling alliances which inevitably evoke opposition combinations and a return to the balance of power with its division of Europe into armed camps awaiting their opportunity for attack.

Mosley's ideas on industry were equally unacceptable to the Tories, whose refusal to recognize the necessity of any modifications—or even alleviations—in the capitalist system as they had grown to know it, was to bring them within a very brief space of time to the inevitability of their great wage-reduction drive. In industry Mosley's ideas had a long way to go before they developed into his "National Policy" of 1931, but they are interesting in that they indicate the direction in which the mind of the insurrectionary young Tory was working. Mosley continues:

> The function of the State should not be the conduct of industry; it should rather keep the ring for the consumer with a minimum of interference... a taunt, which is productive of much unrest, that Labour is a mere chattel on the market, should be met by a frank invitation to Labour to participate as a partner with a voice in the destinies of industries to which it devotes its life. Such measures are compatible with the preservation of that individual initiative on which our industries rest, and, at the same time, would go far towards securing the co-operation of Labour on a basis of joint interest and common humanity.

To understand the complexion of the Conservative Party, when it came into power in the last month of 1922, for the first time—unfettered by alliance with other parties—since 1902, it is necessary to consider the fluctuations and changes in the interests of that bourgeois class whose economic and political philosophy it expressed. In the eighteenth century, Bolingbroke had advocated the revival of the authoritarian national state, and his ideas were, in fact, a reversion to Tudor-Cecil conceptions. It was Peel, who—a hundred years later—transformed the Tories from an eighteenth century party of the landed interest into a modern bourgeois political organization. The Repeal of the Corn Laws celebrated not only the final collapse of the landowning interest as a power in national politics, but the surrender of the landowners themselves within their own party to those vigorous elements of the new *bourgeoisie* who had already for some time been permeating it. For half a century after the Repeal of the Corn Laws the rapid expansion of British industry and finance permitted all sections of the bourgeois class to build up gigantic fortunes, both at home and abroad, and prevented the underlying conflicts of interest within that class from developing into dangerous antagonisms. The trend of Tory thought during that period expressed an idealism which is the product at once of prosperity and of leisure, and while the philanthropy of Shaftesbury declared the conscience of a wealthy aristocracy, the peculiar foresight of the visionary Disraeli attempted to find in the fact of ownership no more than the principle of a responsible trusteeship. As the sands ran out towards the end of the century, and it began to become clear that the owners of wealth were no longer the owners of an England whose interests were at least common with their own, but the owners of mortgage charges over all the civilized and uncivilized world, Joseph Chamberlain made his titanic effort to rally a national party on a national policy. That effort killed great Chamberlain, and it broke the Tory Party. The English bourgeois class were now challenged by the ultimate implications of that system of capitalist economics which had originally brought them into existence. The interests of the capitalist class had at long last ceased to have any fundamental elements in common with the interest of the nation regarded as the basic unit of political action. The master industrialist, who had succeeded the landowner in the leadership of Tory thought during the last decades of the nineteenth century and whose superlative expression had been Joseph Chamberlain, was passing. The family firm was being transformed into the joint-stock company, with stock-owners who are in fact absentee plant-lords, who have never even seen their plant and who would not know the men who work that plant for them if they were to meet them in the street. Property owners were coming to have no longer a direct interest in the land and in the factories of their countries; since property is not, as it once was, cows and sheep and machines and looms, but share certificates and dividend coupons. Capital was ceasing in any sense to be national, and was becoming supremely international, and it was becoming a matter of indifference to the owner of wealth whether he derived his profits from looms in Bombay or in Lancashire, from steelworks in Bohemia or in Middlesbrough, from coal in South Wales or from oil in Mexico. All that he could ask was—Profit. All that he needed was freedom of movement for capital—which he called Free Trade. The Tory Party faced the alternative of whether it would continue to be the party of the producers, the champion of the land and of the factory, or whether it would become the party of property. The two interests had once, at least to a reasonable extent, been the same interest, but when the parting came the Tories took not the "high road" that led to Disraeli's ideal of National Trusteeship, but the "low road" that leads by many devious channels and subterranean passages to the Street that is called Wall. And this continuing conflict of interest between Share-Property and Production, between the interests of International Finance and the national interest, explains the underlying antagonism between Tory aspiration and Tory leadership during the last quarter of a century. Tory leadership, in order to maintain the cohesion of the Tory rank and file, and to give expression to the strong national sentiment of the large body of opinion within the country which traditionally supports Tory policy as it is imagined to be, have been forced to place emphasis on such comparatively minor issues as that of Ireland. When such issues have failed them, they have been driven back on to a revival of an emasculated edition of Joseph Chamberlain's imperial policy—which, once a dynamic conception, is now nearly half a century out of date, and entirely unsuited to the changed demands of a modern national economy. But they have always preferred either to seek alliance with other parties, which has secured them against the necessity of implementing a Tory policy on national lines—as in 1918-22 or in 1931, or to bind themselves by pledges which have protected them from carrying out the very policy which they proclaim to be necessary—as in 1922-3 and in 1924-9. The truth is that the Tory Party has now become completely the Bourgeois-Capitalist Party—particularly since its thorough permeation by Liberal elements during the course of the last ten years. This is confirmed in the fact that the Liberal Party has practically ceased to exist, and so far as it survives at all it can really be said to consist of certain small Scottish and Welsh regional groups, with—attached to them—a number of rather able individuals who find the Liberal Party, during the present period of transition in politics, a convenient middle position, from where they may decide at leisure to which of the two major parties they intend ultimately to attach themselves.

In reviewing the implications of capitalist-bourgeois policy in Britain since the war, it is necessary to define exactly what is meant, in the context, by the terms capital, Capitalism, and the capitalist system. All these terms have come to be very loosely used.

Chapter II

Capital is the accumulation in a community of that surplus of wealth which is not in course of consumption from day to day. The most primitive community is to this extent capitalist, in that it possesses, either in common or divided up among individuals, a surplus of wealth—in use but not consumed—in the form of such things as skins, tents, tools and weapons. A Socialist or Communist community such as the U.S.S.R. possesses large accumulations of capital. Owing, however, to the fact that surplus accumulations of wealth have tended to become concentrated under the control of a minority of individuals, the whole system of the surplus accumulation of capital has come to be identified with the private ownership of wealth, and with the individual right to control the direction and use of those accumulations, with the result that the terms Capitalism and the capitalist system have become synonymous with the conceptions of private ownership in property and of private liberty to dispose of that property as the individual owner may think fit.

Before the Industrial Revolution the processes of production were so laborious that the surpluses, collected by individuals who controlled the means of production and exchange of those days, did not on the whole exceed either the capacity of those individuals to consume in excess of the average member of the community, nor the comparatively modest requirements of legitimate accumulation. For here it may be said that in any community there will always be a necessity for the accumulation of a certain proportion of the daily production of wealth, and its withdrawal from current consumption, in order to provide the necessary reserves of non-consumable wealth (e.g. roads, hospitals, schools, museums, etc.). The real economic problem will always consist, in fact, in appropriating the correct proportions of production which must be applied to the purposes of immediate consumption and of reserve accumulation.

As the Industrial Revolution continued to develop at breakneck speed through the whole course of the nineteenth century, the social struggle developed between the capitalists—the owners of the means of production, who wished to appropriate the greatest possible proportion of the "surplus" of goods produced—that is of profits—to their own uses; and the workers of the machines owned by the capitalists, who wished to have for their own immediate consumption as big a proportion as they could lay their hands on of the goods which they saw passing through those hands. We have shown how the social unrest engendered by this process was ingeniously used by the new capitalist class to strengthen themselves in the purely political field (Reform Act), and how they used their increase of political power against the workers who had been their allies (Poor Law Reforms). The struggle was next extended to the field of cheap food, and by diverting the workers to an agitation for the Repeal of the Corn Laws, the bourgeois capitalists canalized the dangerous social unrest which was finding its expression in the Chartist movement. Cheap food meant cheap wages, and the manufacturers were able to stave off the participation of the workers in a larger share of their surpluses at the expense of the English landowning class, and, incidentally, at the cost of destroying the British agricultural industry. To the extent that the French and other Continental capitalist groups failed to achieve this in their own countries—really because they were opposed by a peasant instead of a landowning interest—Continental Capitalism was unable to develop as rapidly as British, and to this day, in France particularly, a more equitable balance has been maintained within the nation between industry and agriculture, and with it a more equitable distribution of wealth and ownership between the different sections of the community.

As British Capitalism developed, and as surpluses began to accumulate more and more in the hands of comparatively few individuals, a variety of results followed. First, the capacity of the workers, who were excluded from participation in the surpluses in their respective industries, was limited to the consumption of a minimum of the products of industry as a whole. Secondly, the capitalists had either to consume their surpluses or to apply them to uses in new directions. The capitalists could only find avenues for the consumption of their surpluses by the creation of an artificial world of surplus values, the expression of which is bourgeois society as it exists to-day. Thus great houses, yachts which became floating palaces, ostentatious expenditure in horse-racing, gambling both on the stock-markets and at games of chance, all became directions in which capitalist bourgeois society attempted to dissipate its surpluses. Rarities, whose values soared as ever greater accumulations became available for expenditure, jewels, old masters, first editions—attained fantastic values. As one instance, while the coal crisis was dragging out its interminable course the manuscript of *Alice in Wonderland* changed hands for £11,500 while *The Times*, the most sublime organ of bourgeois thought, was agitating to find a purchaser "patriotic" enough to keep this significant document within the British Isles. There must have been thousands of Alices in the coalfields who were at that time living in a wonderland of rather a different kind. But the capitalists who were not interested in shining as the social stars of the gallant bourgeois world, or whose profits were so vast that they could not exhaust them in expenditure there, were forced either to reinvest their wealth in British industries, or to seek alternate outlets for its investment. It was not always profitable to invest in Britain, for the simple reason that the power of the British masses to consume was in inverse proportion to the accumulations which British capitalists had available for investment. Under the capitalist system, in fact, the consuming power of the people—that is the money which entitles the owner to consume so much—was being concentrated in hands which were so few that they were incapable of consuming anything like the total of that which they received, while those who had been deprived of this power to consume, were unable to receive the minimum which they either desired or required. The British capitalist, from being an owner of plant, became more and more a lender of surpluses, and these surpluses he sought to lend all over the world, wherever he could find people ready to pay him interest for their use. As a result there developed a vast system of professional intermediaries in the stock exchanges and the private banks whose business it was to search out new avenues for investment and generally to organize the whole of this investment business. At first the British capitalist found profitable avenues for investment in lending money to the developing industries of America and Germany. Later he had to go further afield into less inviting countries, and he began to lose his way in the jungles of Africa, and in the still more distant forests of South America and Siberia. The proposition seemed a simple one—the new countries opened up would purchase the goods of Britain which they were in process of being lent the money to buy, and they would, for their part, repay the loans—or at least keep up the interest on them—sending to Britain and all over the world the goods which British lending was enabling them to produce. But, unfortunately, the desire of the capitalist for the maximum possible "return" on his money, had the effect of contracting the purchasing power of the new peoples, who were asked at once to buy and to go on paying interest. Surpluses of goods began to accumulate which it became more and more difficult to convert into money dividends, while the rapid improvements in the processes of production—particularly during the last fifteen years, converted what had once been awkward "slumps" into a crisis of the whole system.

The ultimate "mathematical impossibility" of the system of lending at interest—Financial Capitalism—had long been appreciated in economic theory, but it was neither recognized nor accepted by the body of capitalist thought which dominated the political and economic life of the modern world. The Versailles Treaty—with its elaborate system of debt-collecting throughout the world—is indicative of how little the real implications of the capitalist system were appreciated as late as 1919, and, in spite of the popular interest in the writings of economists like J. M. Keynes, it cannot be said that orthodox political parties really took the crisis which was approaching them into serious consideration, until, in 1929, the capitalist house started to tumble over their heads.

After the war, the bourgeois-capitalist parties in Great Britain were concerned to combat the symptoms rather than the causes of the coming crisis. The insurgence of labour frightened them, for labour, having been sustained for a century on a minimum share of the national wealth created, and having participated—if not in an increased proportion of the total national wealth—at least in a fixed proportion of a national income which was annually expanding, was now becoming desperate when it was faced with a reduction in the total amount of the proportion which it had got accustomed to receive. With the inflation of the pound during the war period it had been impossible to resist demands for wage increases, but at no time had these increases been allowed to exceed the proportion of the national income—fluctuating, with the more recent social services, between 48 percent and 51 percent—to which the workers had managed to establish their claim by the end of the preceding century.

With inflation the whole investment system of the City of London had become dislocated and disorganized and a policy had been initiated of restoring the position of the pound sterling as against the dollar, and incidentally, of revaluating the enormous tribute which was payable to British investors in sterling every year from all over the world. The restoration of sterling could not but adversely affect British exports, and bring unemployment to many industries which had been unscientifically expanded during the brief post-war boom, but, characteristically, the interests of the British capitalist class in the stability of the London money-market took precedence over the interests of the nation as producers. As wrote Professor André Siegfried in 1931:

> It is generally admitted to-day that British industry suffered from the economic policy adopted in 1918-19, which aimed at bringing the pound sterling back to parity with the dollar. This policy of credit and prestige was the work of the City financiers.

34 | Chapter II

> The Government adopted it and imposed it upon the industrialists, who were scarcely consulted, and who at first did not realize the severe consequences that it would entail... Experience has now proved that this policy was sacrificing production to commerce. The stability and prestige of the pound sterling was guaranteed and this assisted the financiers, and also the merchants who operate on international margins. ... In the last analysis it is industry that has to pay for saving the pound sterling. (*England's Crisis*, pp. 51-2 and 57.)

In the political field, the emphasis was laid, particularly by the Free Trade school, on the necessity, not only of restoring "financial stability," but of maintaining the Free Trade system in order to allow foreign debtors to continue—through the disposal of goods in the British market—the interest which they were obligated to pay. Thus, while British industry was, on the one hand, handicapped in the export markets by the appreciation of sterling, no protection was accorded to the producer in the home market because it was necessary to enable the debtors of the City of London, one way or the other, to continue their interest payments. The whole export theory—which will be discussed later—is, of course, a fallacy in pure economics, but in the conditions of the capitalist world, it is a very valid consideration, both from the angle of those who desire to continue receiving dividends from other countries, and from the angle of those who seek either profit or livelihood out of home production.

With the development of the policy calculated to restore the power of sterling and the position of the London money-market—that is between 1919 and 1925, the whole question of the internal wage-level became very urgent. Orthodox opinion gradually came to realize that it was impossible to restore sterling and maintain a wage-level which, it was alleged, had become unduly inflated during the war period. It became necessary to undertake a drive to bring wages down to what could be regarded as an "economic" level. In other words the impossible was to be attempted, for while the owner of foreign debts was to receive his dividends in the form of imported goods, which would automatically increase in quantity as sterling appreciated, the capacity to purchase these goods within the country was to be reduced as a result of wage-cuts, and the capitalist who owned productive plants within the British Isles—by these wage-cuts—was to be enabled to produce so cheaply that he would be able to sell his goods either in addition to or in competition with a flow of foreign goods which was to be at least maintained, if not—with the appreciation of sterling—actually increased. The only aspect of this ideally free system which was entirely overlooked was the capacity of the consumer to fulfil his passive functions in the market.

It cannot be admitted that the exceedingly able brains who conduct the policies of bourgeois-capitalist society can have altogether ignored the implications of their post-war policy. But it must here be remembered that capital is essentially international in its outlook. And capital had discovered, long before the war, that there are other countries than England, other continents than Europe, suitable for the investment of surplus profits. Capital has grown accustomed to finding its way to those countries where the social consciousness is least developed—to the South American Republics, to Africa, India, Japan and China. As British agriculture was sacrificed, eighty years before, in the interests of "cheap food" which meant cheap wages at home, so now home industry was to be sacrificed in the interests of cheap wages which could no longer be paid in England, but which could still be paid—in smaller amounts even than English wages had ever been paid—in the sweat-houses of the East.

With a policy which aimed at once at the maintenance of the maximum freedom of movement for capital and the restoration—through sterling—of the London dominance of the capitalist world, was combined a scientific imperialism, which appealed, on the one hand, to the strong sense of Nationalism which has always characterized the British, and, on the other, to that officious sort of idealism, endemic in the bourgeois class, which interprets the historic role of England as that of the carrier of Christianity, order and democratic institutions throughout the world. Thus, while the British Government—relying as it did at that time on a Tory majority in the House of Commons—surrendered to the claims of Irish Nationalism because Ireland is economically a poor country of little interest in the broad purview of Capitalism, all the popular prejudices and enthusiasms which a capitalist Press knows so well how to exploit, have been used to maintain intact the British—and European—position in India and the Far East, and in India it is to the subordinate native capitalist class that concessions have been offered, concessions which, if carried into effect, would only establish in India the sort of amenable local government of the type which has existed throughout South America and other parts of Asia for a century or more.

36 | Chapter II

In Britain, in the meantime, the field was cleared for an attack on that insurgent working class, which was threatening the physical security of the capitalist system in its earliest and greatest stronghold. The same Free Trade policy, which was calculated to perpetuate the interests of financial Capitalism, was thrusting upon the working class that menace of unemployment, through the fear of which they might be most easily cowed. For it is a well-known characteristic of economic history, that the working class becomes most clamant in its demands during a period of expansion, and—conversely—most patient during a period of contraction. Revolution, indeed, proceeds from sheer desperation, but a long process of disintegration separates the misery of a part of the working class from the revolutionary desperation of the whole. And the whole technique of the social democratic State has been evolved during the last thirty—and at greater speed during the last ten—years to prevent misery from becoming desperation, and to divide the merely miserable from the utterly desperate. There is all the difference in the world, then, between defeating working-class insurgence, and provoking revolution. The first, in fact, excludes the second, and we shall examine, later, in more detail, the political methodology by which the first is achieved.

During 1923, the play of political forces which were in movement while the economic readjustments implicit in the restoration of sterling were proceeding, forced the Conservative administration of Mr. Baldwin to go to the country in a "snap" election on the issue of Protection. Mr. Baldwin is the ablest leader which the British bourgeois-capitalist class has produced since the more spectacular Mr. Lloyd George. His mind is so complacently cast in the bourgeois mould, that he is preserved from the dishonesty with which a more acute intellect would be compelled to act in a similar position. Mr. Strachey, in his somewhat unequal book, *The Coming Struggle for Power*, has shown, in a brilliant chapter, how in the crisis of 1931 Mr. Baldwin avoided the imminent embarrassment of an independent Conservative majority and the subsequent pressure of a "right" wing which might have proved irresistible, by agreeing to the rather palpable compromise of a "National" Government, which was destined, in fact, to be a Conservative Government, bound within certain limits which were very convenient to Mr. Baldwin. Similarly, in 1923, the new Conservative leader, confronted with a growing unemployment problem, and the insistent demand of the manufacturing interests for Protection, was enabled, by going to the country with a Protectionist programme for which it had not been psychologically prepared, to leave the unemployment problem to be mishandled by an innocuous Socialist minority Government for a short period of nine months, and to return to power at the end of that time with a party united in the desire to avoid again raising the Protectionist issue. The efforts of the industrialists to obtain a producers' policy had, indeed, been very abortive, and Mr. Baldwin returned to continue the deflationary policy of the City of London, with a picturesque romantic at the exchequer, who has since occupied himself in professing his innocence of finance at the time when he was in nominal charge of the finances of the country. It was perhaps just as well that the Tory Party did not succeed in capturing itself in 1923, for the policy of the Protectionists, in so far as it was national, was completely obsolete, and State intervention to protect industry, without at the same time controlling it, would merely have substituted an internal for an external economic anarchy.

In 1924 the second administration of Mr. Baldwin was in a position to proceed both with sterling deflation and with the attack on wages. It was not until 1931 that the financial interests of the City of London themselves swung round to a "National" and Protectionist policy, and that was only when the system of financial Capitalism, all over the world, had begun to collapse round them, impelling them to the conclusion that, for the present, British industry itself had become the safest avenue for the investment of the remnants of their surpluses.

Chapter III

—The Character of Labour-Socialism—

In the "snap" Election of November, 1923, Oswald Mosley again fought Harrow as an Independent, and was accorded a majority of more than 4,000 over his Tory opponent. Mosley had failed to become infected by the sudden enthusiasm of the Conservatives for Protection, but in this he certainly showed a greater degree of consistency than they. He attacked the whole conception of Protection without either control or organization, which was the keynote to the obsolete proposals of the Tories, in contrast to his own later plans for scientific insulation of the home market. He wrote:

> It is claimed that a rise in price will be offset by a rise in wages. Does anyone wish to start again the mad race between rising prices and wages? Further, it is certain prices will rise; it is not certain wages will rise. In conditions of shortage and restriction any extra profits are more likely to trickle into the pockets of profiteers than into the wages of the workers... We are presented with the inducement of benefiting our Dominions by a preference, but Dominion spokesmen say, as Mr. Joseph Chamberlain said, preference is futile without a tax on meat and wheat, which the Government will not impose. Empire development has been sadly neglected in the past and should be vigorously assisted by transport organization and credit facilities. The last way, however, to promote Imperial unity is by the imposition of taxes which our people resent in order to give the Dominions a preference which they think is useless... If foreign goods enter our markets and so pay taxes, there can

be no protection of industry. If, on the other hand, foreign goods are excluded, there can be no revenue from them to subsidize agriculture. (Harrow, November, 1923.)

When Mr. MacDonald formed his first Labour administration at the beginning of 1924 Oswald Mosley had already established a brilliant reputation in the House of Commons. More than a year before, during the Election of 1922, the *Nation* had written:

> He is a figure of individual strength and purpose, perhaps the most interesting in the later Parliament. Is it a disqualification for politics that a man thinks for himself? Then Mr. Mosley sustains that handicap. Nevertheless, if character, a brilliant and searching mind, a sympathetic temperament, and a repugnance from mean and cruel dealing, fit men for the service of the State, Mr. Mosley should rise high in it. It is hardly a compliment in such days as these to speak of him as a rising man, yet I regard him as something of a star and of no common brightness.

A few months later one of Lord Beaverbrook's papers had referred to him as "the stuff of which Prime Ministers are made," and another Tory paper stated that "Mr. Mosley of all young members now at Westminster shows promise and is the only one who obviously has the making of a Prime Minister." The *Morning Post*, in June of 1923, admitted that "in many respects Mr. Mosley reminds one of Disraeli before he had taken his political bearings." It is not, then, difficult to appreciate the reasons for the storm of fury and hatred which broke over Mosley's head when, in the spring of 1924, he announced his adhesion to the Labour Party. "The aristocracy," said Mirabeau, "always pursue with implacable hatred the friends of the people, but with tenfold implacability—the aristocrat who is the friend of the people." The vitriolic abuse of London Society which pursued not only him but his wife also, the vindictive anger of the capitalist Press which reached its peak in the Smethwick by-election of 1926, the rather undignified intervention of his father, are all incidents which hardly come within the scope of a political study.

Typical of these silly attacks made on Lady Cynthia was the story that during the Smethwick by-election she appealed to the electors to call her 'plain Mrs. Mosley.' In fact the Chairman at one of her meetings, with that inverted snobbery which is characteristic of the Labour Party,

The Character of Labour-Socialism | 41

once introduced her with the proud observation: 'She is just plain Mrs. Mosley to us.' Despite the fact that she was advertised on all posters announcing meetings, etc., by her ordinary name throughout the election, the Press persisted in saying that she appealed to her audiences to address her as plain Mrs. Mosley. In the same category of Press invention was the story that her husband said he would renounce his title, etc. The Mosleys' attitude was an invariable refusal to discuss a question dear to the frivolous heart of our snob-bound Press, which to them had no importance in relation to the serious subjects in which they were interested.

They have, however, a certain significance in that they indicate the sense of potential power which Oswald Mosley, at that date, had already impressed upon his contemporaries. They were, in fact, frightened, and the measure of their fury was the measure of their fear. It was no new thing for members of the aristocracy, nor for wealthy men—men far wealthier than Oswald Mosley—to join the ranks of Labour. This recruiting of the upper *bourgeoisie* to Labour was a particular phenomenon of the post-war period, a phenomenon which surprised the German Socialist, Egon Wertheimer, in his suggestive *Portrait of the Labour Party*. The facility with which men of such undoubted integrity as Lord Haldane and Lord Chelmsford reconciled their Liberal-bourgeois outlook with the policy of the Labour Party is no doubt explained by the fact that the Labour Party in Britain was never a party of social revolution, and, in fact, hardly a Socialist Party, even in theory. Its intellectual background was a continuation of the Liberal-reformist philosophy of the nineteenth century, with all its easy optimism and all its unreasoning belief in the ultimate efficacy of democratic methods to achieve the economic emancipation of the people. Labour thought had, too, a strong strain of Nonconformist religiosity which contrasted strangely with the intense materialism of the Continental Marxists. Its repudiation of philosophic materialism became complete when it was reinforced by the powerful Roman Catholic vote of the Midlands and the Clyde, which introduced into Labour representation those sentiments of passivistic conservatism with which it had formerly imbued the Liberals. The support of the trade unions brought with it a limited realism which was intent on the attainment of immediate economic concessions—themselves insignificant in scope. The trade unions never became revolutionary, nor sought to be, and they were shocked and horrified when a man of the calibre of the late A. J. Cook called out their members, behind their backs, to participate in a General Strike. The trade union leaders thought in terms of the Liberal tradition, and they had, in fact, never emancipated themselves from the slogan of "cheap food" with which the Liberals of an earlier generation had originally directed the revolutionary enthusiasm of Chartism into channels useful to themselves. Labour had recruited a number of ordinary bourgeois "careerists"—particularly from the legal profession—and a number of Liberals, who had foreseen the fate of Liberalism rather earlier than their own leaders, but it had also admitted to influence within its ranks such undoubtedly sincere adherents of pure Socialism as the Buxtons and Sir Charles Trevelyan. In commenting on this phenomenon Wertheimer remarks:

> Without entering into the controversy that rages about them, I would say that far from these men having weakened the Socialist character of the movement, it is they who have given new life and impulse to the Socialist side of the agitation. For them, in contrast to those trade union leaders become sceptic, this newly-discovered Socialism is not a remote ideal, but a standpoint from which to judge every aspect of the daily economic and political struggle. (*Portrait of the Labour Party*, pp. 148-9.)

Such was the Labour Party into which Oswald Mosley passed four years after he had left the Tory Party and had crossed the floor of the House as an Independent. Neither its composition nor its policy in office were particularly inspiring to a young idealism, but it must be realized that the spirit of the Labour machine—in all its genteel servility, its scepticism and its nervous incompetence—was as different from the raw, and often revolutionary, enthusiasm of the mass of its supporters as was cynical cosmopolitanism of the Tory management from the lucid and devoted Nationalism of the Tory rank and file. And Mosley felt the inspiration of a movement that had grown out of the mighty effort of hundreds of thousands of nameless workers, the appeal of a mass heroism "that in its very dumbness is moving."

John Scanlon, a Clydeside shipyard-worker of the extreme Left, writes with sympathy of "the tragedy" of Oswald Mosley, in his book *The Decline and Fall of the Labour Party*:

So far as Mr. Mosley was concerned, I feel sure that his motives were of the highest. Just as Mr. Oliver Baldwin in his book describes how he left his own class because he realized their futilities and joined the Labour Party because he believed they were different, I feel sure that these also were the motives of Mr. Mosley. But if he came in believing that here was a great democratic force struggling for freedom because they believed in the dignity of the working class, he must soon have been cured of that illusion. (*Decline and Fall of the Labour Party*, p. 182.)

Mosley, in an article addressed to his constituents in April, 1924, proclaimed in ringing tones the two alternatives which seemed to confront his generation:

The fight of the future, will be no sham fight, but a struggle of grim reality upon the result of which may depend the fate of millions. In all countries the forces involved are mustering to the fight. Two distinct and conflicting mentalities are preparing to battle for the mastery of the world:

The mind of progress, inspired to great exertions by the agonies which surround it, infused by the grandeur of belief in the destiny of man, and determined at all hazards to win through to a nobler order of the world.

The mind of reaction, confronting with gloomy and inert pessimism the pain and squalor that it believes to be inherent in human nature, dismissing with derisive laugh the idealistic vision of a more human and splendid future... (*Middlesex and Bucks Advertiser*, 18th April, 1924.)

Years later, in May, 1929, Mosley contributed to *The Labour Magazine* an article entitled "From Tory to Labour," in which he attempts to give some account of his psychological transformation during the first five years of his political life:

I entered Parliament in 1918, as a Coalition candidate, a member of the conservative Party, but a follower and admirer of Mr. Lloyd George. That statesman had stated in incomparable language the practical conceptions and the higher aspirations of the war generation. No man before or since has ever so entirely captured the imagination of Young Britain—or more completely betrayed it. We came back from the war with a great determination. We were determined that the world should never again suffer what we had suffered; we were determined that as a result of that suffering Britain should be roused from the torpor of a century to build the finest civilization mankind had ever known... We were concerned only to build a new and nobler world on the ashes of the old. We held ourselves as a generation set apart by a great ordeal and consecrated to a mighty task...

That was the temper in which we approached the problems of the post-war world. You may search in vain my election address of 1918 for any mention of reparations or of 'hanging the Kaiser.' You will find instead, great schemes of social reform and ruthless Socialist measures, designed to cut through the great vested interests to the reconstruction of Britain. High wages and shorter hours as the bases of a prosperous home market; transport and electricity 'controlled and developed by the State'; housing schemes carried out by the community; the abolition of slums and back-to-back houses; the compulsory acquisition of necessary land; educational facilities from the cradle to the university; drastic schemes for health and child welfare; these were the proposals of my election address. Not far short of this was the programme of Mr. Lloyd George and the Coalition leaders at the outset of the campaign. It was not until a few days before the poll, in his famous Bristol speech that he surrendered to the reparation clamour. It was his first great surrender—the first of many.

You may be surprised that on a programme, in effect as Socialistic as that which the Labour Party now advances, I was adopted by a Conservative Association and returned by a majority of nearly 11,000 by a Conservative constituency. That was the temper of the times. The young men, the new men, the men of the war, were in charge. Not until we got to Westminster and the old games did the old men resume the reins. The first shock was the first sight of our colleagues. The young men were in a minority and the 'hard-faced men' were in a great majority. The profiteer outnumbered the fighter...

At home no attempt was made to use the great machine of war for the greater purposes of peace... The productive machine so painfully and laboriously erected was scrapped or sold at knock-down prices to the profiteers. Abroad, the tragedy of Versailles was in full swing. Spurred forward by a shower of minatory telegrams from the 'hard-faced men,' Mr. Lloyd George produced his final masterpiece of European ruin. Everything for which we fought—peace abroad and reconstruction at home—was thrown to the wolves of the great vested interests...

That was enough for me and at the opening of the Autumn Session of 1920 I crossed the floor to take my place as an Independent on the Labour benches. Then, so far as I was concerned, the storm burst. My rising in debate evoked at once a howl of abuse from the 'hard-faced men.' The great barrage descended to prevent other 'class traitors' crossing over to the trenches of the enemy. I was at first very much surprised at the fury of my reception in the House and in the Press. My opening speeches in opposition were rather gentle protests against what seemed to me an extraordinary and temporary aberration of my class and party. I had very speedily, in self-defence, to develop a certain ferocity in debating method, for which I have since been much blamed, as relying unduly on satire, invective, and the more brutal methods of controversy. Without those weapons, I could not have survived. It is a 'wicked animal which defends itself when attacked,' but it was only by assailing with personal ridicule the noisiest of my assailants that I could get a hearing at all. It was not until years later that I could advance a reasoned argument in the House of Commons without first beating down the interruptors by such methods. However, those were good Parliamentary days. We of the small band of Opposition spoke every night against a record majority and an extraordinary array of Ministerial talent in debate... It was grand practice! Having survived it, I do not regret it!

... Soon after I crossed the floor, the Coalition and the Conservative Party finally surrendered to the great interests. The workers encountered the full shock of their Deflation Policy... The last great illusions of the war were lost. Bonar Law and a pure Tory Government were returned to power, 'not on a policy but on a yawn.' Lethargy was to be the balm for England's wounds...

I honestly believe that I hold much the same broad opinions as when I entered Parliament in 1918. Inevitably one learns in more than a decade something more of economics and of life. A man who boasts that he has passed a lifetime without changing an opinion, boasts that he has lived his life without learning anything. But, substantially, my opinions are the same that I held and that the country supported in 1918. Yet I have occasionally been called an extreme influence in the Labour Party. We were all 'extremists' in the sense that we wished to get things done, until the young grew tired and the old ways and the old men crept back. My fear is not that the Labour Party will do more than a united nation demanded ten years ago. My fear is rather that in the face of the united opposition they will encounter, they will not do as much.

Mosley's last sentence might well be taken as the text, not only for the history of the movement which he had joined, but of the whole Social Democratic movement throughout Europe. It is not our purpose here to consider at any great length the reasons why the European Social Democratic movement has not only failed to achieve that peaceful transformation of society which it offered as a substitute for revolution, but has failed also to maintain even those economic and political advantages which the workers had managed to wrest from the capitalists, before Social Democracy attempted to assume the leadership which it has so signally betrayed. Two recent books, Strachey's *Coming Struggle for Power* and Scanlon's *Decline and Fall of the Labour Party*, have been devoted to a detailed and pessimistic examination of those causes which are alleged to have occasioned the debilitation of the Labour-Socialist movement in England. The hysteria of democratic propagandists of the type of Professor Laski can hardly disguise the fact that it is not Fascist violence, but the angry disillusion of the people, which has brought about the collapse of the Social Democratic Parties and of democratic institutions in general in Italy and Germany. Lastly, Mr. Trotsky, with the unsurpassed brilliance of his dialectic, has analysed, in his *History of the Russian Revolution* and other works, the historical and psychological causes which trepanned the Social Democrats of Russia.

We can only interpret the failure of the British Labour-Socialists *to achieve change*, by reverting to our consideration of the bourgeois mind, which we have defined as the psychological expression of the capitalist state of society. "Without learning from the masses there can be no revolutionary statesmanship," writes Trotsky, but it was not from the masses that Labour had learnt, nor wished to learn, but from that bourgeois society of which political Labour was itself a part. The leaders of the modern British Labour movement were themselves petty bourgeois, and in their youth they had all of them been infected with the inhibitions of Liberal and Nonconformist bourgeois thought. "They seldom saw workmen," says Scanlon, "except from platforms. They lived middle-class lives and took their impressions from middle-class people." They were thoroughly representative of the orthodox ideas of bourgeois Liberalism, and if they pretended to adhere to the economics of Marx, they were appalled by the political methodology of Lenin or of Mussolini—or for that matter of Collins and Griffiths. They were bourgeois most essentially in that they were "men of the mind," sedentary men, not "men of the hand"—"fact men," like the workers and the soldiers who have built big changes in Italy, in Russia, and in Germany. The typical bourgeois ideals of "liberty," "freedom of speech" and "law and order" had saturated their soft bodies. Most characteristic of all, perhaps, is the emphasis laid by these talkers on "freedom of speech" as the fundamental foundation of all political action. They whined for "gradualness," which was the echo only of the professedly bourgeois Mr. Baldwin's pathetic plea for "safety first." Never the tittering laugh of Lenin, never the grim soldier's humour of Mussolini, never the boyish drive of Collins, could rouse these careful British bourgeois to the great ecstasy of action. "The policies of a revolutionary government ought never to offend anybody unnecessarily," said the lawyer Demianov, an important official in the Ministry of Kerensky. "It is always a mistake in politics to provoke catastrophe, for if one avoids it, whatever turns up is bound to be better than the catastrophe one might have precipitated," is the answer of Mr. A. L. Rowse to the question: "Where Stands Socialism To-day?"

According to the Clydesider Scanlon, MacDonald had already begun, before the war, to divert the Labour movement into the channels of bourgeois orthodoxy. Not for him were the crude "cloth-cap" politics of Hardie, with the old Chartist flavour that they had about them. "Mr. MacDonald had other ideas. He moulded his style, not on Keir Hardie, but rather on Gladstone and the other great political leaders." Mr. Scanlon continues:

> Whatever else the Parliament of 1923 was, it was not the Parliament conceived by Hardie and the pioneers. They had conceived of a body of strong, dignified, self-reliant, intelligent working men entering Parliament, proud because they were workers who knew and felt the struggles of the working class, and because they knew and felt the struggle, were alone capable of ending it. They understood the injustice of the capitalist system because they had suffered under it; they understood its futilities because they had studied and believed there was a better system. (*Decline and Fall of the Labour Party*, p. 42.)

Mr. Scanlon goes on to show, in his entertaining book, how a party which was psychologically bourgeois proceeded to merge itself in the bourgeois world of Parliamentary politics. Economically the individuals who made up the Parliamentary Labour Party were, of course, by no means all of middle-class origin. But the mind of the Party was bourgeois in the sense in which we have defined the term, and they were proceeding to implement the bourgeois political tradition in an atmosphere which was the very home and breeding-ground of the bourgeois philosophy of life. It is not to be wondered at, in view of its composition and environment, that the Party found its political activities directed into strictly "constitutional" channels, but it is at least rather pathetic that the individual members of the party should have succumbed so easily to the attractions of a society which they had spent their lives in denouncing, and into which they had been elevated by the efforts of their followers in order that they might "revolutionize" if not destroy it. Mr. Scanlon recalls that:

> Mr. Winston Churchill was able to state, with obvious satisfaction and with truth, that those who believed that they had fashioned a machine for working-class emancipation had only succeeded in building a ladder by which men climbed to place and power.

There was a majority who did not climb so far, and who found themselves late in life apeing the manners of a world of which they had

always been instinctively the unrecognized members.
Again, Mr. Scanlon:

> It must be remembered that the bulk of Labour members were men who had gained administrative experience on municipal work or in their trade union or co-operative society... In Parliament, however, experience in these things counts for little. Members had to be taught how to bow and the number of times to bow when they entered and left the Chamber. They had to be taught when to speak with a hat on and with it off, and there were also terrible dangers lurking in the path of any member who addressed another as an honourable gentleman when that gentleman was, in fact, a right honourable gentleman or honourable and gallant. Nor must they say 'Hear, hear,' in moments of emotion, but instead must make a noise which sounded like 'Hah.' Until these accomplishments had been acquired the leaders felt that the world would never be safe for democracy, and so Professor Lees Smith was brought to the House and a class in deportment was formed. (*Decline and Fall of the Labour Party*, p. 65.)

Such was the party in which Oswald Mosley was destined to spend the next six years of his political life. He entered the party full of high hopes and great visions. He had yet to learn that he was engaging not in "the fight of the future," but in the most shameful sort of "sham fight." Egon Wertheimer heard Mosley speak, not long after he had assumed his new allegiance:

> Then the new man spoke; what he said remained for me—who at that time, dictionary in hand, was endeavouring to tear its secret from a leading article in *The Times*—for the most part darkling and unintelligible. But all the more unforgettable was the impression, the visual and oral impression, which the style of this speech made upon me. It was a hymn, an emotional appeal, not to the intellect, but to the Socialist idea, which obviously was still a subject of wonder to the orator, a youthful experience. (*Portrait of the Labour Party*, p. ix.)

The coming years were to bring Mosley defeat, the abortion of effort,

50 | Chapter III

and a bitter disillusion. At the end of those years, when the great adventure of the New Party had ended in disaster, and Oswald Mosley was faced with the prospect of political extinction, he could write:

> We are going to keep a little powder for the day when we need it most. Our time will come, and even if it should never come, we shall yet have been right to have done what we have done and will have no regrets at our decision. *Better the great adventure, better the great attempt for England's sake, better defeat, disaster, better far the end of that trivial thing called a Political Career than stifling in the uniform of Blue and Gold, strutting and posturing on the stage of Little England, amid the scenery of decadence, until history in turning over an heroic page of the human story writes of us the contemptuous postscript*—'These were the men to whom was entrusted the Empire of Great Britain, and whose idleness, ignorance and cowardice left it a Spain.' We shall win: or at least we shall return upon our shields. (Last number of *Action*.)

The comment of the Social Democrats upon their own defeat at the end of these same events is scarcely less characteristic. It is quoted from the recent volume *Where Stands Socialism To-day?* which was published to set out the official attitude of the Socialist Party in the year 1933.

"We may have been ineffective; but we have been on the right track all the time. Make no mistake about that." (*Where Stands Socialism To-day?*, p. 98.) The italics are their own.

Chapter IV

—Mosley Emerges—

So far as it is legitimate—for purposes of practical clarity—to divide the complicated and unending process of psychological and economic interactions known as history into clear-cut periods, it may be said that the ten years which intervened between the close of the German War and the first sharp jerk to the neck of the capitalist-bourgeois world in the financial crisis of 1929 constituted such a period. This period was characterized by the failure of the principal capitalist world-powers—America, Great Britain and France—to recognize the nature of the crisis through which the whole modern system of society was passing to its inevitable and inescapable end. "The war to make the world safe for democracy" had, in fact, revealed with tragic emphasis the fundamental economic fallacies upon which capitalist society—and democratic institutions as the political expression of that society—were based. The war marked the final failure of democracy to evolve a viable foundation for human relations, and the fact that a purely military and economic victory was proclaimed as a great triumph of the democratic theory was as illustrative of the incorrigible fatuity and ignorant complacency of bourgeois-capitalist thought as was the conception of "a return to normalcy" which epitomized the policies of the governing classes in the three great capitalist countries during the ten years immediately following the conclusion of armed hostilities.

The peoples of the three Western democracies were unfortu-nate in that very strength of their economic mechanisms which saved them from being confronted by the violent crises which overtook their weaker neighbors. Russia had gone first, and Russia was the weakest link in the chain-net of world-capitalism. The first impact of modern war had been sufficient to undermine the unbalanced edifice of her new national capitalism, and her democratic institutions, stillborn and immature as they were, were washed down the drain of social revolution. Germany—one of the strongest units in world-capitalism—had suffered a military defeat, and was destined to go through a process of desperate mauling by her adversaries before the Nazi Revolution broke through the ruins of the capitalist state to overthrow the flimsy idols of democracy. The policy towards Germany of the advocates of a "return to normalcy" is the best historical indication of the disintegrating character of the forces inherent in bourgeois-capitalist society—forces which make it mathematically impossible for that society to preserve itself. The attempts to smash Germany as a unit of national capitalism, and at the same time to retain it as an organic part of a capitalist world-whole, would appear to be motives of policy which were mutually exclusive, and yet they form the principal theme of Allied policy during the years following the war. It was obviously in the vital interests of the bourgeois-capitalist system—regarded as an international framework within which national inter-relations were to continue to be conducted—to adapt policies in such a way as to nurture and preserve their own opposite numbers in Germany—those bourgeois-democratic elements who had assumed power with the attainment of the Weimar Constitution. German democracy was always a weed—and an unnatural one at that—and it could not long stand the vicious spraying of French policy. The French, in fact, deliberately destroyed the only political system in Germany, which might have collaborated in the preservation of the existing capitalist-economic and social-democratic political system of Europe. In Italy the situation was different. Here was a power which had emerged victorious from the war, but her strength as a national capitalist unit was by no means so great as that of the other Western democracies, placed firm on great reserves of national wealth and foreign investment. The political class in Italy, who had, it is true, a long tradition of action and government behind them, were unable either to restore the balance of the capitalist machine or to sustain confidence in the normal institutions of democracy. There was to be no protracted attempt to "return to normalcy" for the Giolittis, the Nittis and the Factas of Italy. The old men faltered on their unsure way. Young and insurgent forces rose out of the streets, and had, within four years of the end of the war, pushed them out of power and begun to make an end of democratic institutions within the Kingdom of Italy.

The three Western democracies not only weathered the first post-war phase of the crisis in Capitalism, but their primary institutions remained unchallenged and no movements developed to capture, by force, the accepted organs of political power. It was a bad time for the young manhood of those three countries. In Russia, in Italy and in Germany, the war generations—each in their several ways—were seizing, or had seized, the mastery of their own destinies. For better or for worse, the older men, who had been responsible for the making of the pre-war world and who had let it slide to its ultimate agony, these older men had been flung aside, and were attending, in impotent prostration, the painful preparation of a new and mighty drama, the very theme of which was strange and alien to the temper of the bourgeois mind. In America, in Britain and in France the setting was quite different. The older institutions had withstood a desperate strain, the old governing classes had kept their power. Men, by their own bland subtleties, explained the triumphant changes which they saw transforming the whole life of lands beyond their own borders, as changes which had no relation to the problems with which they themselves were faced. They set themselves to "return to normalcy"—to get back to the old conditions which they thought that they understood so well. The post-war period became, therefore, quite definitely an era of the old men in all three of the great Western democracies. Young men came to be excluded from dynamic activities which might have rallied them as the war had rallied them, because the forces of "normalcy" were too strong for them, and they failed to take their part in an effort to attain a "stability" which touched no chord of the corporate consciousness of their generation. This state of things—this spiritual abortion of the post-war generation—was productive of what was assumed to be a "decadence" in the youth of the post-war years, and which was proclaimed as such by their self-satisfied elders. In Britain the young men and women of the middle classes, living in a period of personal economic uncertainty, and finding outlets neither for their energies nor for their emotions, were diverted into avenues of self-indulgence and eroticism, which have provided material for the mass of decadent literature which mirrors a "decadent" phase of national life. The cocktail-shaker became the symbol of a generation which had found self-expression neither in the Fasces nor in the Hammer and Sickle, and "bottle-parties'" absorbed the energies of potential StormTroop leaders. The fate of the young men and women of the working classes was worse, if only because they were deprived of the shabby joys and tinsel occupations which made endurable the individual lives of their more fortunate fellows. Thrown upon a labour market, where they found scarcely ever less than two million people competing for the jobs which they themselves were seeking, they dropped into the dreary life of the unemployed queues, and waited for the pittance which was to keep them alive as the unused and unneeded slaves of a system which could find for them no useful functions to perform. Even the steerage-passages which, in more prosperous times, it had been the habitual practice of British Capitalism to offer to the sons of its workers, were not now made available, and in the mournful streets of the great industrial cities a well-paid police—with its proverbial good humour—was ready to steer young workers from the pursuit of revolution to the pursuit of the electric hare.

The methods which in each country were adopted in order to achieve a "return to normalcy" were, in each case, quite characteristic of the country concerned. While England sought above all a financial stability which should ensure the restoration of the traditional dominance of the City of London in international finance, America developed a policy of credit expansion, which it was thought might achieve a state of permanent prosperity for capitalist industry. The British deflationary policy began to debilitate the whole economic life of the country from the moment that it was initiated, and the slow strain was dragged out to the final snapping of the strands in 1931. As is now generally recognized, it was a policy which favoured the owner of wealth as against the creator of wealth—whether the latter were the wage-earners or their actual employers, the men of enterprise. The American policy of credit expansion favoured the businessman and for some years the wage-earner also, but owing to the failure of the modern capitalist state to evolve a mechanism for the control of speculative activities, credit was used extensively for the purpose of gambling in the probable results of creative effort, with the inevitable effect that the tendency of production to outrun the capacity to consume received a stimulus which culminated in the severe financial crises of 1929 and succeeding years. While the British had been slowly contracting consumption and hence ultimately production for certain reasons of financial policy, the Americans had committed the cardinal error of unduly expanding production without giving any scientific attention at all to the problem of expanding consuming capacity to meet the increased production. In the unregulated chaos of American economic life it had been left to the fortuitous conditions of high wages and such devices as hire-purchase to maintain a balance, the need for which appears scarcely even to have been understood by the leaders of American political life.

In France, where the conception of the national state had always been more developed than in Britain or America, and where the forces of an uncontrolled Capitalism had never been given such free play, a policy had been adopted which elevated the purely political interests of France above all other considerations. The *rentier*—in spite of the powerful influence which he possessed owing to the widespread ownership of capital in France—was ruthlessly sacrificed—and the French then proceeded to consolidate their power on the Continent of Europe, by the accumulation of a great hoard of gold, and by quite unscrupulous financial pressure against the more orthodox capitalist countries. It may at least be said that French policy set the national interests of France before the financial interests of any particular class, and the healthy spread of small property within the economic structure of France allowed them to enter the final stages of the crisis of Capitalism without suffering those dramatic occasions which have befallen their neighbours. But just as in internal policy they set the interests of France before the interests of the *rentier*, so in international politics they have set the interests of their country before those of Capitalism as a whole, and to the extent that the interests of France may be said to be bound up in the maintenance of a system of relations which has grown out of the post-war structure of international Capitalism, to that extent will France prove ultimately to have suffered from the policy pursued. The Continental policy of the two Napoleons is certainly an anachronism in the conditions of modern Europe—even although that anachronism may have dominated the political history of Europe during the last fifteen years—and as a national French policy it can hardly be expected to be able to survive the fundamental transformations through which Europe is now passing. But French bourgeois democracy has always been a convenient facade behind which the Frenchman clings pertinaciously to those ideals which have always been peculiar to himself. A country is not unfortunate which prefers its destinies to be directed by the officers of its General Staff rather than by the partners in its finance-houses, and as the scene shifts the French will probably adapt themselves to the conditions of a new economy with less discomfort and with more grace than certain other countries. Whether they will accept with the same ease the international modifications implicit in these changes is more doubtful.

It has been necessary to summarize at some length a view of the broad tendencies in the three great Western democracies during the ten years of the immediate post-war phase, in order to gain perspective for the consideration in more detail of the political field in Britain, and of the preparatory role which Oswald Mosley was playing during those crucial years. In the Labour Party, Mosley participated to the full in the protracted and wearisome rear-guard action which was being conducted against the financial and industrial policy of the Conservative Party. This fight was the most spectacular part of his activities during this period, although it had, in effect, ceased to be more than a demonstration, since the Socialists had capitulated to Tory strategy as early as 1924, when Mr. Snowden, very shortly after his appointment to the Exchequer, had declared that he "was guided by the Report of the Cunliffe Committee." (*Hansard*, Vol. 170, Col. 706.) In this laconic phrase was announced the complete surrender of Social Democracy in England to the powerful encirclement of capitalist finance, a surrender of all revolutionary intent as complete—though less dramatic—as the occasion upon which Ebert and Scheidemann called in the generals to protect them from the anger of a Spartacist mob. Of Snowden's surrender Mosley was to write later:

> At the time of the appointment of the Colwyn Committee I asked Mr. Snowden that its terms of reference should include the relation to the debt question of the general policy of deflation recommended by the Cunliffe Committee. This was peremptorily refused, as the Labour Chancellor was "guided by the Report of the Cunliffe Committee." Yet the Cunliffe policy of deflation has been responsible for nearly doubling the real burden of the national debt... Acute deflation with the object of returning to the gold standard at pre-war parity has been the policy of this country since the war, in pursuance of the recommendations of the Cunliffe Committee. Deflation, in fact, achieves its object through the creation of unemployment. Credit is restricted and industry slowed up. By this process a surplus of unemployed is created which competes for jobs and thus helps to reduce the wages of those in employment. By the reduction of wages the internal price level is reduced and the foreign exchange forced up until the objective of pre-war parity is reached. The falling price level entails a steady history of industrial losses and bankruptcies. Every manufacturer has to

buy his raw material and labour in a higher price level than that in which he sells the finished product. Consequently they draw in their horns and wait for prices to touch bottom, with the result of trade stagnation... Yet in the concluding phase of a policy which, in the opinion not only of Socialists but of most modern economists, has doubled the burden of the national debt, has forced the two greatest industrial struggles of history upon the workers, and has entailed unparalleled wage reductions, Mr. Philip Snowden wrote in the *Financial Times* of 23rd December, 1926: "Eighteen months' experience of the operation of the gold standard has not brought the disastrous consequences which some people feared..." The adherence of the Labour Chancellor to the Cunliffe recommendations and the gold standard objective has throughout prevented the great crime of Toryism in the creation of unemployment and the reduction of wages being fully brought home to its authors. Labour was not guilty of this crime, but the attitude and commitments of our financial pundits made it difficult to challenge Tory policy effectively and to drive home the lesson in the country. Another example of this difficulty can be found so late as the Debate on the Treasury Vote, 27th June, 1927, when Mr. Graham made the statement in answer to Mr. Churchill's cross-examination that he was "an enthusiastic supporter of the gold standard." Mr. Churchill followed up this admission with the sardonic observation that the right hon. gentleman is now "nailed securely to the cross of gold." (Mosley, "The Labour Party's Financial Policy," in the *Socialist Review*, September, 1927.)

During the five years between 1924 and 1929 Mosley had quickly advanced towards the leadership of the more vigorous sections of opinion within the Labour Party. His great election fights at Ladywood and Smethwick had made history, and everywhere he went, either as an exponent of Socialist theory or as a protagonist in the long fight against wage reductions, he was hailed by excited and enthusiastic crowds. "He was one of the most brilliant and hopeful figures thrown up by the Socialist movement during the last thirty years," was the verdict of John Wheatley two years after Mosley had joined the party (*Daily Herald*, 14th December, 1926). When the droll comedy of the Campbell case

Chapter IV

forced the first Labour Government into the General Election of 1924, Mosley went up to Ladywood to challenge the Chamberlains in their family stronghold. The correspondent of the Conservative *Birmingham Evening Dispatch* writes:

> He confessed to me that his idea in tackling Ladywood under the Labour Party banner was to endeavour to win a victory that *would* be a victory—a victory that would not merely give him a hardly-won seat in the House of Commons, but would entitle him to his spurs in the movement to which he is a recent convert. It is an open secret that on turning Labour, Mr. Mosley received over fifty invitations from divisional Labour parties to become Labour candidate. Of these fifty at least eight represented safe seats for him, and the majority were more promising from the Labour point of view than Ladywood. But Mr. Mosley chose Ladywood because it offered him a stern fight in the very stronghold of Chamberlainism against the most vital representative of that tradition. Among the candidatures offered to Mr. Mosley were many, of course, for mining divisions. "In a mining constituency, however," says Mr. Mosley, "I should merely have to address a meeting and then return on polling day to watch the voting. That is not my idea of a fight. Every convert to Labour or any other party should be required to win his spurs, and a hard battle at the polls is the real test." (*Birmingham Evening Dispatch*, 15th August, 1924.)

The result of the contest was one of the most amazing in the whole history of English election fights, as recounts an eye-witness:

> The count was certainly the most exciting political experience I remember. They counted and recounted from 9 p.m. to 5 a.m. First Chamberlain was in by two, then Mosley in by two, then Chamberlain in by seven. Thus the fortunes fluctuated until it was decided to put the whole of the votes back *en bloc* and start entirely afresh. This resulted in Chamberlain obtaining a majority of seventy-seven, but most of those present felt that the counting was not entirely satisfactory. During the whole of this time, eight hours, the air was split with cries, songs, cheering, etc., from the supporters of every party in the gallery.

At the end there was question of the expensive process known as a "judicial scrutiny," but Mosley would have none of that, saying:

> I do not think it right, in the present state of Labour finances, to have a great sum of money expended on one seat. I think it is definitely wrong to spend a large sum of money on one seat... Whatever happens on this occasion it must be unsatisfactory. A long delay and drawn-out process through the Law Courts, if it gives us the seat in the end, is not so satisfactory as a straight win on the night of the poll.

And so it was left.

Neville Chamberlain got away with a majority of seventy-seven, but he was careful, at the next election, to abandon the family seat at Ladywood for the more salubrious middle-class atmosphere of Edgbaston. So, although Mosley had not won the seat, he had been successful in chasing the Chamberlains out of Ladywood, and that in itself was no mean triumph. But to secure the vote he did, in a Conservative stronghold, at an election when Labour was losing seats all over the country, was a great personal victory which entrenched him in the goodwill of the rank and file of the whole movement. When two years later, in the autumn of 1926, Mosley went up to Smethwick to contest the by-election there, his campaign became at once an event of national importance. The whole enthusiasm of the working class was behind their protagonist in the first important by-election after the General Strike, and all the venom of the capitalist Press was directed against the man who was regarded as at once a traitor and a menace to the capitalist class. "Oswald Mosley," wrote Mr. H. C. Charleton, M.P., in the *Railway Review*, "is the man whom the Tories hate more than any other man on our benches," and *Truth* observed, during the election:

> I suppose that Mr. Mosley expected little mercy from the party he left when he went over to Socialism. But he can hardly have expected the vicious personal attacks that are being made on him in the anti-Labour section of the London Press. If I were an elector of Smethwick, this sort of thing would certainly lead me to vote Socialist... The limit seems to have been reached by the *Daily Express* when it persuaded Sir Oswald Mosley to take a hand in the campaign against his son by means of an

interview... as political ammunition Mosley Senior seems to be what used to be called at the front a dud. So far as the *Daily Express* is concerned he has shaped rather like a boomerang. (15th December, 1926.)

The same process occurred when the mild and devoted Oliver Baldwin became a Socialist, and it is indicative not only of the vindictive vulgarity which is to be expected from Press lords, but of the contemptible methods to which those responsible for the working of the Tory machine are prepared to sink so soon as they become either frightened or incensed. As it was, the electors of Smethwick passed their verdict on Press "barracking" by giving Oswald Mosley the handsome majority of 6,582. As Mosley subsequently commented:

> This election has made history—it has been a combat between Labour and Pressocracy, over which Labour has triumphed. Democracy has refused to believe the dope poured out by scores of newspapers in the hands of two or three Press millionaires.

So soon as he was back in the House of Commons, Mosley threw himself with renewed strength into the fight against the financial and industrial policy of the Government. During the long-drawn-out mining crisis in 1925 and 1926 he had spoken at many meetings. He said at Liverpool in October, 1925:

> It is the Government's financial juggling, and the forcing up of the exchange that has hit the industry... We are told that we could successfully compete with foreigners if they (the miners) would accept smaller wages. Directly this is done in this country the same would happen in other countries... By the stand the miners took they saved not only England, but they saved the workers of the world. They had the economic sense to realize that if they took the first precipitatory step, down would come the whole fabric of civilization.

In another speech at Carlisle during the same month he emphasized the wide implications which would follow the success of the policy to reduce wages:

The Tories denounced the organized workers as Bolsheviks, just because they refused to sell their labour at a price which meant starvation to themselves and families. A reduction of wages would not even put industry on its feet, as the Tories claimed. The reduction of wages would only take away from the workers power to buy goods, and this was the mad, suicidal tactics international capitalism invited them to embark upon.

In the Budget Debate of April, 1927, it was left to Mosley to deliver the principal attack on the financial policy outlined by Mr. Winston Churchill. He proceeded to analyze the results of the return to the gold standard, in terms which are generally recognized as valid to-day, even by that Chancellor who had been responsible for the development of the policy, but which were then regarded as new, and in many respects heretical, by such orthodox leaders of Labour economic thought as Mr. (now Viscount) Snowden and the late Mr. William Graham.

Having pointed out that the *rentier* class had benefited, according to the estimate of Mr. Keynes, to the extent of approximately £1,000,000,000 by the financial maneuvers of the Conservative Party, Mosley proceeded both to an analysis of the economic effects of deflation, and to a spirited defence of the miners against the insolent claim of the Chancellor that it was the mining crisis, and that alone, which was responsible for the declining state of the country's trade and the unsatisfactory position of the Budget.

It was the development of the home market—not by the obsolete methods of Tory Protection, but by sweeping and revolutionary methods "in accordance with the dictates of modern thought and the elementary postulates of human justice"—which Mosley now urged with all the determined energy of his character and all the insistence of his formidable oratory. In November, 1928, in the Debate on the King's Speech, he was still hammering this crucial issue before a House which was prepared neither to learn nor to move. In reference to unemployment, he said:

> All the old palliatives were produced with, perhaps, one additional palliative—the transfer of men from one district to another. We now have the extraordinary theory that if you take a man who is unemployed in Durham, and put him down in Birmingham, where there is considerable unemployment, you

are assisting the aggregate of employment if that man from Durham puts a man, who is in a job in Birmingham, out of that job. That is what it comes to. We are not increasing the aggregate of employment by a single man; we are merely putting one man out of a job to make room for another. Until you can expand your market, until you can increase your demand for goods, and thus increase the demand for labour, you have not begun to deal with the problem that confronts us... I believe that there are few things more fallacious than the conception of the right hon. member for West Swansea (Mr. Runciman). He seemed to think that the only criterion for British industry was the number of goods we could send abroad for foreigners to consume. That fallacy arises from this simple fact that we have got to export to buy the foodstuffs and raw materials we require, but need not export much in excess of that. In recent years we have exported sufficient to buy £300,000,000 worth of imported articles and to pile up in 1927 the favourable trade balance of £97,000,000 which was largely spent in creating industries abroad and which might better have been used to create them in the suffering districts of our own land. Of course, we have to maintain and stimulate our export trade, but do not let us make a fetish of export trade. Do not let us think it is the sole criterion of British prosperity. It is to the home market, therefore, and to the raising of wages and purchasing power that we must increasingly look, and we must, of course, anticipate some transfer of production from the export to the home trade. (*Hansard*, 8th November, 1928.)

Three weeks later, in a debate on the De-Rating Bill, Mosley returned to the problem of the home market, and to the "export fetish," with which at that time all parties in the House continued to be obsessed. He went on:

I believe, that in this instance the remedies proposed (under de-rating) are altogether ineffective. For instance, the Minister of Transport, speaking last night, claimed that the maximum benefit to coal from the reduction of railway rates amounted to 7½d. a ton, and I think it is agreed that the actual reduction in the overhead charges on coal itself, consequent upon colliery de-rating, does not amount to more than 3d.; so that at the very most you are saving some 10d. a ton to the coal trade, upon which trade, according to the estimate of the secretary of the Mining Association, Mr. Lee, you placed a burden of at least a shilling a ton by the return to the gold standard a year or two ago. But even if it be true that the assistance given to the export trade is material, I would point out to the party opposite this extraordinary conclusion to which their policy is now leading. It has always been the policy of the party opposite to tax the goods which the foreigner supplies to us. It is now the policy of the Conservative Party to subsidize the goods which we supply to the foreigner. I wonder what the hon. and gallant member for Bournemouth (Sir H. Page-Croft) thinks of this new-found philanthropy of the Conservative Party for the foreign consumer, this elaborate subsidy to our exports in order to supply the foreigner with a cheaper product.

At this point there was the usual sort of interruption with which the Tories were accustomed to greet any particularly penetrating analysis of their own mental processes by the hated member for Smethwick. Mosley was at last able to continue:

I would suggest, that, in a situation such as that with which we are now confronted, where we are exporting enough goods, not only to buy all the food and raw materials that we require, but also to import £300,000,000 worth of manufactured articles each year and to maintain a favourable trade balance of some £90,000,000 a year for foreign investments—I would suggest that, in a situation such as that, a subsidy to exports and to exports alone, which this measure amounts to, is not justified, and that really our problem is not to maintain and yet further to swell our totally artificial export trade of pre-war days, but rather to organize measures for the reconstruction and development of our home market, which are altogether lacking from the proposal that is now before us. (*Hansard*, 29th November, 1928.)

Mosley's exposure of the "export fallacy" was contrary to the doctrines of the financial pundits of the Labour Party—bred as they had been in

Chapter IV

the Liberal school of *laissez-faire* economics. He was already coming into conflict with the masters of the party machine, and raising against himself a hostility, which was first to attempt his exclusion from any position of influence or responsibility in a future Labour Government, and which later was to bring about the abortion of his work and of his conceptions of a Socialist policy of dynamic action. In 1925 he had already formulated drastic proposals for stimulating the consuming power of the home market in a pamphlet entitled *Revolution by Reason*.[2] Here, in reply to Mr. Baldwin's announcement that "all the workers of this country have got to face a reduction of wages," Mosley restated his own interpretation of the economic problem:

> The policy of wage reduction proves especially fatal in international competition. Wage reduction in Britain, resulting in lower competitive prices in the world markets, is inevitably encountered by wage reductions in other countries. The final frenzy of Capitalism sets in. The lower wages fall in their mad competition, the smaller becomes the market for which they are competing. By their competition they are destroying the very market for which they are striving. By reducing wages and so removing the workers' power to buy, they are destroying the capacity to purchase the goods which industry has to sell. Can any policy be more suicidal? Conservatism sometimes accuses us of "feeding the dog upon its tail." Their own policy reduces European civilization to the absurd position of a little dog chasing, but for ever failing even to catch, its own tail.

He was elaborating proposals for the scientific development of "consumers' credits," and he was careful to guard himself against the charge of inflationism:

> Such expansion of credit will not result in inflation. By inflation is meant an increase in the supply of money without an increase in the supply of goods. An increase in the supply of money accompanied by a corresponding increase in the supply of goods is not inflation.

---

[2] Later elaborated by John Strachey in a book under the same title.

Mosley then pursues this theme:

> Money in the hands of the workers means demand upon the great staple industries in which men and machines are now idle. It is a steady demand, a calculable demand which we can prepare to meet in advance. If this demand is allied to Socialist planning, we have assurance that goods will be produced to meet it, that inflation will not ensue and that prices will not rise... As already suggested, the great capitalist monopolies might refuse to respond to the new demand which we propose to create. They might restrict output and try to force a rise in price. Against them we could employ the economic power acquired by the workers in the socialization of the banks. We could do more. By the strategy of Socialism here adumbrated we should have forced the exploiter into an exposed and indefensible position. If Capitalism refused to respond to the demand thus created, we could proceed to summary socialization with overwhelming popular support. We should have called the great bluff of Capitalism. They cry: "Show us markets and we will serve the community." If, in fact, they strove not to serve but to exploit when markets were provided by the community, they would be convicted out of their own mouths. Summary socialization would be a much easier matter in respect of industries clearly convicted of anti-social conduct in face of a definite emergency and opportunity. In a recent and analogous case overwhelming popular support was forthcoming for summary measures of Socialism. The Bill introduced by Mr. Wheatley on behalf of the late Labour Government, to deal with profiteering in building materials, was one of the most popular measures ever introduced to Parliament.

Turning to orthodox Socialist theory in contrast to his own creative proposals, Mosley continues:

> We shall not find salvation in mere redistribution, although the process is vitally necessary in order to redress the tilted balance of industry and suppress the futility of luxury demand. The workers' position will only be greatly improved by an increase

in the net total of wealth production directed to working-class uses. When we have begun this major operation we shall have greater prospect of success in the minor attempt to transfer existing demand. This transfer of existing demand involves the closing down of luxury industry and the transfer of labour to useful industry. In the present enfeebled condition of the industrial body the shock would be severe. In a prosperous condition of full productivity the temporary dislocation would be more easily sustained. Then by the instrument of direct taxation existing income could be more easily diverted to social uses.

Mosley then proceeds to examine exchange problems in relation to his credit proposals:

By a fantastic inversion of the facts, it is asserted that the Birmingham proposals would cause a fall in the exchange and thereby would damage our export trade… If the exchange should fall from psychological reasons resulting from engineered panic, exports would not be handicapped, but, on the contrary, stimulated. If a fall in the exchange value of sterling was not accompanied by a rise in the domestic price level, exports would be assisted. If our measures to prevent price rise were at all successful, our export trade would be in an exceptionally favourable position. We should be faced with the exact reverse of the present situation, where the pound purchases more abroad than at home, with the result that imports are assisted and exports handicapped. If, on the contrary, the pound purchased more at home than abroad, exports would be stimulated and imports checked. But we need not enter at length into the dreary labyrinth of exchange. To do so is to mistake the shadow for the substance, a process dear to our present financial dictators. The exchange is not the body of industry, but merely the thermometer which registers the condition of that body. The Conservatives have triumphantly 'pegged' the thermometer, while leaving everything else to flux and chaos. They cry: "This is stability and health," while they have merely broken the instrument which records the state of the industrial body…

In reference to the current "export mania," he adds:

> By no means all our present imports represent foodstuffs and raw materials. We import completely manufactured articles to the value of £300,000,000 per annum, most of which could be made at home. Our essential supplies can be purchased by far less exports than are at present sent abroad. The natural revulsion from the crude fallacies of Protection has resulted in a fetish worship of the present dimensions of our export trade by minds which have just succeeded in grasping the elementary fact that we must export in order to import certain necessities which cannot be produced at home.

During the five years which elapsed between 1924, when he joined the Labour Party, and 1929, when he accepted office in the second Labour administration, Mosley had proceeded far beyond the orthodox canons of official Socialist thought. In 1927 he had given an emphatic lead to those sections of the Socialist Party who were becoming increasingly alarmed at the financial theories of Mr. Snowden.

"The ranks of the city are now divided." So he wrote in "The Labour Party's Financial Policy."

> The advanced section, headed by Mr. McKenna and Mr. Keynes, face the orthodox and reactionary ranks which are led by Mr. Montague Norman and the heads of the Treasury. To the uninitiated it thus seems a little unfortunate that the ex-Labour Chancellor should appear, judging from his article in the *Banker*, to be an ardent supporter of Mr. Montague Norman. It will be little less than a disaster if in this struggle Labour support is accorded to the reactionary elements in the city. It will certainly be a fantastic negation of the purposes of our party.

But if his financial proposals envisaged a dynamic departure from orthodox theory, his views on the development of Empire trade were no less shocking to those who had been weaned and bred in the Liberal tradition of Free Trade. For a long time official Labour policies had contained pious platitudes with regard to the Empire. Mosley proceeded to drag them into light and to give them the form of real proposals.

Chapter IV

Speaking in a debate on unemployment:

> Hon. members opposite talk a good deal about the Dominions, and I am very glad that they do, because, obviously, there is a possibility of a very large market for this country in the Dominions, but I suggest to them that we are asking the Dominions for something for nothing. There has been no Dominions policy since Joseph Chamberlain went down on his great Protectionist cry in 1906, and it is idle for hon. members opposite to pretend that the Tory party have got any policy of any kind. In 1924 they did not propose a tax on food. It was a tax on wheat and meat that alone was of any use to the Dominions. That went down in 1906, and nobody in this country has had the courage even to propose it since. In 1924 hon. members opposite had a different suggestion. They did, I believe, go so far as to suggest a tax on tinned lobster, but the Dominions in return suggested that the British Empire was too large an institution to be held together by something so frail as the grip of a lobster's claws.
> If I may get back to my main argument, I think we can all agree that it is the export of wheat, meat and wool which is of importance to our Dominions and that, if we want a market from them, we must take some measures to produce a market here for these staple products of theirs. What policy is there on the other side of the House? On this side of the House there is the approved and declared policy of the Labour Party to buy direct from the Dominions the staple food-stuffs and even raw materials, to enter into direct agreement with such bodies as the Co-operative Society of Canada, the Wheat Pool of Canada, for the bulk purchase of its commodities. That co-operative society controls to-day 70 per cent of the wheat produced by Canada. Canada exports about 300,000,000 bushels a year, and I believe our total imports are not much more than 250,000,000 bushels. By a policy such as that you can enter into direct negotiation and agreement with the main staple trades of the Dominions and, by doing so, can reduce instead of increasing the price of food in this country... There is only one Dominion policy and that is the policy of buying direct from the Dominions, a policy which gives them a market and gives us cheap food. That is the

only Dominion policy which now holds the field. (*Hansard*, 8th November, 1928.)

Mosley had entered the Labour Party, moved, perhaps, partly by the emotional appeal which the whole Labour movement seemed to offer to the young men of his generation, but mainly because he sought an avenue by which to approach the application of a new and dynamic policy of action to the problems of the nation. He was now coming near to the hour of his disillusionment, when the leaders of British Social Democracy walked cautiously to those seats of power, which it was their intention most carefully to retain.

Chapter V

—Mosley in the Second Labour Government—

It was, perhaps, that intuition which is the only true genius rather than a Machiavellian foresight which led Mr. Baldwin, in the spring of 1929, to relinquish the reins of government to Mr. MacDonald. Certainly in no election in British history has a great party made less attempt to win a majority than did the Conservatives when they went to the people on the dim credit of the De-Rating Act, and suggested that the nation should seek recovery in the cultivation of the broccoli. Mr. Baldwin of his kind is a genius, who rises superbly above the patent cynicism of a Giolitti, or the desperate wire-pulling of a von Papen, and as England has developed, probably to its highest potentiality the art of democratic government, so it has produced in the late evening of that art its most finished practitioner in Mr. Baldwin. The very fact that Mr. Baldwin does not begin to understand the economic and spiritual problems of the modern world, is the necessary basis for his direction of the last automatic maneuvers of self-preservation which are the inevitable reactions to the present of that order of society of which he is the supreme expression. Every small movement that he makes is perfect: he does not caper about in the aeroplanes of an alien generation like the exhibitionist MacDonald, nor does he indulge in the megalopolitan frolics of Lord Beaverbrook. He is redolent of England, and representative of all that was most lovable in the quiet English business-man of a period that is past. His genius is that he *is*, that it is not necessary for him to pretend. He is the perfect intuitive animal, and in his own environment his instinct is faultless. And the tragedy of Mr. Baldwin is that he has appeared at a period when England does not require to be conducted from 1890 to 1900, but must be led out of one epoch into another. The tragedy for England is that the genius of

Mr. Baldwin is of such a quality, that the country may continue to allow him to maneuver for too long.

In May, 1929, the political stage in England was set after the design of this very great producer, as it had been in 1922, in 1923, in 1924, and was to be in 1931. A professedly Socialist Government came into office, supported and maintained there by a Liberal Party, the basis of whose very tenets was about to suffer dramatic and complete destruction. A Conservative Opposition occupied the perfect strategic position of awaiting the impending failure of a Liberal-Labour majority to cope with the cumulative decline in the export trade and the resultant accentuation of the conditions of unemployment. On the premises of bourgeois-capitalist thought which the economists of all parties in the House accepted—Messrs. Snowden and Graham no less than Mr. Lloyd George and Sir Herbert Samuel—Mr. Baldwin was right, and he was destined to be proved to be right.

Since the complete collapse of Social Democracy in England—so dramatically emphasized by the failure of the Labour administration of 1929-31 in office—Socialists have been at pains to explain to themselves the failure of their party to carry out any parts of the policy of Socialism which their leaders had adumbrated for so long. Mosley had appreciated the contrast between Socialist promise and potential performance, before he took office in the Labour administration of 1929, and we shall return to an examination of the efforts which he made to rescue his colleagues from their determined destiny and to galvanize them into the reality of action. It is easy to philosophize after the event, and to find inevitable historical tendencies in events which at the moment presented all the intricacies of actuality. John Strachey, a Left critic of Labour-Socialism, has done this with effect in his analysis of the trends of post-war Social Democracy, in his book *The Coming Struggle for Power*:

> To anyone," he writes, "who has had personal contact with Labour leaders the idea that if another thirty or forty Labour members had been elected in 1929, thus securing a majority, the whole conduct of the Labour Government would have been transformed is grotesque. It is laughable to suppose that in that event Mr. MacDonald would have sprung forward, a British Lenin, and begun the gigantic and hazardous task of destroying British Capitalism and replacing it with a Socialist economy... None of this, however, was visible to the average British worker

who voted Labour. All he knew of Mr. MacDonald was that he was an imposing gentleman who came down to great Town Hall meetings and declared that he was in favour of Socialism. "So that's all right," said the worker; "he shall have my vote." True, there were no signs at all of Socialism when Mr. MacDonald, having got the votes, became Prime Minister. But, then, he didn't have a majority. And he always said that you have got to have a majority before you could begin to bring in Socialism. True, the local "Reds" say that Mr. MacDonald never meant "all that about Socialism," anyhow. But how can one tell that? Anyhow, he never had a majority, had he?'

The force of this argument for the workers, who, in the nature of things, cannot know the real intentions of their leaders, cannot be overestimated. Communist propaganda has hurled itself for these ten years past upon the hitherto impregnable rock of that great excuse—"Well, they never did have a majority, did they?" If, therefore, the election of another forty trade union officials to Parliament would have made no difference at all to the economic situation with which the Labour Government had to deal, it would have transformed the political situation. It would have destroyed the great excuse... Thus, in the case of a politically advanced nation like Great Britain, it can perhaps be laid down as one of the conditions for the existence of a Social Democratic party that it should never obtain a Parliamentary majority. (*The Coming Struggle for Power*, pp. 298, 303-4.)

Strachey is, of course, correct in his appraisal of the character of political Labour, but where he is mistaken—like so many intellectuals of his type, who lack any intimate awareness either of the life of the working class or indeed of life itself—is in his conception of the working class as an organic whole, having a functioning class-consciousness and definite class aims. A nation—which is an organic being—has, at times, an emotional mass-consciousness of its own. A crowd may have it for the half-hour or the half-day that it is in being. A class may have it only to the extent that that class is a "ruling" class, an organism of function, made up of a comparatively small number of individual units, with a developed intelligence of self-interest and a consciousness of community of object, and even then the majority of individuals forming that class act instinctively, and are inevitably under the direction of the minority among them who are possessed of political foresight and ability. When we speak of the "bourgeois class" we are, as has been stated earlier, speaking, in fact, of those strata of society who are benefiting under, and therefore endeavouring to maintain, the capitalist system of economics—the intellectual expression of which is the "bourgeois" state of mind. The "working class" in Britain is to this extent bourgeois itself, in that a large proportion of individuals within this class live and hope and dream in terms of the bourgeois state of mind. There is no revolutionary slave class, but a vast aggregation of individuals who have in part achieved the economic standards of the lower middle classes (ownership of shops, small house-properties, War Savings Certificates, etc.), or who aspire to achieve those standards. Even the organs of their economic and political self-consciousness, the trade unions and co-operative societies, have become typically capitalist structures managed by capitalist methods within the economic inhibitions of the capitalist system (i.e., the huge investments of the trade unions and co-operatives in "gilt-edged" investments naturally inclined them towards conservatism in finance). The fact that the "working class" cannot be regarded as a conscious integral whole is perhaps best illustrated in the truism that each political party has been dependent on a "working class" vote for the attainment of power. There is in fact no "great revolutionary working class" in Britain, and there never has been. Politics cannot become so simplified. There are certain active elements among the manual workers as well as among other sections of the nation who see the futility of reformism, and demand a vigorous effort to transform the whole social-economic system, and there are periods when some passing evil stampedes the anger of great masses of the population, but only in the emotional fashion in which war will stampede them in another direction. The Socialist party has, it is true, expressed revolutionary ideals in that "fantasy" sense which Strachey defines so well, but so has Liberalism in its time. The pompous dukes of the great Whig country houses of the eighteenth century lived on the glamour of the desultory *coup d'etat* which they called the "Glorious Revolution" of 1688, and the French attorneys and bourse operators of the Third Republic derive the same prestige from the events of 1789. In Italy, Poland and Spain and other Continental countries the connections between Liberalism and Revolution were at one time more valid.

The real revolutions of the nineteenth century were in fact the national renascence which Garibaldi and Cavour carried through in Italy, and the formation of the modern German Reich for which Bismarck was responsible. Both in Italy and in Germany *things were different* after these two great historical processes had been completed, and therefore these processes may be called revolutions. Neither France nor Britain, owing to the longer periods during which their national integrations had been in process, and owing to the different circumstances which conditioned different methods, had need of these great crises of integration which composed European history during the nineteenth century, and their own revolutions were nothing more than dramatic phases in their slower and more even periods of development. In Britain the expansion which followed a successful process of integration was achieved—owing to circumstances of geographical position—without major aggressions against other developing national organisms. In France a similar process provoked the Napoleonic Wars, and the delayed integrations of Germany and—to a lesser extent—of Italy, resulted in international conditions which culminated in the recent war.

A revolution is a far more complicated process than a mere social upheaval, for the latter is generally the expression of faults in the political mechanism of a particular country, and does not necessarily imply any fundamental transformations as a result. The numerous "revolutions" of 1848 and the abortive Communist "revolutions" in Central Europe during the period 1918-20 are examples. The Russian Revolution was a true revolution, but scarcely in the sense in which its Western admirers see it. It was, as Trotsky has so clearly pointed out in his first volume of the *History*, a revolution directed against the domination of a foreign Capitalism and a foreign culture over the Russian land. The history of Russia since the time of Peter the Great had been what Oswald Spengler defines as a pseudo-morphosis—that is the imposition upon the body of the Russian people of the elements of an alien and extraneous culture. There has never been in history any real expression of the soul of the Russian people. Kievian Russia was a Byzantine cultural colony with a Norse aristocracy, and later medieval Russia was a Tartar protectorate. Petrine Russia became the social and political expression of the individual genius of German soldiers and colonists and European adventurers from all countries, and upon it was later imposed the structure of Franco-British financial Capitalism. The Russian ruling caste had for half a century been bolstered up by the finance of the Entente powers, and the Russian Emperor fought for the Entente almost in the same sense as the Nizam of Hyderabad fulfilled his obligations to the suzerain power in India. Russia was, in fact, a vassal state of European colonial Capitalism in the same way, although in a less obvious degree, as India was of British Capitalism. This delicate fabric could not withstand the impact of modern war, and upon the ruins of its fantastic structure rose up the primitive Russian peasant in all the majesty of his barbarian wrath. It was, in fact, a *Russian* Revolution as well as a "social" revolution, and in this lies its supreme importance. The raw Russian mass starts out to build its destiny—the destiny of a new people in a new land—without even those inhibitions borrowed from older homes or those restrictions of gradualness which controlled the development of the American people during the nineteenth century. We have, therefore, to expect something really new, and something really peculiar to the Russian genius. The Russians borrow the equalitarian theory of Marxism to clothe the peasants' communal jealousy and primitive lack of individualism, and their little-disguised worship of the machine seems to derive from the most infantile traits of the human mind. It is not odd that the factory expert and the gunman from the slums should have succeeded the Orthodox priest and the Baltic baron as the masters of the country. On this, Trotksy wrote:

> The laws of history have nothing in common with a pedantic schematism. Unevenness, the most general law of the historic process, reveals itself most sharply and complexly in the destiny of the backward countries. Under the whip of external necessity their backward culture is compelled to make leaps. From the universal law of unevenness thus derives another law which, for the lack of a better name, we may call the law of *combined development*—by which we mean a drawing together of the different stages of the journey, a combining of separate steps, an amalgam of archaic with more contemporary forms... The law of combined development of backward countries—in the sense of a peculiar mixture of backward elements with the most modern factors—here rises before us in its most finished form, and offers a key to the fundamental riddle of the Russian revolution. (Trotsky, *History*, pp. 25, 70.)

It has been necessary to diverge at some length to consider the political character of the "working class" in Britain, and also to reflect upon the forms of revolution in general, in order to appreciate the fallacies of the position occupied by British Socialism at the end of that period which was to mark the final failure of the bourgeois-capitalist parties to "return to normalcy." It is indicative of the peculiar mediocrity of thought which has characterized British Social Democracy throughout its existence that it could find, even in "fantasy," the historical need for "social" revolution in Britain, or for that matter in the industrial countries of Western Europe which were in a similar stage of development. The tendency of the Left sections of the party to admire or to follow the Russian experiment was even more extraordinary, and is only paralleled by the ridiculous fear of the Right bourgeois parties in regard to Bolshevism. It has been observed that the Russian Revolution was of supreme importance to Western Europe in that it meant a complete transformation of *national* life across the whole of the sub-Continent immediately adjoining Europe, but it had little immediate relativity to the conditions of life in Britain or in any other near European country. There was neither the need for nor the inclination towards purely "class" revolution among the manual workers of Britain, but what those workers did require was leadership in a policy of action which would ultimately have the effect of a *national* revolution transforming the economic and political life of the country in accordance with its needs as an organic unit of corporate life. The action necessary for the carrying through of such an organic revolution had already been achieved in Italy and was preparing in Germany. In Britain, political developments had given the opportunity for such action to the Socialist Party, but its leaders were psychologically incapable of appreciating either the significance of their opportunity or the importance of the moment. Mosley, and possibly Wheatley, saw the way with rare constructive foresight, but their liberal-democratic traditions and the inhibitions of their bourgeois environment bore down the others to an inevitable abortion of all the hopes and all the efforts of a generation.

Following the failure of the General Strike, and the complete abdication of official Labour to the conception of the permanence of the capitalist system which was consummated in the Mand-Turner Report, the Left elements in the Socialist Party had attempted to rally revolutionary opinion in the country. The abortive Cook-Maxton campaign was the practical expression and the end of this attempt. Scanlon, the familiar of Wheatley and Maxton, has given some account of this campaign, and it is worth quoting, as instancing the incapacity for leadership and for effective action which is inherent in the democratic

Chapter V

methodology, saying:

> When it came to a programme, the Communists wanted a long list of items outlining to a penny what should be the workers' pay, and all the unemployment allowances for men, women and children. Wheatley laughed at this coming from a body of revolutionary workers and informed them the Cook-Maxton campaign was being launched to rouse the workers to demand all they produced and not merely the odd coppers; and as this was apparently too advanced for the Communists, they would have to go on without them. Much to Willie Gallacher's annoyance and regret, the campaign did go on without them, but it was not the campaign that Mr. Wheatley had in mind. He was quite frankly for a campaign which would have for its object the setting up of a group in each district pledged to support only those Labour candidates who would work for a Socialist programme. If the Labour candidate was not suitable, then he would be opposed. He believed, then, that there was no hope of Socialism, or even social advance under the then leadership, and there was no hope of a different leadership until at least 50 per cent of the members on the back benches had been replaced by others who did believe in Socialism. Mr. Maxton took a different view. He believed the Movement would resent anything which damaged the prospects of a Labour Government at the first election. Mr. Wheatley took the view that the worst thing that could happen to the Labour Movement would be a Labour Government composed of the then leaders. He believed that they would do nothing to justify the aspirations of the workers, and because of the disappointment and disillusionment the Movement would be set back twenty years.
>
> ... The question of what was actually to be said at the meetings, as it happened, was never seriously discussed. Each of us had in our own minds what ought to be said and, therefore, both Mr. Cook and Mr. Maxton took what they believed was the best line under the circumstances. Mr. Cook wanted to prove that, according to the materialistic conception of history, the T.U.C. Peace in Industry Policy was bound to fail. Mr. Maxton apparently took the view that if the rank and file

insisted on a Socialist policy then even Mr. MacDonald would supply the demand. Mr. Wheatley's conception of what should be said and done was different from both.

... The campaign went on, but no attempt was made to form a rival organization. Mr. Maxton still stuck to the view that the Movement must not be divided, as the consensus of opinion among the active rank and file was that the Labour leaders should be given a chance to become the Government, and it would be time enough to judge them after they had failed. (*Decline and Fall of the Labour Party*, pp. 110-14.)

In the meantime, Mosley, without waiting "to judge them after they had failed," was attempting to inspire the Labour leaders with the intent of action. A Committee of the National Executive of the Labour Party had been appointed to draft an election programme. Scanlon gives a dry account:

All would have been plain sailing, in the production of this programme, as the supply of scissors and paste with which former programmes had been made was far from exhausted, but in the interval Sir Oswald Mosley had been elected to the Executive, and being new to politics, had demanded a programme which the workers would be able to understand. What was worse, he wanted a series of definite proposals outlined, in which there would be no equivocation, as he believed the workers preferred to have their programmes outlined in clear, simple language. In this demand he was supported by Mr. Charles Trevelyan, and for a time these two succeeded in annoying the elder statesmen who knew much better what was good for the workers. Mr. MacDonald, for instance, had never made an important statement in his life which could not be interpreted in three or four different ways, and had increasingly gained the confidence of the workers the more obscure the statements were... Under Hardie's blunt leadership the party had never more than forty members; by Mr. MacDonald's method it had actually been the Government of the country. Mr. Henderson, too, lost patience with Sir Oswald and once (in biblical terms, of course) referred to him as the rich young man.

In the end the two rebels yielded, although still unconvinced that the best type of programme was one which appeared to mean one thing, but if necessary could be made to mean something quite different. The plan was finally produced, and when it was laid before the Conference at Birmingham, Mr. MacDonald, in explaining it, said that always there would be Socialism in the background. Everybody liked this explanation without understanding that Socialism would be so far in the background.

The plan was known as 'Labour and the Nation,' but, unlike the Russian plan, it contained no time limit. Five years, twenty years or a hundred did not matter. It was such a good plan, however, that everybody free from prejudice could have found something he liked, and if there was anything he disliked there was always something to show that the dislike had arisen because it had not been taken in conjunction with something else. It was like taking gin without bitters. In fact, it was more a running buffet than a set meal, and the ordinary member of the party could take a nibble just as the mood seized him.

As for the Cabinet, they decided that none of it was good enough for them. Mr. MacDonald possibly had good reasons for this. Just as certain animals after much labour produce their young, only to eat them or ignore them, so Mr. MacDonald had lost all affection or interest for the child of his labours. (*Decline and Fall of the Labour Party*, pp. 119-20.)

On the subject of the national programme, Mosley could write afterwards:

A small Committee from the National Executive of the Labour Party was appointed to draft an Election programme. The main protagonists were, on the one hand, MacDonald and Snowden, and on the other, Charles Trevelyan and myself. Henderson was, as usual, floundering about in between. MacDonald and Snowden desired a long and woolly document containing every proposal the Labour Party had ever made for reform on earth or in heaven. We, on the other hand, desired a crisp, practical programme of measures which Labour would carry in the life of one Parliament. Our argument was that we should thus concentrate the enthusiasm of our supporters on immediate and practical proposals and also by a precise definition would set a limit to the fears of those who were doubtful what Labour would do in office and thought we would uproot every institution in the country within five minutes. In fact by setting out a precise programme we could at once create more enthusiasm among our own supporters and disarm the alarmist tactics of the Tories.

MacDonald disliked being bound to anything concrete, and this led him to oppose us. In the first instance, MacDonald brought to the Committee a long and woolly document, and I brought a short precise document. As a result of the controversy MacDonald's draft, which was referred to the National Executive, was rejected; a great rebuff to a Party leader.

As a compromise, the National Executive turned on Tawney to produce 'Labour and the Nation,' which was really an Old Gang document, and a triumph for the Old Gang, although it was certainly better than MacDonald's original effort, the woolliness of which was beyond belief.

We were then faced with the acceptance of that long, vague and meaningless programme or a split at the Party Conference at Birmingham in 1928.

This ground was peculiarly favourable for me to fight on, as it was my own Birmingham stronghold where we carried half the seats in the city at the subsequent election against the Chamberlain domination of over half a century. Rather than split the party on the eve of an Election, I did not fight, and 'Labour and the Nation' became the accepted programme of the party.

... The broad facts of the dispute are well known. They illustrate my struggle within the Labour Party to develop a hard, concrete, practical, in essence Fascist, programme against the vague promises of ultimate utopia from which they invariably retreated in office to the lowest depths of the Capitalist Hell. (In a letter to the author, 21st August, 1933.)

When the second Labour administration was formed in May, 1929, the high expectations which not only the rank and file of the party but also wide sections of the general public had formed as to the influence which

Mosley would occupy in the new Government were disappointed. Even Wheatley, the only personal success of the previous Government, was overlooked, and the intellectual patriarchs of the Socialist and trade union movement were flanked in all the minor offices by gentlemen whose irreproachably bourgeois outlook enabled them to be distinguished not at all from the Liberals who were prepared to maintain them in office. As a gesture to the public a new department had been set up to deal directly with the unemployment problem. At its head was Mr. J. H. Thomas, who, in the true English tradition, had been accorded the nominal post of Lord Privy Seal. Three minor ministers were delegated to assist the railwaymen's leader. It was not without significance that they were three of the most vigorous critics of official Labour policy. Mr. George Lansbury, a veteran of the Left, Mr. Tom Johnston, the able editor of the formerly extremist *Forward*, and Sir Oswald Mosley, were at once gagged as effective critics of Government policy, and loaded with the potential discredit for a failure which they were to be given neither the responsibility nor the authority to overcome. Sir Oswald Mosley, in name, occupied the decorative and medieval post of Chancellor of the Duchy of Lancaster—a very subtle revenge on the leader of revolutionary thought in the Midlands. He was, in fact, assistant minister to Mr. Thomas, with all the practical inhibitions which the occupancy of that post implied. Mosley's position was obviously a very difficult one, but while he showed again—as he had done at the Birmingham Conference—his willingness to work with others and to compromise very far for the sake of unity and in the tradition of loyalty, he soon made it clear that he was not prepared to accept without a fight the total surrender of any policy of reality and action.

It is not the purpose of this book to recapitulate the recent and familiar incidents of the period of the Labour Government of 1929-31, but rather to consider the broad flow of events and the development of Mosley's mind in reaction thereto, until that moment when he found that he had been thinking and acting in terms of Fascist thought rather than that he had reached a certain stage of political crisis where he decided arbitrarily to become a Fascist. For our purpose we cannot do better than revert to the invaluable work of Mr. Scanlon, who, it must be borne in mind, is a devoted follower of Mr. Maxton, and who writes therefore from the point of view of activist Socialism, so far as any section of the Socialist Party can be said to retain any shreds of an activist policy.

From the outset the Government did not attempt to consider the

Mosley in the Second Labour Government | 83

elaborate schemes, prepared by Mosley at an earlier date, for attacking the unemployment problem from the point of view of the stimulation of consumption. They confined themselves to the easier (and for that matter the minor) part of any concerted campaign against unemployment—the preparation of work schemes, which in varying degrees had been pursued by the Conservatives and advocated by the Liberals during the whole of the post-war period. "It was considered better," comments Scanlon, "to work on things which were bound to fail rather than risk defeat on something which might succeed." Mr. Thomas floundered off into these work schemes, and chased such hares as a scheme for building a bridge over the Zambesi, and special contracts for bulk purchase of British goods by Canada—which proved ultimately to be no more than the manipulation of the normal trade between Canada and this country. Even the structure of the new department over which Mr. Thomas presided was hopeless, and such work schemes as received approval were delayed rather than accelerated by the existence of the department. When the first year of the new Labour Government's period of office had passed Mr. Thomas was still clattering around in a helplessness which might have been pathetic had it not been vulgarized by the crude irresponsibility of his optimism. In October of 1929 he had told the Annual Conference of the Labour Party at Brighton in reference to unemployment that "I am confident that when February comes the figures will improve." In May, 1929, when he took office, the figures of the registered unemployed had been 1,132,297. By the end of that year 1,770,051 were on the register. However, in November, "speaking from a close examination of the facts, he had no hesitation in saying there is a trade improvement," and on January 18th of 1930, he "struck the note of optimism based on past experience." By the end of February he "thought the bottom had been reached," and in March "he saw fresh signs of hope." In his May Day speech he went so far as to say: "I frankly admit there is a cloud on the horizon, but I do believe the worst is past. I believe there is a silver lining." By August he had abandoned all pretensions to seriousness, and had become quite flippant. "Do not be too keen," he said, "about this humbug of breaking records. I broke all records in the number of the unemployed." In an age which was not so tolerant Queen Marie Antoinette had been condemned for an observation which was not quite so feckless, but Mr. Thomas remained to bob up once more as one of the leaders of the National Government—forgiven by those trade unionists of whom he was himself so typical, applauded by Tories to whom he gave a comfortable feeling that they were keeping in step with revolution by listening to his after-dinner speeches.

It was not to be expected that the hard dynamic Mosley would bear long with Mr. Thomas, as wrote Scanlon:

> His restless energy soon made it evident that he could not long remain as an assistant to Mr. Thomas. Mr. Thomas had too few ideas, Sir Oswald too many. Whilst Mr. Thomas was making his futile speeches Sir Oswald was busy piling memorandum upon memorandum on Mr. Thomas's desk. Work schemes by the score were prepared, but all the memoranda found a resting-place in the Lord Privy Seal's waste-paper basket. For the first few months there was no evidence in public that all was not well. Sir Oswald accepted his share of the criticism of the Labour back benches and more than his share of the jeers of the Conservative back benches; but he voted loyally with his party... As the figures of unemployment mounted steadily and nothing was done effectively to check the rise, Sir Oswald's patience could no longer be kept in control. He was still young enough to believe that reputations in British politics are only made and maintained by doing things; Mr. Thomas, much more astute, knew that British political history taught that reputations were maintained by doing nothing, but by making the proper kind of speeches...
>
> It was therefore with perfect expressions of cordiality that Mr. Thomas acknowledged receipt of all memoranda prepared by Sir Oswald, and for six months Sir Oswald, in a spirit of loyalty to his chief, continued to send them, although perhaps with less cordiality than they were received. But as the months stretched out and nothing at all was happening, except the steady rise in the numbers at the Labour Exchanges, Sir Oswald decided that he must place his plans directly before the Cabinet. This was intimated to Mr. Thomas, who, it must be said, offered not the slightest objection. He knew his Cabinet, and he probably knew that if Mr. MacDonald, Mr. Snowden and himself did not agree with Sir Oswald's ideas there was no further need to worry. The only difference so far as Mr. Thomas was concerned would be that he would not now be obliged to read them before putting them in the waste-paper basket.

Armed with his chief's consent, Sir Oswald prepared that scheme which for long excited the newspapers, and was known to them as the Mosley Memorandum. It was submitted to the Cabinet in the joint names of Mr. George Lansbury, Mr. Tom Johnston and Sir Oswald. Mr. Lansbury and Mr. Johnston will not feel slighted when I say that the document was the work of Sir Oswald. For weeks and weeks it lay with the Cabinet and nothing whatever had been done about it. Then began an exchange of notes between the Prime Minister and Sir Oswald, which became more and more acid as the weeks stretched into months.

The memorandum had been there for many weeks before a single mention of it appeared in the newspapers, and then one morning the *Manchester Guardian* contained a harmless paragraph in the London Letter; and by that evening the *Evening Standard* had transformed this innocent paragraph into a first-class political sensation. By the following day every newspaper in the country treated it as a serious matter, and members of the Parliamentary Labour Party, many of whom knew of its existence weeks before, also treated the memorandum as being of first-class importance.

The complacency of M.P.s was badly disturbed, and for a time the party was divided into two—Mosleyites and anti-Mosleyites. Tempers were ruffled, and at the many party meetings held at that time the stout defenders of the Government, the men who still believed Mr. MacDonald, Mr. Snowden and Mr. Thomas could do no wrong, poured scorn on the group who had closely allied themselves with Sir Oswald.

As it happened, the merits of the Mosley plan itself were seldom discussed, because, as Mr. MacDonald himself said, it was now a Government document and as such could not be discussed until they had given their decision one way or the other. All the discussions ranged round the question of 'this young bounder Mosley creating dissension in the party.' In a party where motives always played a big part, the motives of Sir Oswald in putting forward the document were discussed, rather than the policy of the document itself, and, as was to be expected, the very worst motives were imputed. It was much easier to say that Sir Oswald was simply out to get leadership of the party than to try to prove the document was unsound. Wheatley with his Socialist schemes had been disposed of in this way; why not Sir Oswald? (*Decline and Fall of the Labour Party*, p. 183 *et seq.*)

Mosley finally resigned from the Government, and in his famous "Resignation Speech" during a Debate on Supply, made a detailed defence and exposition of his position, as the Conservative *Scotsman* wrote:

> His speech was the outstanding feature of the Debate. His economics might be questionable, but his criticism of his old colleagues without any personal bitterness was deadly, and one sensed a feeling on the Ministerial back benches that a Government with no policy of its own had let go the only member who at least tried to apply his mind to the problem. (29th May, 1930.)

The *Yorkshire Post*—the leading Tory journal of the Midlands—gave as its opinion that:

> Sir Oswald Mosley had increased his stature by his speech. The good taste with which he delivered it was remarked by all parties. The full mind with which he spoke was shown by the fact that he spoke without notes. He held the attention of the House all the time, and although he damaged the Government considerably by the force of the facts which he marshalled, he did not make a studied attack, and he avoided personalities. Listeners felt as he proceeded that here was a man who was the equal of the best, and the superior of most of the Front Bench colleagues whom he had just left. That was the main lesson of the night. (29th May, 1930.)

The speech suggests so many of the ideas which Mosley embodied a few months later in the "National Policy" put forward by the New Party, and which he elaborated further in his Fascist programme, that it would be superfluous here to make a detailed analysis either of his general approach to the economic problem, or of the proposals which he set out to meet the situation which presented itself at that time. It is interesting, however, in that it demonstrates the "Fascist" cast of his mind, and shows the peculiarly English characteristic of the subconscious pursuit of a new political ideology through purely economic channels. His resignation speech and the New Party policy were purely economic programmes. It was only after the great spiritual disillusionment with the old world and with the old Parliamentary methodology, that he turned to the ideology of Fascism and substituted it for the ideology of Social Democracy. A similar crisis can, of course, be identified in the mental and spiritual evolution of Mussolini, who had struggled for years to develop his inspiration within the framework of Social Democracy, until—impatient at the abortion of his efforts and at the "inactivism" inherent in the Social Democratic technique—he resolved, when, indeed, he was not only of about the same political stature as Mosley, but also about the same age, to seek his own masterful way out of the problems which assailed his own mind and the mind of his generation.

When Mosley rose to speak he addressed the crowded Chamber steadfastly from his heart:

> The Prime Minister, in his speech, pointed out a fact which none can deny, that world conditions have been vastly aggravated since the arrival in power of the present Government, and that no one can suggest that the Government are responsible for these conditions. None can deny that fact, but this I do submit, that the more serious the situation the greater the necessity for action by Government. We must, above all, beware, as the world situation degenerates, that we do not make that situation an excuse for doing less rather than a spur for doing more.

Mosley then turned to the inadequacy of the administrative mechanism for dealing with the unemployment problem on emergency lines, and he proceeded to outline his own recommendations—recommendations which he was later to elaborate and expand:

> It is admittedly a complex organization. I was told that to carry such an organization into effect would mean a revolution in the machinery of government. My only comment is this. The machinery which I suggested may be right or may be wrong— after a very short administrative experience, it is probably wrong—but this I do suggest, that to grapple with this problem

it is necessary to have a revolution in the machinery of government. After all, it was done in the war; there were revolutions in the machinery of government one after the other, until the machine was devised and created by which the job could be done. Unless we treat the unemployment problem as a lesser problem, which I believe to be a fallacious view, we have to have a change in the machinery of government by which we can get that central drive and organization by which alone this problem can be surmounted.

Mosley then proceeded to divide the problem into that of "the long-term reconstruction of the industries of this country, and the short-term programme to bridge the gulf before the fruition of the long-term programme." He continued:

I think we can all agree, whatever our views upon the permanent reconstruction of Britain, that it cannot be done in five minutes. It will be a matter of three years at least, and possibly five years, before you can arrive by long-term measures at an appreciable effect upon the unemployment figures. If that view be agreed to, it is evidently necessary, in addition, to have a short-term programme to deal with unemployment in the interval, which should at the same time contribute to the economic advantage of the country.

He then proceeded to examine the exaggerated hopes reposed in the conception of "Rationalization," which had become the latest political panacea of the capitalist parties, and which had particularly appealed to the imagination of Mr. Thomas:

The Government throughout have pinned their hopes to rationalization. For my part, I have always made it perfectly clear that, in my view, rationalization was necessary and inevitable. It has to come in the modern world. Industries which do not rationalize simply go under. It is agreed among most people that rationalization is necessary, but do not let us proceed to the easy belief that rationalization in itself will cure the unemployment problem.

He then went on to examine four big groups of trades to which methods of rationalization had been applied, and in which—over a period of five years—while production had been increased by 20 per cent, employment had declined by 4 per cent.

Mosley then turned to "the export fallacy," which still gripped the minds of a vast majority in all three parties:

> I submit that this hope of recovering our position through an expansion of our export trade is an illusion, and a dangerous illusion; and the sooner the fallacy is realized, the quicker can we devote ourselves to a search for the real remedy... The intensified competition all over the world is making more and more illusory the belief that we can again build up in the world that unique position which we occupied many years ago.
>
> I should be interested to hear if these figures and calculations can be challenged. If they cannot be challenged, we have to face a shift in the whole basis of the economic life of this country. I believe, and have always urged, that it is to the home market that we must look for the solution of our troubles... If our export trade on its pre-war basis is no longer possible we have to turn to the home market. We must always, of course, export sufficient to buy our essential food-stuffs and raw materials, but we need not export enough to build up a favourable trade balance for foreign investment of £100,000,000 a year, or to pay for the import of so many luxury manufactured articles as to-day come into the country. We have to get away from the belief that the only criterion of British prosperity is how many goods we can send abroad for foreigners to consume.

Mosley then went on to elaborate his theories of the control of imports:

> I want now to suggest that that policy of controlled imports can and should be extended to other trades, for this reason, that if we are to build up a home market, it must be agreed that this nation must to some extent be insulated from the electric shocks of present world conditions. You cannot build a higher civilization and a standard of life which can absorb the great force of modern production if you are subject to price

90 | Chapter V

fluctuations from the rest of the world which dislocate your industry at every turn, and to the sport of competition from virtually slave conditions in other countries... I only suggest at this stage that there is, in the analysis which I have presented, some ground for disbelief in the current view that is now so widely accepted, and if there is any force in this analysis, or in these arguments, the attempt to deal with unemployment by an intensification of the export trade is doomed to failure, and the belief that it can be done is a dangerous delusion which diverts the mind of the country from the problems which should be really considered and the things that really matter.

Mosley went on to explain at considerable length his "short-term" policy which it was estimated would put 700,000 to 800,000 men into employment within a reasonably short space of time. These proposals were a balanced combination of methods calculated to remove the old and the very young from competition in the labour market, while at the same time stimulating the purchasing power of the internal market, and schemes for the vigorous pursuit of public works, the plans for which had lain fallow during Mr. Thomas's period of administration. These proposals were not expensive, when both the concurrent relief in unemployment payments—a constantly rising item, and the state of the financial market were taken into consideration.

Finally, Mosley concluded with an attack on the enthusiasm for the investment of British capital abroad, at a time when it was assumed not to be available for investment in its country of ownership. £16,000,000 of new capital had been invested abroad during the first fortnight of May, a fact which had given rise to expressions of gratification on the part of Mr. William Graham, the Socialist President of the Board of Trade. Mosely asked:

Why is it so right and proper and desirable that capital should go overseas to equip factories to compete against us, to build roads and railways in the Argentine or in Timbuctoo, to provide employment for people in those countries while it is supposed to shake the whole basis of our financial strength if anyone dares to suggest the raising of money by the Government of this country to provide employment for the people of this country? If those views are passed without examination or challenge the position of this country is serious indeed. In conclusion let me say that the position which faces us is, of course, very serious. Everybody knows that; and, perhaps, those who have been in office for a short time know it even better. It is not, I confidently believe, irreparable, but I feel this from the depths of my being, that the days of muddling through are over, that this time we cannot muddle through.

"The rounds of cheering," commented the correspondent of the *Morning Post*—a veteran of the lobbies, "in which the explanation terminated were—ominous sign—common to all three parties." The *Daily Telegraph* wrote that:

> His ideas might be right or wrong, but here was evidence of hard work, of independent, concrete thinking, and of a real political conscience, and the House, after the soft abstractions of the Prime Minister, rejoiced to feel solid ground under its feet... After to-day's speech no one can think of Sir Oswald Mosley as a dilettante in politics. This industrious and able man, if he keeps his health and his industry, must be regarded as a candidate, some day, for the highest honours. (29th May, 1930.)

The Radical *Star* stated that "enthusiastic Labour M.P.s were hailing Sir Oswald as a future Prime Minister," while the *Daily Herald*—under the heading "A Future Premier?" said that "everybody is still talking about Sir Oswald's great personal triumph. I heard a most naive remark in the Lobby just after the Division. An elderly Tory M.P. said: "I wish he had never left our Party. That man will be Prime Minister some day." (30th May, 1930.) The shrewd old *Morning Post* correspondent was the best judge, and the general acclamation of Mosley's speech was to prove indeed "ominous" of an equally general agreement to ignore his proposals, and "ominous" of the fate of the New Party policy of "social compromise" during the succeeding year.

The crisis between Mosley and the official Socialist leaders dragged out its desultory course through the remainder of the summer. But with the approach of the Annual Conference of the Labour Party at Llandudno, which had been fixed for the beginning of October, it was obvious that matters must come to an issue. It is not possible to follow these events more impartially than in the account of the Clydesider

Chapter V

Scanlon, whose group had little sympathy either for the impotent drift of the Government or for the direct realism of Oswald Mosley. Scanlon recounts:

> Sir Oswald, took his first step in open revolt against the Government. He decided to go right over the heads of a reactionary Government and over the heads of stupid Parliamentary colleagues, and appeal direct to the advanced wise men in the local Labour Parties, who had sent the stupid ones to Parliament. Several thousand copies of the memorandum were printed and copies sent to the secretary of each local Labour Party, with a request that the local party should consider it, and if they agreed with its contents give instructions to their delegates to support it at the Annual Conference.
>
> This was a bold dramatic stroke. By telling the workers outside what was going on, Sir Oswald had committed what was the unforgivable sin. To discuss with the workers what is happening behind the scenes is regarded with almost the same horror as would be the actions of a crook by his pals if he discussed the actions of his gang before a meeting of detectives. Sir Oswald ought to have known that the duty of local Labour Parties was to make the constituencies safe for democracy, and their privilege was to pay the political levy, safe in the knowledge that their trusted leaders, Mr. MacDonald, Mr. Snowden and Mr. Thomas, would never let them down.
>
> There was only one thing saved Sir Oswald from expulsion there and then, and that was the fact that he had acquired a surprisingly large following in the local Labour Parties. These people, poor souls, were being jeered at in the workshops and mines. With brutal candour they had cursed the voters who were foolish enough to believe that the Liberal and Tory Parties could ever do anything for the workers. 'Wait till we get a Labour Government,' they said, 'and things will be different.' The only difference, alas, had been in the figures of unemployment, and now these Labour enthusiasts were willing to clutch at anything which would save them from the jeers of their workmates. Accordingly they supported the memorandum in such large numbers that Sir Oswald was saved from

disciplinary action.

At the Conference itself, Mr. MacDonald made a wonderful speech. He said nothing whatever, but he said it so eloquently that the delegates were deeply moved... It must be admitted that the atmosphere of the Conference lent itself to anyone who was prepared to play on the emotions of the delegates. The Conference opened in tragic gloom. It was that week-end when a member of the Cabinet and several engineers crashed in the disaster to the R101, while cruising to France on its voyage to India. It was on this note of tragedy caused by the death of Lord Thomson that Mr. MacDonald began his speech, and soon all the delegates were feeling the nearness of the presence of death. Thus, what might easily have been a critical Conference was turned into a house of mourning, and a speech which might easily have fallen flat created scenes of enthusiasm. In other circumstances, of course, another speech would have been delivered and with equal success.

It was in this atmosphere that Mr. Maxton had to rise and make a criticism of the work of the Government, and it is scarcely surprising that he failed. By the time Sir Oswald rose to make his speech the Conference had returned to normality, and the volume of cheering which greeted his rising showed the amazing hold he had acquired on the mind of delegates. Next to the Prime Minister he was the most popular man at the Conference, and for the first time all the dislike of the Right Wing had been transferred from Maxton to Sir Oswald. His speech was a masterly indictment of the Government and a clear, lucid explanation of his own scheme. Then occurred another of those amazing things which make one despair of the stability of any human mind, once that mind has been committed to politics. Mr. George Lansbury, who had signed the memorandum and had asked, with Sir Oswald, that its work schemes should be adopted, was the official spokesman of the Party Executive against the memorandum. With Cabinet Ministers of the Left and Right against it, and with the Maxton group indifferent, the amazing thing is that Sir Oswald's plan received any support at all. Conference, however, recorded a big vote in its favour, and then proceeded to show its appreciation of the efforts of Mr. Thomas by turning him off the

Chapter V

Executive.

Thus, in spite of the emotional atmosphere created by the death of Lord Thomson, it will be seen that delegates were demanding something more from their Government than the Premier was prepared to offer. Sir Oswald's vote was the biggest challenge ever delivered to the governing machine. But for the fact that the issue was regarded as a vote of confidence or no confidence in the Government, Sir Oswald's vote would have been very much bigger. Delegates who were weary of the Government's inactivity and would have liked to show their disapproval hesitated to show the country that they had no confidence in their leaders. Loyalty, as usual, carried the day. (*Decline and Fall of the Labour Party*, p. 188 *et seq.*)

The resolution had been in the following terms:

This Conference considers that the 'Mosley Memorandum' is of so much importance that it ought to be seriously considered by the Parliamentary Party. The National Executive is therefore instructed to go fully into the proposals of the memorandum and to issue an early and comprehensive report to all affiliated organizations.

The voting was as follows, on the card vote system:

For the resolution... 1,046,000.
Against the resolution................................... 1,251,000.

Of this, Scanlon commented:

If the Prime Minister carried all before him when he had the platform, Sir Oswald could justly claim that once the Conference settled down to business, the tide turned completely for him. In the Press and the Labour Movement itself the discussions now centred round the question of how long it would be before Sir Oswald became the party leader. Even without a crash in the party's fortunes it was easy to see that changes must come soon. The controllers of the Labour Party, mostly old men, could not stay the inexorable march of time any more than ordinary mortals. No other leader was in sight. Mr. Wheatley was gone. Mr. Maxton had none of the pushful qualities which carry a man to leadership in Labour politics, and nobody from the trade unions showed the slightest sign of being able to take charge. Therefore every prophet fixed on Sir Oswald as the next party leader. Even Socialists, who had no particular love for Sir Oswald, were saying nothing could stop it. All the prophets, however, had overlooked the one man who could stop it—Sir Oswald himself. (*Decline and Fall of the Labour Party*, p. 194.)

Oswald Mosley had already abandoned—in spirit—the party who would have liked to follow him, but did not dare. He had reached the point, as another had done before, where he realized that the social democratic machine was an organ neither of revolutionary action nor of action in any meaning of that word. The big, grey woolly ghost of the "Bourgeois Mind" permeated alike the lobbies of the House of Commons and the corridors of Labour and trade union conferences, and the live acid of Mosley's spirit could not, and would not, mingle with it.

"I wish he had never left our party," said the elderly Tory M.P.; "that man will be Prime Minister some day." "Even Socialists, who had no particular love for Sir Oswald, were saying nothing could stop it." About this time one of the latter, John Strachey, had a "premonition," as he writes in *The Menace of Fascism:*

I recollect the spectacle of Mosley sitting silent and alone, brooding with an indescribable bitterness, as the elderly, portly trade union officials and nervous pacifist intellectuals filed out of a party meeting at which they had demonstrated their undiminished confidence in Mr. MacDonald. A stab of premonition flashed through my mind. How had the Italian Social Democrats looked at the Congress of the Italian Socialist Party which expelled the editor of the *Avanti*? Had they not been sure that they had finished with that tiresome fellow Mussolini? I do not know if Mosley's premonitions were of a more detailed character.

The Beginnings of Fascism: After a New Party Fight at Birmingham

Chapter VI

—The New Party: Attempt at "Social Compromise" —

Between the publication of *Revolution by Reason* in 1925 and his effort to secure an "activist" Socialist policy in 1929 Oswald Mosley had, along his own lines and in accordance with the peculiar conditions of the British problem, been developing that rationalization of Modern economic theory and pragmatic idealism which now forms the basis of action in those European countries which have already become Fascist. It is perhaps characteristic of English political life that the economic bases of Fascist thought should have been widely propagated, and scarcely less widely accepted, before the political implications of these new tendencies and of this new attitude of mind had been either considered or foreshadowed. Thus it was that Oswald Mosley, and a good many other average Englishmen, found themselves Fascists through the sheer logic of their own processes of thought, but even when they made this discovery they hesitated to admit it to themselves. They pressed for a "reform of the parliamentary system" which should make it possible to implement the drastic economic revolution which they had discovered to be essential if the life of the country were to be reconstructed and if social values were to be adjusted. It was natural therefore that, at first, Oswald Mosley and his associates should work for the reform of the parliamentary system through Parliament, and that they should not lightly abandon their conception of an economic revolution carried out through Parliament and by means of the familiar hallowed democratic methods. They were destined to fail, and their failure confronted them abruptly with the realization that revolutionary changes cannot be carried through a machine which has been so evolved and developed as to place the maximum of obstruction in the way of any sort of change. If any man in England could have carried effective revolutionary changes through the ordinary mechanism of the party and parliamentary system, it was Oswald Mosley. At the Llandudno Conference he had been successful in achieving "the biggest challenge ever delivered to the governing machine," and within three weeks of the Conference he proceeded to carry the battle against the party system into the House of Commons. Mosley had behind him the moral support of substantial sections of the Labour Party, both inside and outside the House. At the same time the most influential individuals among the younger Tories and some of the younger Liberals had entered into very intimate relations with him. The plan was rapidly developed of forming a national group recruited from among the younger—and more independent—members of all three parties, which would be prepared to challenge both the Government and the older parties on a policy of immediate national action. A policy drafted by Mosley and his closest associations in the Labour Party received the approval of representative elements from among the younger Tories in the House of Commons, and concerted action was to follow. It is not the purpose of this book to enter into the somewhat sensational incidents of this period, nor would the subject of our study desire that the oscillations of individuals, who have since proved able to reconcile themselves with an environment which they then found both intolerable and hopeless, should be openly discussed. "In the beginning everyone betrayed us," said a great Fascist leader in reference to the early history of Fascism in his own country, and the Fascist realist can leave these men to the mediocrity which they prefer with the reflection that they were the victims of that "bourgeois mentality" which we have already examined at some length.

In the debate on the King's Speech on 29th October, 1930, Mosley made a long and studied statement of policy. He was followed by many of the younger members on both sides of the House, and the occasion became, in fact, a debate on Mosley's policy—which received approval on all sides. The utter contrast between the conceptions of the younger members of more modern outlook and the upholders of parliamentary self-sufficiency is perhaps best illustrated by quotations from the speeches of Major Walter Elliot and Sir Donald Maclean. First, Major Elliot:

> The danger that is now before us is that not merely one party but all parties are discredited as long as the present deadlock in

The New Party: Attempt at "Social Compromise" | 99

this House persists. There is a feeling of impatience, not merely with the Government, but with Parliament itself. That is one of the gravest features of the present situation, and it is not improved by the pettifogging proposals which are brought forward in a King's Speech such as we have to consider this afternoon; it is not improved by the proposals which are being the subject of so much old-fashioned logic chopping from one side of the House to another... It was a long-continued complaint of the Opposition about us that the Tories were the stupid party. This Government is not only to be the stupid party, but the incompetent party. The Government have displayed during the past year an amount of incompetence which would be absolutely incredible if it had not actually occurred before our eyes, and in the speech which is now before us they propose to continue on the same course, without even facing the facts... We say that the difficulties before the country are not being faced in this Speech, and, until they are faced, there will be no reality in our debates and no recovery from our position.

Sir Donald Maclean, who followed Sir Oswald Mosley and Mr. Oliver Stanley, complained that "they were too pessimistic," saying:

Anyone would imagine that the world has passed into an entirely different phase after the war, that there had been nothing like it in the history of the world. Anyone would imagine that there was in that war some peculiar quality which completely changed human nature. If they would take the trouble, not to read for the first time, but to renew their acquaintance with the results on Europe, and to a lesser degree on other parts of the world, of the Napoleonic wars, they would find something like the very remedies they are suggesting to-day put forward as a solution of the difficulties of that period.

Sir Donald went on to recommend economy as the fundamental solution of the national problems, and his conclusion is so characteristic of the dominant thought in the bourgeois parties that it is worthy of quotation:

If those who are interested in this subject look at history, they will find written large for all who seek it, this truth—that other nations, which, in comparison to the size of the world in their days, were as great and as powerful as ours, have fallen, not so much by the attacks of those who sought to destroy them by military means as by the crushing weight of extravagant, useless, unnecessary national expenditure. From the time of the decline of Rome to the decay of Spain, and right down to the crash of Russia, this has been so... I say once again that history will make no excuse for this House of Commons, founded as it is on the principle of the control of the public purse, if it fails in its bounden duty to the nation in this time to see that rigid economy in every Department is the spirit of public expenditure.

Mosley first attacked the Government policy of referring the unemployment problem to yet another Committee of Inquiry:

We cannot govern in this state of affairs by the simple process of putting this country into commission. Sooner or later a decision must be taken and action must ensue. It is a painful and unpleasant moment, but it has to come, and we cannot continue simply to dodge from one inquiry to another in every difficult problem which confronts the country.

Mosley then proceeded to give an analysis of what he considered to be the five primary causes of the crisis in the export market. They were (1) "the local industrialization of markets which we had previously commanded"; (2) "the arrival of new competitors on a scale and with advantages we did not conceive in our original position"; (3) "the development of sweated or backward labour in competition with white labour"; (4) "the arrival of the great producers' organizations"; and (5) "the steady fall in the price level due to the inadequacy of the new gold supply in relation to the new production of the world, and, still more than that, the deliberate hoarding and sterilization of gold by some of the great users of the world."

In regard to (3) he touched on one of the most formidable of modern developments which threatens the whole standard of living, and ultimately the very civilization, of the white peoples:

The New Party: Attempt at "Social Compromise" | 101

That factor was not serious so long as industry maintained the artisan basis. There was great force behind the old Free Trade case so long as industry rested on skilled workmanship and artisanship. I remember in India finding that even in an Oriental market the relatively high paid labour of Lancashire was defeating Indian labour paid about five shillings per week by reason of superior skill and application. The new factor cutting right across the old Free Trade case is the development of mass production methods. When you reduce every industrial operation to the simplest process, you are turning the industrial system into a system even more suited for Oriental labour than for white labour. I remember standing in Ford's works at Detroit watching a man turning a screw to nip a piece of wire which had been placed under the screw by another man. He did that for six or seven hours a day and got £5 or £6 a week for it. Any man can be trained to that job in five minutes, and the coming of these mass production methods puts the Oriental and backward type of labour on a parity for the first time with white labour. Inevitably the development of these backward countries by Capitalism will lead to increasing threats to the white standard of life.

In regard to (4) he laid emphasis on a phenomenon which was to gather impetus during the following two years:

There is a fourth factor, the arrival of the great producers' organizations, those great combinations with a power of dumping and undercutting in the struggle for markets which was never possessed by any organization before the war. And they have this incidental reaction upon markets, that they are able to maintain prices for a very long time against the falling price level such as we have had during the past few years; but when they collapse, when one of the giants collapses, there is a tremendous downward rush of prices, as in the last year, which dislocates the whole industrial mechanism of the world.

Mosley turned again to the problem of the home market:

Chapter VI

> Are we not driven to the conclusion that if we expose our home market to these shocks, to that world chaos which I have striven to describe, that it is impossible to build in that home market a civilization higher than that which prevails in the rest of the world? And unless we build that higher civilization here with a higher purchasing power, what hope have we of absorbing the production of modern machinery which now cannot find an outlet? Can that civilization be built if our home market is exposed to price fluctuations, to dumping, to the competition of sweated labour, to all these electric shocks from the rest of the world which are daily dislocating our industrial areas? I do not see how you can build up that home market if you expose that market to those conditions and those shocks.

Having examined the conditions which made the Tory policy of simple tariffs seem antiquated and impotent to cope with the existing situation, Mosley continued to elaborate the policy of insulation by import control, bulk purchase and Commodity Boards, which he had advocated on previous occasions. He proposed, also, the centralization of the Empire's gold reserves, and the use of the Empire's annual production of gold to assist in introducing order into the existing unsatisfactory conditions of gold-distribution. He concluded with an appeal for rapid action by the nation:

> It is no use using soft words upon this subject. It is no good going to international conferences and saying: 'We are in a terribly weak position; will you please stop hoarding gold and placing tariffs against us?' It is no use telling us that we must wait until every other country in Europe has come up to our standard before we do anything in this matter. It is no use telling us that we must wait until every anarchical force has been brought under control. It is no use saying that we must wait for the organization of our trade until all the backward people in the world have come up to our standard of Socialism. If we wait until the sweet, small voice of the President of the Board of Trade at Geneva has drowned the strains of 'Giovinezza' in every Fascist capital, we shall have to wait for a very long time. If this kind of policy goes on we doom ourselves to wait until a series of unlikely things happen over which we have no control.

The New Party: Attempt at "Social Compromise" | 103

In the meantime we expose our industries and our trade to all these factors of chaos which are operating in the world market, to the dislocation of our industry by factors over which we have no control, and in the meantime we have to face with equanimity reductions in our standard of life in order to maintain our competitive position.

We drift back to the wage struggle of 1926 and worse; we drift to disaster in helplessness and disorganization because we shrink from the higher and the proper use of power. Meanwhile in Parliament we recite the classic cases of Free Trade and Protection like sixth-form boys reciting prize essays which they had not even composed. At the end we go to the country on a general election shouting the meaningless slogans of a century-old controversy, which has no more in common to the modern age than whiskers and crinolines. True that in the dust and clamour of the nineteenth century hustings we may obscure the failure of two Front Benches and two Parliaments. But in the turmoil England sinks quietly to her final lethargy. For my part, I believe if once we could realize that the old basis of our trade has gone, and gone for ever, that we have got to think again, and think harder than before, that we have to face modern problems with modern minds, we should then be able to lift this great economic problem and national emergency far above the turmoil of party clamour and with national unity could achieve a solution adequate to the problem and worthy of the modern mind.

Mr. Oliver Stanley, the intellectual leader of the younger Tories, followed with a speech which was sensational in that it accepted Mosley's main thesis, and underlined and supported many of the latter's arguments:

If the Government and the Chancellor of the Exchequer are right, and this is just such a crisis as we have seen before, then, perhaps, the only thing to do is to sit down and amuse ourselves for a little while with electoral reform or a Trade Union Bill, and wait until the economic blizzard is past and the sun comes out again, and Parliament can get down to the sole function of present-day government—the discussion of how the cake is going to be cut. Some of us take a very different view. Some of us do not think that this crisis is similar to any that we have ever been through before. Some of us do not think that the economic blizzard is ever going to pass unless we do something to make it pass. Some of us think that, unless we do something to make it pass, there will not only be no cake, but no bread, to cut in the future. We believe that the fundamentals have altered, that the whole condition and conception of our trade is different, that the case cannot be met by mere optimism and patience, but only by cunning and by method.

I accept the analysis which the hon. baronet the member for Smethwick (Sir O. Mosley) has given of the difference which exists between our trade conditions to-day and before the war... Whatever the reasons are, whether they are good or bad, whether the world can, in fact, survive split up into a hundred economic units, whatever the ultimate result may be, we have to face this fact. Five years ago there were signs that possibly the general trend of world opinion would change, that barriers might be lifted. Can anyone suggest that this is the case to-day? Can anyone deny that the last five years have seen an accentuation of that system? Can anyone deny that, for the next generation at least, we are faced with a world in which our goods will be largely denied access to markets?

If that be so, if the hon. Baronet's analysis be correct—and I believe it to be correct—then the whole basis of our old prosperity has vanished, our whole conception of our industrial future has been falsified. We have built up a population, we have built up an industrial system, we have erected a fiscal machine, we have created a standard of life, on the basis of our being the workshop of the world. We find to-day that the world does not want workshops. It wants markets... It is not pleasant to have to realize that your advantages have gone, that, having once enjoyed industrial supremacy, you have to come back into the ranks, and that, when you used to talk in terms of inevitable industrial supremacy, you talk now in terms of possible industrial equality.

A further unpleasant fact to face is that we are not going to get over our difficulties by refusing to face them. We realize the dangers and difficulties that lie in the path of an attempt to alter

The New Party: Attempt at "Social Compromise" | 105

our fiscal system, but we see the dangers and the difficulties that lie in the path before us to-day. We see the dangers and difficulties of trying to keep an unemployed population of 2,200,000... We have to face those dangers and to brave those difficulties. A new world faces us, and we have to adopt new methods... You are not going to compress the solution of a nation's difficulties into the headline of a morning paper. Socialism, Individualism, Cobdenism, Protectionism—let us cut the 'isms.' It is only by doing that that we can avert the catastrophe that is looming over our heads. We may differ as to machinery, but I believe that there is a general belief among people, irrespective of party and irrespective of theory, on two fundamental points. The first is the growing and ever-increasing importance of the home market as compared with the export markets on which we depended in the past, and the second is the absolute necessity, if we are to maintain that portion of exports which are necessary for our existence, of using and organizing our great consuming power to buy off the nationalist tendencies in the countries with which we deal.

Mr. Stanley proceeded to examine in detail and to give his general support to Mosley's proposals for the insulation of the home market. He concluded with an expression of sympathy for the Government, the terms of which are not without a certain element of irony when we remember the subsequent performances of the National Government of which Mr. Stanley was destined so soon to be a member:

If their difficulties have been great, their opportunities have been supreme, because they have behind them to-day what you never have in times of prosperity, a country which is frightened, a country which is anxious, a country which is prepared to get its help, to find its salvation, at the hands of anyone who is prepared to give it to it... The Government, if they had had courage, if they had had vision, might have cut right across the old historic traditions of this country. They might have achieved something which would have altered the future of this country for generations. They might have united behind them vast sections of the population which to-day are itching to have their hands at each other's throats. Their opportunity has been supreme.

The remainder of the speeches in that debate which came from men on either side of the House who had claims to any independence of outlook were couched in the same tones, from the dry Tory wit of Colonel John Buchan to the brilliant analysis of Mr. W. J. Brown, the somewhat emotional secretary of the Civil Servants' Union. The stage was set, and the situation was ripe, for an effective revolt of the independent elements in Parliament, on a scale which would have seriously embarrassed all the older party leaders. But if Mosley had been mistaken when he believed that British Labour-Socialism was capable of initiating a policy of action, and again when he believed that it was possible to carry through what was in essence a "Fascist" revolutionary economic policy within the framework of the democratic system, he made a still greater mistake when he contemplated the possibility of welding a dynamic political force out of the heterogeneous collection of democratic politicians who infested the lobbies of the House of Commons.

As Scanlon writes in reference to his own party:

> As for the majority of the back-benchers, there was still no indication that they had ceased to believe in their gods. The only people they seemed capable of disliking were those few who still persisted that the Government should have some regard for the pledges given to the poorest of the poor. Smug and complacent, they allowed the parliamentary game to be played as though everything were as comfortable in the country as it was in the House of Commons... Those who had ever understood Socialism had now definitely turned their backs on it, and had not the courage or intelligence to go for the only other alternative—a well-organized Capitalism... Whatever excuses could be offered for the first session, none could be offered for the second. When Parliament began its work on 20th October, 1930, the British working class was passing through a period of hardship the like of which had not been experienced in the mind of living man, and as Mr. Fenner Brockway pointed out in the House during the debate, the Cabinet had decided to devote the major part of the parliamentary year to discussion 'on electoral reform for 1933, and land taxation for 1934. (*Decline and Fall of the Labour Party*, p. 195 *et seq.*)

"If they had had courage, if they had had vision," Mr. Stanley thought, "they might have achieved something which would have altered the future of this country for generations." Unfortunately the democratic system produces and gives responsibility to men who are singularly deficient in just those two qualities which Mr. Stanley named.

A few days after the debate on the King's Speech, on 7th December, a manifesto was issued, bearing the signatures of seventeen Labour M.P.s, and also that of Mr. A. J. Cook, which set out a policy on the lines which up till then had been adumbrated by Mosley. In addition to Mr. Cook, Left activism was well represented by the names of Mr. Aneurin Bevan, a young Welsh miner, the aforementioned Mr. W. J. Brown, Mr. Oliver Baldwin, Mr. John McGovern, Mr. Phillips Price, Mr. J. F. Horrabin, Mr. John Strachey, Mr. W. G. Cove, and Mr. John Batey. The manifesto was ostensibly issued to influence policy within the party, but it invited "any in our party and in the nation who agree with the substance of such policy to state their agreement," and it was the basis of substantial agreement with important elements of opinion outside the Labour Party. The weeks dragged on and the preparation of an elaborate party policy was undertaken. This eventually was published and circulated as the "National Policy" of the New Party, and it bore the names of Messrs. Bevan and Brown, in addition to those of Sir Oswald Mosley, Mr. John Strachey and Mr. Allen Young. But while the "National Policy" was still in proof, the seventeen had dwindled to six, who finally resigned from the Labour Party at the beginning of March, 1931. Of these six, only Sir Oswald Mosley, and his wife, Lady Cynthia, with Mr. Strachey and Dr. Forgan, actually functioned on the council of the New Party. Mr. Bevan never definitely resigned from the Labour Party, and Messrs. Baldwin and Brown, after resigning, ultimately made their peace.

But if certain Labour members, confronted with the inability of Mosley to carry his maneuvre against the older parties to an ultimate success, were forced to humiliate themselves before the machine which they had professed to despise, the more cautious Tories had saved themselves from similar embarrassment. When some of them had already shown themselves very daring—for Tories—a resounding crack of Mr. Baldwin's whip had sent them slinking back to the soft lap of maternal Conservatism. Mosley, having once made up his mind, proceeded to the formation of the New Party without either the promise or the expectation of their support, but some of them had the grace to show a mild and lingering sympathy when the New Party—which had now become rather a forlorn hope—was finally launched. Three letters appeared in *The Times*, which were, in fact, at once the apologies of three very gallant gentlemen and the obituary notices of the policy of "social compromise."

In retrospect, it may be said that the New Party had failed before it had been launched, although the few who had followed through the whole design and found themselves directing its machine, continued to express high hopes both to their friends and to themselves. Its policy is best considered at length later, when we proceed to analyse the development of Mosley's ideas on national policy in his book, *Greater Britain*. It is sufficient to recall here that the New Party was formed six months before the country was faced with acute financial crisis, in order to warn the electorate that such a crisis was approaching, and to advocate a policy calculated to meet that crisis. The National Government surrendered in a hurry to the conditions which Mosley had anticipated, and they adopted in partial and belated fashion, elements of the very policy which he had been outlawed for advocating. Other parts—and very substantial parts—of that policy have since been borrowed by the Labour Party, when, after the landslide of 1931, they found themselves under the necessity of finding some substitute for the obsolete forms of Liberalism to which they had for so long adhered. The New Party policy was a policy which was sound enough in all the circumstances of the period during which it was evolved, and no one who was associated either with that party or with that policy need regret the hopelessness of the effort. Destiny itself was playing an unkind game with Oswald Mosley during the year 1931. At the time that the New Party was officially launched according to pre-arranged plan, and while he and his few colleagues were taking their formal steps of resignation from the Labour Party, Mosley himself was lying seriously ill with pneumonia. He had got up too soon after a sharp attack of influenza, in order to motor out of London to rally an adherent who was losing heart at the last moment. The result was that his life was despaired of for some days. In the meantime Lady Cynthia Mosley had to carry the brunt of the work, although she was herself in indifferent health, which ultimately was to fail her altogether. That heroic figure appeared at all the great meetings which had been booked previously for her husband. There seemed something symbolic and supremely noble in her as she faced the angry audiences of disappointed Labour supporters in the North, and filled the place, not only of her husband, but of all the clever men who had been clever enough to keep out of the New Party. Cynthia Mosley, during those anxious, bitter weeks, gave the pattern of real greatness.

Mosley was, during the summer of 1931, faced with the necessity of building up a normal democratic machine to fight the other democratic machines in a coming general election. He himself—and sometimes his party—was already accused of Fascist tendencies, but the very composition of the party made it impossible for Mosley to adopt either the ideology or the methods of Fascism, even had he himself become convinced at that period that he could not logically avoid a full confession of the Fascist creed. The party of "social compromise" was a party of men who had agreed to agree in principle, but who were always unable to agree in detail. At the same time the imminence of complete failure—which under the circumstances must be inevitable—in the event of a General Election, did not help to stimulate the enthusiasm of several important members of the council, who had been bred, and who thought completely in terms of the social-democratic tradition. The party had gathered to itself, also, a number of distinguished "intellectuals," who, even more than the Parliamentarians, felt the pull of the social democratic conscience. The result of the Ashton by-election in the mid-summer did not fail to produce an "ideological" crisis within the party. Allen Young, a capable ex-Socialist and the personal secretary of Mosley, had been the candidate of the New Party in this contest. The election created great interest, and the enthusiasm at the New Party meetings had caused unjustified hopes. In Manchester, long-forgotten "young" Tories telephoned to make inquiries, and a rather middle-aged one actually sat in the dim light of the New Party lorry the night before the poll. Allen Young secured over 4,000 votes, which was quite a creditable performance under the circumstances, but it cast before ugly shadows of the prospects of New Party candidates in the event of an early General Election. The circumstances of the defeat created a strong impression on John Strachey. He gives a vivid picture of his impressions in his book *The Menace of Fascism*:

> I recollect the figure of Mosley standing on the town hall steps at Ashton-under-Lyne, facing the enormous crowd which entirely filled the wide, cobbled market-square. The result of the election had just been announced, and it was seen that the intervention of the New Party had defeated the Labour candidate and elected the Conservative. The crowd consisted of

most of the keenest workers in the Labour Party in all the neighbouring Lancashire towns. (Four or five million workers live within a tram-ride of Ashton.) The crowd was violently hostile to Mosley and the New Party. It roared at him, and, as he stood facing it, he said to me: 'That is the crowd that has prevented anyone doing anything in England since the war.' At that moment British Fascism was born.

The defeat which steeled Mosley to face up to the ultimate realities of the position into which the clear logic of his own thought was leading him had quite a different effect on some other members of the council of the New Party. It was obvious that they were neither prepared to face the hard realities with which the Fascist alternative confronted them, nor the obloquy which pursues those who have detached themselves from one of the great political machines without at the same time having obtained the support of a no less-powerful alternative machine.

As Strachey writes:

> The actual breaking-point came upon that touchstone of the modern world, our attitude to Soviet Russia. I was asked to write a memorandum defining the New Party's attitude to Soviet Russia. I wrote an unequivocally pro-Russian document. Mosley equally unequivocally rejected it, and gave, quite frankly, his real reason for doing so. If the New Party adopted a pro-Russian attitude, all hopes of support from the Conservatives and capitalists would be gone. (*The Menace of Fascism*, p. 164.)

We quote this statement at some length, not only in order to demonstrate the trivial pretext which the social democratic element had chosen as an excuse for covering their retreat, but in order to repudiate Strachey's statement with regard to Mosley. Mosley's attitude to Russia was and is frankly opportunist. He would be prepared to treat Russia on the same basis as any other foreign country, and he considered it no more necessary to make announcements into the air with regard to his policy in power towards Russia than it would have been to make a similar announcement with regard to possible future policy towards any other country. A number of industrialists are notoriously in favour of closer relations with Russia in their own sectional interests, and the question of

The New Party: Attempt at "Social Compromise" | 111

attracting the approval of industrialists can therefore hardly be said to have arisen. Mosley was laying emphasis, at this time, on a policy of greater co-operation with the Dominions, and he was always inclined to discount the assumed interest of the workers—except in a few areas where local employment might depend to a limited extent on Russian orders—in any policy directed towards the development of special relations with the Soviet Union.

So it was upon the Russian issue that Messrs. Strachey and Young[3] resigned from the New Party. The fact that they were not followed even by many of their own intimate friends among the rank and file would appear to indicate that the Russian pretext struck few sympathetic chords within a party membership which had been largely recruited from the Left. It would, perhaps, be unfair to suggest that the issue was raised to cover a purely personal "strategic retreat," but it may at least be said that the pretext was characteristic of the woolliness of the typical social democratic mind, and of the total incapacity of that mind to confront the basic realities of the existing political and economic situation in Great Britain.

As it was, the flight of the social democrats relieved Mosley of the last necessity of attempting to conciliate the fluctuations in the mental condition of these highly-sensitive individuals, and he could proceed without the embarrassment of the constantly threatened "split" to develop his own more realist conceptions. The tactics of the "split"—so characteristic of the disintegrative processes of democracy, were to play no part in the building of the hard core of a Fascist Party.

In the meantime the financial crisis—which Mosley had so long anticipated in terms of crisis in the balance of trade—broke like a tornado over the astonished heads of complacent financiers and all the smug advocates of "Freedom for Capital." The occasion was the German financial crisis, with the serious reactions in this country, resulting from the irresponsible activities of city groups in financing short-term loans to Germany. The facts are too recent to require recapitulation, but the methods whereby the results of serious faults in capitalist practice were

---

[3] Allen Young was of a different calibre to Strachey. A gnarled little Clydeside worker, who had established himself as an economist of great penetration, he failed to reconcile his revolutionary economic conclusions, with his orthodox democratic idealism. He turned away from the grim realities of action—the victim of a hyper-sensitive conscience.

manipulated to justify a "national" attack on the standards of living of wide sections of the community should be studied as the supreme example of the genius for maneuvre within the democratic framework which the bourgeois class have developed as the substitute for direct control. The May Report on Economy, which had tended to precipitate the panic, served now both as a weapon of terrorism and as an excuse for surrender within the rival political groups in the House of Commons. The ingenuous pretence of scared social democrats that the crisis was the result of "a bankers' ramp" was, of course, entirely irrelevant—as Mosley pointed out—to the fundamental issues of the moment. The English bankers were not likely to precipitate a crisis—and their own embarrassment—in order to overthrow a social democratic Government which had always shown itself completely subservient to themselves. The complete independence of any given national unit which Capitalism had developed during the preceding decades—and particularly since the German War—and the dominance which the international banking machine enjoyed, in an emergency, over any national unit was now demonstrated in the crudest possible form. Loans from Paris and New York, required to afford even a few days', or weeks', stability to the pound sterling, were conditioned by a reconstruction of the Government and an abrupt reversal of the social policy which successive parties in the State had been pursuing for the last thirty years. The proud British democracy was at last shown with the most brutal directness that the whole of their vaunted system of self-government was nothing more than a futile sham. But so great was the panic engendered by the immediate situation, and stimulated by those interests who hesitated no longer even to disguise the reality of their power, that those varied forces which go to constitute public opinion in Britain allowed themselves to be stampeded into an orgasm of patriotic emotionalism without realizing any of the significance of their great surrender.

Within the Labour Party the well-known social democratic tactic of the "split" was carried through with a degree of facility which demonstrated the perfect working of the British machine by contrast with the more clumsy convolutions of its Continental parallels in similar emergencies. While a few leaders and a small proportion of the rank and file remained to give the other parties a sense of national (and "class") cohesion, by occupying the nominal leadership and other important positions within the new Government, the majority—although already committed to practically all parts of the policy which they were to begin

The New Party: Attempt at "Social Compromise" | 113

immediately to denounce—broke off to rally the rank and file of Labour, and to perform the useful function of ensuring that the disillusioned battalions of the workers were not diverted into extreme and uncontrollable paths.

On 8th September, 1931, James Ramsay MacDonald, the veteran leader of British Socialism, faced the House of Commons at the head of a National Government. "My colleagues are with me now," he could say with pride, as he pointed to the serried ranks of Conservatives and Liberals at his back. Quite all his colleagues were not there, for four members of this emergency Government were Marquesses—possibly on the assumption that Marquesses still have a market value in New York.

The occasion was a memorable one, and any student of contemporary history—particularly of the history of European social democracy—should read and re-read the report of the debate which followed.

"Little did we think," said the Prime Minister, "when we bade each other good-bye on 31st July last, that the next meeting of the House of Commons would show this revolutionary change... but may I say, first of all, that this is one of those extraordinary incidents which happen in politics, and which are really a test of democratic government. Every now and again things happen which require courage to face." (Interruption.)

"Let this House be in no doubt about the situation," continued this erstwhile prophet of Marxism. "I wish I could afford merely to talk magnificent generalities about it."

"The specific, and indeed the only problem," Mr. MacDonald went on to explain, "was to restore waning confidence, to stop the drain, to secure the loan necessary to give us a chance to rebuild our defences.

"An attempt is being made, I see, to represent the crisis as no crisis at all. I have said that it did exist. We must not be deceived, moreover, in giving proper proportion and proper weight to the imminence of the crisis because of the fact that it was of long origin... Nor must people imagine, or get away with the criticism, that what is being proposed to be done now is of the nature of a permanent cure for the whole system. The position when this is over has to be carefully and thoroughly examined and reviewed so that evils can be remedied and faults removed from it. But that is not for this moment. Criticisms of the banking system—these have to be examined... Who said that for the first time? Who is alone thinking of that now in relation to our difficulties? None of these things can be overlooked. None of these things will be overlooked when the lack of confidence recently shown in this country, and which has brought us into our recent troubles, has been overcome."

Having excused the suggestion of an hon. member that the country should "get rid of him" as "a little bit of humour," the Marxist leader went on to explain the details of the situation as a result of which the complete surrender of the pretensions of social democracy had become necessary.

"The financial situation," he said, "had worked itself out, all things had been considered carefully, out and in, backward and forward, up and down, and analysed; but it was perfectly clear that what had to be secured and what was the first goal that had to be reached was a loan. When it was put to the representatives of the other political parties they said to us: 'Will this scheme secure the loan? If it does, we will support it. If it does not, we shall not.' Again, with full consent, representatives of the Bank of England were consulted as to whether in their opinion the scheme proposed would produce the loan. Remember, we were asking for it. If our terms did not give assurance, we should not get it. (Interruption.) Nor have you ever got it under any other system.

"There was nothing different between these consultations and those which precede the floating, say, of a limited liability company. People interested ask questions. They want to find out what provision is made for this, and what provision is made for that. If they feel secure, they subscribe. If they do not feel secure, they do not subscribe. That is exactly the position...

"I wish to state, specifically and emphatically—and this has been reported to my colleagues before—that never in the whole process of the negotiations carried on by the Chancellor of the Exchequer and myself, with the approval of the Government, and reported to it immediately after each interview, did the banks interfere with political proposals. They simply confined themselves to giving us expert advice as to the effect of the proposals on the possible yield of the loan. (Interruption.) I hope that hon. members before they laugh at the matter will ponder over it. Some people may say that these ways of raising money are humiliating, and those who cannot bring their minds to bear upon actual facts, and who know very little about the Constitution, may describe it as unconstitutional, but that is precisely what has happened for generations in every public, private, or State loan that has been raised in the money-markets in the whole world.

"And, certainly, suppose they were objectionable as some hon.

The New Party: Attempt at "Social Compromise" | 115

members think, suppose every time we saw a banker he said: 'You must make this political change,' we could not have changed the system during the day or two which were left.

"In view of the far-reaching negotiations which must be begun pretty soon as regards reparation settlements and so on, which can only be begun to be discussed when the very best of goodwill has been created between France, America and ourselves, I am sure that those who have experience of the conduct of foreign affairs will see to it that in this campaign against the banks nothing will be repeated like what was said the other day, which was quite untrue, against the magnificent helpfulness and goodwill shown by New York and the American bankers from beginning to end of the whole negotiations."

After prophesying that, but for the negotiations which had enabled Britain to retain for a few more days a slippery grip upon the gold standard, "one day it would have been twenty shillings and the next day ten shillings, and it would have tumbled without control," the Prime Minister proceeded to a last grand repudiation of every principle which he had advocated during the preceding thirty years.

"It is no use," he said, "sitting complacently talking about considerations which have nothing to do with this crisis, and in spite of the fact that country after country in Europe has undergone it for precisely the same reasons as are beginning to show in our finance. (Interruption.) Over-borrowing, over-spending! The hon. member knows perfectly well that in different circumstances and down different ways, but from precisely the same things, the same methods, the same shortcomings, borrowing to pay debts, expenditure out of proportion to capacity, one piled on top of the other, country after country has suffered a financial collapse, and the people who suffered were not the wealthy people most of all, but the great mass of working people. People may say that this is a scare, but I challenge anyone to say where the deterioration once begun, where the tumbling once started, is to be stopped. The experience of other nations shows that it stops only at the bottom. That I decline to face, and will continue to decline… I appeal to all classes and conditions to go cheerfully with the Government over the hard and broken road along which our security, our honour and our well-being have to be found. Far better for all of us to go with tight belts into stability than with loose ones into confusion."

The attitude of the New Party at this juncture had never been in doubt. They had consistently opposed and attacked the policy of deflation in all its implications, even to the Anomalies Bill which had been introduced by the Labour Government—and supported by their rank and file—in what were to prove their last days of office. The New Party members were determined not to rally to the scaremongers in a last desperate effort to maintain the deflationary policy. At the same time Mosley was unwilling to embarrass the older parties in this crisis of their own making, and he stated as much in the first few sentences of his speech in reply to the orthodox party leaders. He even went so far, on the following day, as to support the Government in taking certain emergency powers on the grounds that "the only possible way to get out of our present difficulties is to act quickly, and it is impossible for rapid action to take place if there are Parliamentary delays and obstruction of the old-fashioned order."

Mosley was, however, ruthless in his analysis of the pretensions and policy of the new "National" Government.

"I would," he said, "put before the House the view that this crisis, this event of the last few weeks, is not in itself a crisis at all. It is merely the realization of the fact that crisis exists by people who for months, and some of them for years, have refused to face that obvious fact. It is the panic of all the woolly-headed people who refuse to face the facts, the menacing facts of the situation; it is that panic and that alone which led to the events of the last few weeks. The position of Great Britain as an industrial and financial nation is certainly no better and is very little worse than it has been for the last year or year and a half. It is the sudden waking up to the fact of industrial crisis which has led to the present revenue and financial crisis. That industrial crisis has been referred to very briefly to-day. But the ugly facts and figures of that crisis have not been mentioned at all. We have dealt purely in terms and figures of finance.

"... I would like to quote one or two figures which give the whole reason for the crisis. If we take the first seven months of this year and compare them with the first seven months of 1929, we find a 45 per cent drop in the exports of this country. That is really your crisis. That is why you have panic on the markets of the world. Even if you make all allowances for slight monetary changes in the interval, that figure is startling and almost appalling. In the same period imports have fallen by only 30 per cent. It is the comparison between imports and exports... which is the really alarming aspect of the situation. Imports for this year have more than doubled exports. In 1929, only two years ago, they were

The New Party: Attempt at "Social Compromise" | 117

little more than 50 per cent above exports. In manufactured goods we now import as much as we export.

"That extraordinary change in the balance of trade, illustrated in those very few and obvious and simple figures, accounts, and accounts entirely, for the present financial panic. In view of progressive deterioration of the industrial position, what is the use of trying to balance your Budget on the present basis of revenue when, unless you have an active industrial policy, your revenue is bound again to collapse within a measurable distance of time? That is why the one thing which I want to urge upon the House is the immediate adoption of some constructive industrial policy. I put forward my suggestions for an industrial policy over eighteen months ago. I also put forward an analysis of the position leading to the present crisis which has since proved correct. So, perhaps, the remedies might be looked at now with a little more favour than they received at the time when I suggested them. The point is this: Some plan and some policy from some quarter to meet the industrial situation has to be adopted unless things are to get worse... I believe that the adoption of a constructive industrial policy is far and away the most important duty of a Government or a House of Commons. I believe that it is a far greater factor in actually holding our exchanges than the balancing of the Budget. What, after all, is more important to the foreign investor? Is it to see £100,000,000 or even £200,000,000 added to the £9,000,000,000 or so of our National Debt at present, or is it to see British industries go down and unemployment rush up past the 3,000,000 mark? If anybody were investing money in Britain, would he not be more worried by the collapse of our industries and the absence of any policy to remedy it than by any temporary deficit in our Budget?

"... Many people seem to think that we are the only country in the world faced with the prospect of a Budget deficit. As a matter of fact ours is the only country in the world which is taking any steps to meet it. Deficits are the fashion nowadays. All the best countries have deficits. America, the strong boy of the world, has an enormous deficit, far bigger than the one confronting us. France, I think, has always a deficit. I am not sure, but at least I looked through a long list of the most respectable and powerful countries the other day, and I find that nearly all have big deficits. There is no collapse of their exchanges, no withdrawal of foreign deposits, no efflux of gold because they have deficits. Why? Because their industrial position is strong, and the investor has confidence... Therefore, the view that I have to put before the House is this: That it is far more important to give the world—and Britishers—confidence in the industrial future of this country than to try to balance the Budget upon a basis of revenue which will soon prove illusory.

"Suppose that we adopted the view that it is far more important to have industrial recovery than to balance our Budget, and that we might, in fact, despite all financial respectability and prudery in these matters, have for the moment a deficit, provided that we were sure that in a few years we should emerge from the present position by reason of a policy of industrial reconstruction. We then should adopt the method of balancing our Budget advocated by Mr. Keynes and other economists, which is simply to continue to borrow—I know that it shocks hon. Members—to continue to borrow to provide for the Unemployment Insurance Fund, or I would prefer to say, borrow to provide constructive works to give employment in place of it, to suspend the Sinking Fund, and to raise the remainder by a revenue tariff, or, as I would say, a protective tariff.

"But may I try to develop this theme as seriously as the situation demands? Suppose that we balance our Budget in that way, would the resulting situation be so terrible? A deficit is regarded as a dangerous thing because it is inflation, but does any hon. member suggest that we are in danger of inflation in a period in which prices are sharply falling? It is true that a measure like that might tend to arrest the fall of prices in this country and maintain our price level above the world level; that there would be a disparity between the two and a consequent strain upon our exchange and a possible efflux of gold. But the very measures which have been suggested counteract that tendency, in that a strongly protective tariff tends to keep the trade balance much more favourable to us, and measures of expansion at home, such as borrowing for the reconditioning of British industry or even for constructive work of the kind which the Liberal Party used to suggest, provide a more attractive outlet for British capital and prevent some of it going abroad.

"The fact that such capital resources are available is clear from any study of recent figures. Capital issues have dropped from £30,000,000 a month in 1928 to £13,000,000 a month at present. That means £17,000,000 a month, or over £200,000,000 a year, which, if brought back into active use, would provide employment for some 1,000,000 men in this country. I suggest that if a protectionist policy, stimulating the home market and raising revenue, accompanied... by stringent guarantees as to efficiency of industry, as to low prices, as to good wages

The New Party: Attempt at "Social Compromise" | 119

and the whole of the scientific machinery which some of us suggest for ensuring that you will get the benefit of protection without its evils—if a policy of protection of that kind, which I might describe as scientific protection... a policy of scientific protection of that kind, linked with a policy for the reconstruction, reconditioning and restoring to world efficiency of British industry, would, I believe, be an alternative to the policy of mere cutting down and additional taxation which has been suggested."

Mosley then turned to the methods which had recently been applied to meet the actual conditions of the financial crisis.

"We have not heard to-day," he said, "any of the strong, manly posturing about the foreign investments. There has not been one word from the Labour benches about the mobilization of foreign investments. Have they looked into it again? It was done in the war. We have, I believe, some £4,000,000,000 of foreign investments, and I believe that foreign deposits in this country total about £400,000,000. If we were able by any means to do what we did in the war by getting into our hands one-tenth of these foreign investments, we should not have had to go cap in hand to the markets of the world. We should not have had to hold out the hat of Britain as a supplicant. We could have said to Wall Street or to any other stock exchange: 'We have £400,000,000 of dollar securities, and unless we get the loan we want, they go on to Wall Street to-morrow morning and you will get the biggest bear raid in your market that you have known for the last two years.' And you would have got your loan. If you want a policy of vigour and of virility to face world finance, there it is. I venture to suggest that you could have secured the loan which you have secured and which has pegged your exchange, without humiliation to Britain, by the use of the financial strength which Britain possesses. I suggest, further, a policy of scientific protection of home expansion and of the use of our capital resources. The reconditioning of our industries accompanying such a policy as that would within a short period have placed this country in the forefront of the industrial nations of the world."

Mosley concluded with an answer to MacDonald's final apostrophe.

"It seems to me," he said, "that Britain in her crisis is being asked to turn her face to the wall and to give up like an old woman who knows that she has to die. I want to see this country at least make an effort. I do not believe and never have believed in the cure of fasting, but in the cure of effort. I believe that the way out is not the way of the monk, but the way of the athlete. It is only by exertion, it is only by endeavour, by a great attempt to reorganize our industries, that this country can win through, and I venture to suggest that the simple question before the House in this debate is whether Great Britain is to meet its crisis lying down or standing up."

The first National Government endured some weeks. It was not aware of the great panic-power of its appeal, and hesitated to go to the country. Finally the international financial situation and the pressure of the Tory Right Wing forced MacDonald to take the jump. Britain lay down to be jumped on, and the National Government was returned by a majority the size of which its most acute advisers had never dared to anticipate. If they had been members of the advertising fraternity engaged in the sale and distribution of actual patent medicines to invalid proletarians, the party organizers would have appreciated even more than they did the terrific potency of the fear motif in "selling ideas" to the democracy.

The New Party was not in a position, after six months of active existence, to throw up overnight the vast machinery necessary to fight a general election at short notice. As a gesture they put eighteen candidates into the field. Most of them lost their deposits. Oswald Mosley, himself, polled about a third of the votes accorded to the entire party. The total vote cast for the New Party was in the neighbourhood of half that given to Communist candidates. Both the Fascists in Italy and the Nazis in Germany had, in their early phases, made electoral efforts which were even less auspicious. The organs of the capitalist Press proclaimed that Mosley was finished. A few—less envenomed—lamented the passing of a figure of great Parliamentary promise. Mosley, meantime, had begun again—from the beginning.

Chapter VII

—Fascism and the Crisis of the West—

During the last months of the German War an obscure Munich schoolmaster published a work of nearly a thousand pages under the title *Untergang des Abendlandes*. The work appeared in England in 1926 as *The Decline of the West*. Few major books have aroused such hostile criticism nor deserved such profound respect. While the professors of the German democracy were combining to produce composite attacks upon every angle of the magnificent monolith of Oswald Spengler's thought, history was taking the course which he had foreseen under their very noses.

Spengler's portentous pessimism was, in fact, the ultimate expression of the despair in the heart of the bourgeois classes of Europe. The world-fear which had been voiced by Schopenhauer and by Nietzsche in the preceding century was by Spengler *shown* to have a basis of inevitable reality. The shallow intellects of minor professors and publicists were summoned to refute his smallest facts, and to conjure away the impending night of his great prophecy with the facile rainbow of an optimism which was toned to a pale grey by the daily events of the world in which they were all living. Spengler's interpretation of world history is a colossal monument to the European mind, which may well remain the epitaph of his "Faustian man," if that man fails to grip the future.

By the side of Spengler's work "the outlines of history" of little democratic optimists like Wells become the splutterings of well-paid journalists. Yet Spengler must remain the last great intellectual titan of a world-class which could analyse, but which could not confront, its destiny. He came to the edge of the abyss of the old world, and he looked back upon the heights and down into the depths, but he failed to appraise the potentialities of that strange product of old chaos—the New Man. He hesitated before the grim crudities of Bolshevism, and turned in despair from the Russian man. He failed to foresee the new character of a Fascism which was already growling in the streets of his own Munich, and which within three years was to grasp the power in Italy. Spengler anticipated only a new "Caesarism," which his critics who were presently to feel the weight of unattended revolution, were inclined, under the awning of the Weimar Constitution, to regard as the most fantastic of prognostications. Spengler must be regarded as the ultimate and the greatest expression of the bourgeois mind, and as such he belongs to the past rather than to the future. His latest work, *Man and Technics*, is an abdication in despair. But at the same time his interpretation of past history remains valid, and constitutes a base from which modern man may begin to interpret his own present and to modify his own future.

Spengler has interpreted history as a series of *cultures*, which blossom finally into the mature phase, which he differentiates as *civilization*. Each of these *cultures* have had their own character, their own soul, and their own symbolic forms of expression. In spirit and in dynamic each *culture* has differed profoundly from others which have come before and after it. Each culture has been influenced in varying degrees by those which have preceded it, and each culture has influenced its successors. But fundamentally each has been very different from the other, and each has proceeded to its own strange and inevitable destiny. Materially these cultures are governed by certain basic conditions of Nature, in the same way as the life of plants is controlled by the character of the soil in which they have been seeded. The economics of the early stages of a culture based on the primitive activities of men are productive of political and social conditions, which are found to be repeated in the parallel stages of other cultures. It is therefore possible to draw close comparisons in the history of the material development of all known cultures. They are found to pass through the same social-political stages—through a period of early "god-emperors," and then through the stage of monarcho-feudalism, followed by the phase of absolute monarchy, and then the spell of oligarchy (parliamentarism or bourgeois-feudalism), to the ultimate disintegrative phase of democracy, which precedes a last popular-Imperial or "Caesarian" interval before a final collapse. Spengler has gone far to establish the validity of his theories in examining the history of all known cultures, but in relation to the modern world his definition of the course of the Apollinian (or Classical), the

Magian (or Arabe-Byzantine) and the Faustian (or European) are the most significant.

The period of democracy is the period of the blooming of the *culture* into the *civilization*. As the foliage flourishes the roots are already beginning to decay. It is the phase of *mass*. Money-economy and big capital have destroyed the old traditional bases of the life of a community. The State is no longer based on the peasant, the lord and the priest. The ideals which derive from the patriarchal monarchy or republic appear to be utterly ridiculous and alien to the shifting and shiftless populations of great cities. Power derives from the control of a mass of money, and no longer from hereditary rights and the fixed ownership of tangible assets such as land (or ships as in the case of the Venetian and Genoese Republics and the various maritime states of the Classical-Apollinian culture). Public opinion is the expression of the fluctuating passions and hopes of vast city masses and not of fixed classes of static peasants, steady burghers and impassive nobles. In the mass there is a continual mingling, a feverish confusion, a lack of orientation, which corresponds to the vast and uncontrolled fluctuations in the ownership of wealth in the economic sphere. There are no longer noble houses, but banking houses. There are no longer classes, but "the masses." The land has ceased to be the basis of the life of a community. The land has no interest except for the dwindling number of its occupiers.

Instead the giant city—the "megapolis" of Spengler—sucks into its iron belly the insignificant units who swarm in from all the outlying lands of the old "culture." The Americans have coined the euphemism of "The Melting Pot" to describe this process. And the process has always been the same, whether it be the hiving of Armenians, Gauls and Arabs in the dark tenements of Rome, or the amalgam of Russians, Saxons, Spaniards and Bulgarians in the slums of Byzantium, or the rough-and-tumble of English, Irish, Scots, Italians, Poles, Jews, Ukrainians and Chinese, in the backlands of Chicago, Pittsburg and New York.

When economic and social life has become a mass mingling, politics are also mass-politics, whether it be in the Forum of Rome, the Hippodrome of Byzantium, or in the hysterical General Elections of Britain and America. The day of Lincoln and of the Gracchi is already past. It is the day of Al Smith and of Clodius. Parties lose their *class* significance and become mere aggregations of individuals, mere rival gangs maneuvring for the control of money-power, who are forced in order to carry the day for themselves, to appeal occasionally and spasmodically to the shallow interest of the city mobs. Such are the Conservatives and the Liberal-Socialists, the Republicans and the Democrats, the Optimates, and the Populares. Gang-politics produce gangster-politics. The intellect of the cities and of city politics is exhausting itself, and intellectual politics utterly discredit themselves. "Men of action"—physical men "of the blood" in contrast to the exhausted intellectuals—alone have the capacity to master events and to arrive at the control of the uncontrollable megalopolitan state. It is the phase of the Pompeys and the Caesars, the Mussolinis and the Hitlers, even of the Roosevelts. This phase represents the bankruptcy of the "city-mind." The end of all intellectual aspirations has arrived. It is only men "of the blood"—"the fact-men"—who can confront chaos. Whether these "fact-men" may only delay the coming of chaos as in the history of past civilizations, or whether they may give the time which modern man needs in order to know and discipline himself and arrive at newer forms of continuing, remains the great riddle of the present epoch. Spengler, in a memorable passage, has contemplated the fate of the intellectual and the destiny of the man of action, and his conclusions are the more impressive since he himself writes as an objective "thinker:"

> Destiny has made the man so or so—subtle and fact-shy, or active and contemptuous of thought. But the man of the active category is a whole man, whereas in the contemplative a single organ can operate without (and even against) the body. All the worse, then, when this organ tries to master actuality as well as its own world, for then we get all those ethico-politico-social reform-projects which demonstrate, unanswerably, how things ought to be and how to set about making them so—theories that without exception rest upon the hypothesis that all men are as rich in ideas and as poor in motives as the author is (or thinks he is). Such theories, even when they have taken the field armed with the full authority of a religion or the prestige of a famous name, have not in one single instance effected the slightest alteration in life. They have merely caused us to think otherwise than before about life. And this, precisely, is the doom of the "late" ages of a culture, the ages of much writing and much reading—that they should perpetually confuse the opposition of life and thought with the opposition between thought-about-life

and thought-about-thought. All world-improvers, priests, and philosophers are unanimous in holding that life is a fit object for the nicest meditation, but the life of the world goes its own way, and cares not in the least what is said about it...

For in the last resort, only the active man, the man of destiny, lives in the actual world, the world of political, military and economic decisions, in which concepts and systems do not figure or count. Here a shrewd blow is more than a shrewd conclusion, and there is sense in the contempt with which statesmen and soldiers of all times have regarded the 'ink-slinger and the bookworm' who think that world history exists for the sake of the intellect or science or even art. Let us say frankly and without ambiguity: the understanding divorced from sensation is only one, and not the decisive, side of life. A history of Western thought may not contain the name of Napoleon, but in the history of actuality Archimedes, for all his scientific discoveries, was possibly less effective than that soldier who killed him at the storming of Syracuse...

All grand events of history are carried by beings of the cosmic order, by peoples, parties, armies, and classes, while the history of the intellect runs its course in loose associations and circles, schools, levels of education, 'tendencies' and 'isms.' And here again it is a question of destiny whether such aggregates at the decisive moments of highest effectiveness find a leader or are driven blindly on, whether the chance headmen are men of the first order or men of no real significance tossed up, like Robespierre or Pompey, by the surge of events. It is the hall-mark of the statesman that he has a sure and penetrating eye for these mass-souls that form and dissolve on the tide of the times, their strength and their duration, their direction and purpose. And even so, it is a question of Incident whether he is one who can master them or one who is swept away by them. (*Decline of the West*, II, p. 16 *et seq.*)

Facing the naked realities of the modern world, with its hungry Communism and its angry Fascism, the tremulous bourgeois mind is forced to deny the validity of the intellect. Spengler continues:

In the historical world, there are no ideals, but only facts—no truths, but only facts. There is no reason, no honesty, no equity, no final aim, but only facts, and anyone who does not realize this should write books on politics—let him not try to *make* politics.

In nerveless horror the intellect contemplates that supreme expression of the power of intellect—"the world-city." The men of intellect abdicate before the problems of its chaos, and it is left to the ruthless "fact-men" to cope with its formless anarchy. As Spengler writes:

> The stone colossus, Cosmopolis, stands at the end of the life's course of every culture. The culture-man whom the land has spiritually formed is seized and possessed by his new creation, the City, and is made into its creature, its executive organ, and finally its victim. This stony mass is the *absolute* city. Its image, as it appears with all its grandiose beauty in the light-world of the human eye, contains the whole noble death-symbolism of the definite thing-become.

Each great culture has been consummated in the dreadful magnificence of its megalopolitan phase. The story of Frankenstein repeats itself. Paris and Berlin, London and New York, are but the time-symbols of a ripening civilization, as were Rome and Alexandria, Byzantium, Baghdad and Samarra, in the "contemporary" phases of older cultures. Again, Spengler:

> The block-tenements of Rome, such as the famous Insula Feliculae, rose with a street breadth of only three to five metres to heights that have never been seen in Western Europe, and are seen in only a few cities in America. Near the Capitol, the roofs already reached to the level of the hill-saddle. But always the splendid mass-cities harbour lamentable poverty and degraded habits, and the attics and mansards, the cellars and back courts are breeding a new type of raw man—in Baghdad and in Babylon, just as in Tenochtitlan and to-day in London and Berlin.

The consciousness of the horror and the fascination of the megalopolitan life has become the theme of a vast modern literature, particularly since the last war, when men have come to realize the remorseless power of the Machine, which is chawing into pulp the whole cultural life of the Europe which they can remember and regret. As Eugen Diesel writes of Berlin:

> Between these disconnected streets and squares and buildings, with all their individual qualities loom the endless districts in which the millions live and work and have their being. These districts are almost always without form or character; they do not even stand in any particular relation to a definite core or centre of the city... Nothing helps to make more human the square blocks of stone of which these depressing neighbourhoods are built. They have nothing warm or vital about them; the basis of everything is the trades union and the statistical chart, or in the better districts the state of business. The fact that they are often decked out in the most florid style of "Berlin Renaissance" only makes them the more unpleasant. An atmosphere of sinister oppression and mechanical existence broods over them. In such districts Berlin will eventually be able to house eight and even ten millions of people... It has always been the place where chaos has acquired form, as chaos. And now that Germany along with the rest of the world is a chaos, Berlin has really come into its own. (*Germany and the Germans*, pp. 102-7.)

In England a whole literary generation takes up the refrain of Mr. T. S. Eliot in *The Waste Land*.

> Unreal City
> Under the brown fog of a winter dawn.
> A crowd flowed over London Bridge, so many,
> I had not thought death had undone so many.

And again:

> He who was living is now dead
> We who were living are now dying
> With a little patience.

Chapter VII

Falling towers
Jerusalem Athens Alexandria
Vienna, London
Unreal.

London Bridge is falling down falling down falling down.

Yet it is the men of the intellect, "the intellectuals," who know and feel the squalor of the city's disintegration, who constitute themselves, in the political field, the most desperate defenders of an uncontrolled formlessness of all moral and intellectual life. Like intelligent bluebottles on the muck-heap of all culture, they sun themselves in its foul odours and swell fat upon its ordure. Not only religion, but all formative thought, all virile effort, become for them the subjects for tittering ridicule. All morality, all courage, all natural vitality, is by them dissected with the logic of hopelessness. Lolling among the cushions of their philosophy, titillating themselves with the needles of refined sensation, they allow their relaxed minds to contemplate an ultimate futility which they themselves diffuse. Of Jean Cocteau's book, *Opium—the Diary of an Addict*, a leading English intellectual review can write:

> The book is a *pastiche* of ideas, epigrams, conclusions and impressions. They were written during the time when the author was in a clinic, recovering from the effects of opium smoking. His mind was therefore in a peculiarly relaxed condition. He stands up for the drug, separating it from all other drugs, as gold lies apart from all other metals.

Spengler goes on:

> No wretchedness, no compulsion, not even a clear vision of the madness of this development, avails to neutralize the attractive force of these daemonic creations... Once the full sinful beauty of this last marvel of all history has captured a victim, it never lets him go. Primitive folk can loose themselves from the soil and wander, but the intellectual nomad never. Home-sickness for the great city is keener than any other nostalgia. Home is for him any one of these giant cities, but even the nearest village is alien territory. He would sooner die upon the pavement than go

'back' to the land. Even disgust at this pretentiousness, weariness of the thousand-hued glitter, the *taedium vitae* that in the end overcomes many, does not set them free. They take the city with them into the mountains or on the sea. They have lost the country within themselves, and will never regain it outside.

Spengler proceeds to define that "tension" which the life of the city creates, in contrast to the serenity—the equable balance—which comes from a continuing contact with the life of the natural world:

> What makes the man of the world-cities incapable of living on any but this artificial footing is that the cosmic beat in his being is ever decreasing, while the tensions of his waking-consciousness become more and more dangerous. It must be remembered that in a microcosm the animal waking side supervenes upon the vegetable side, that of being, and not vice versa. Beat and tension, blood and intellect, destiny and causality are to one another what the country-side in bloom is to the city of stone, as something existing *per se* to something existing dependently. Tension without cosmic pulsation to animate it is the transition to nothingness. But civilization is nothing but tension. The head, in all the outstanding men of the civilizations, is dominated exclusively by an expression of extreme tension. Intelligence is only the capacity for understanding at high tension, and in every culture these heads are the types of its final men—one has only to compare them with the peasant heads, when such happen to emerge in the swirl of the great city's street life... Intelligence is the replacement of unconscious living by exercise in thought, masterly but bloodless and jejune. The intelligent visage is similar in all races—what is recessive in them is, precisely, race.

Finally Spengler confronts the end—that racial sterility which derives from a moral despair and an intellectual impotence drifting through the bright streets and the dank alley-ways of the Megapolis:

> And then, when being is sufficiently uprooted and waking-being sufficiently strained, there suddenly emerges into the bright light of history a phenomenon that has long been

preparing itself underground and now steps forward to make an end of the drama—*the sterility of civilized man*. This is not something that can be grasped as a plain matter of causality (as modern science naturally enough has tried to grasp it); it is to be understood as an essentially *metaphysical* turn towards death. The last man of the world-city no longer *wants* to live— he may cling to life as an individual, but as a type, as an aggregate, no, for it is a characteristic of this collective existence that it eliminates the terror of death. That which strikes the true peasant with an inexplicable fear, the notion that the family and the name may be extinguished, has now lost its meaning. The continuance of the blood-relation in the visible world is no longer a duty of the blood, and the destiny of being the last of the line is no longer felt as a doom. Children do not happen, not because children have become impossible, but principally because intelligence at the peak of intensity can no longer find any reason for their existence. Let the reader try to merge himself in the soul of the peasant. He has sat on his *glebe* from primeval times, or has fastened his clutch in it, to adhere to it with his blood. He is rooted in it as the descendant of his forbears and as the forbear of future descendants. *His* house, *his* property, means, here, not the temporary connection of person and thing for a brief span of years, but an enduring and inward union of *eternal* land and *eternal* blood. It is only from this mystical conviction of settlement that the great epochs of the cycle—pro-creation, birth, and death—derive that metaphysical element of wonder which condenses in the symbolism of custom and religion that all landbound people possess. For the 'last men' all this is past and gone. Intelligence and sterility are allied in old families, old peoples, and old cultures, not merely because in each microcosm the overstrained and fettered animal-element is eating up the plant-element, but also because the waking consciousness assumes that being is normally regulated by causality. That which the man of intelligence, most significantly and characteristically, labels as 'natural impulse' or 'life-force,' he not only knows, but also values causally, giving it the place among his other needs that his judgment assigns to it. When the ordinary thought of a cultivated people begins to regard 'having children' as a question of *pros* and *cons*, the great turning-point has come. For Nature knows nothing of *pro* and *con*. Everywhere, wherever life is actual, reigns an inward organic logic, an 'it,' a drive, that is utterly independent of waking-being, with its causal linkages, and indeed not even observed by it. The abundant proliferation of primitive peoples is a *natural phenomenon*, which is not even thought about, still less judged as to its utility or the reverse.

When reasons have to be put forward at all in a question of life, life itself has become questionable. At that point begins prudent limitation of the number of births. In the classical world the custom was deplored by Polybius as the ruin of Greece, and yet even at his date it had long been established in the great cities; in subsequent Roman times it became appallingly general. At first explained by the economic misery of the times, very soon it ceased to explain itself at all. And at that point, too, in Buddhist India as in Babylon, in Rome as in our own cities, a man's choice of the woman who is to be, not mother of his children as among peasants and primitives, but his own 'companion for life,' becomes a problem of mentalities. The Ibsen marriage appears, the 'higher spiritual affinity' in which both parties are 'free'—free, that is, as intelligences, free from the plantlike urge of the blood to continue itself, and it becomes possible for a Shaw to say "that unless woman repudiates her womanliness, her duty to her husband, to her children, to society, to the law, and to everyone but herself, she cannot emancipate herself." (Shaw, *The Quintessence of Ibsen*.)

As Spengler says:

> The primary woman, the peasant woman, is *mother*. The whole vocation towards which she has yearned from childhood is included in that one word. But now emerges the Ibsen woman, the comrade, the heroine of the whole megalopolitan literature from Northern drama to Parisian novel. Instead of children, she has soul-conflicts; marriage is a craft-art for the achievement of 'mutual understanding.' It is all the same whether the case against children is the American lady's who would not miss a season for anything, or the Parisienne's who fears that her lover would leave her, or an Ibsen heroine's who 'belongs to herself'—they all belong to themselves and they are all unfruitful. The same fact, in conjunction with the same

arguments, is to be found in the Alexandrian, in the Roman, and, as a matter of course, in every other civilized society—and conspicuously in that in which Buddha grew up. And in Hellenism and in the nineteenth century, as in the times of Lao-Tzu and the Charvaka doctrine, there is an ethic for childless intelligences, and a literature about the inner conflicts of Nora and Nana. The 'quiverful,' which was still an honourable enough spectacle in the days of Werther, becomes something rather provincial. The father of many children is for the great city a subject for caricature; Ibsen did not fail to note it, and presented it in his *Love's Comedy*. (*Decline of the West*, p. 98 et seq.)

Behind "the intelligent woman" minces the man who is no longer man. In the formless life of the city, where all life is unnatural, all "relaxations" may be deemed natural. The sex-perverted man of the great cities is of a very different type to those homosexuals who are common among more primitive peoples. Here, scarcity of women, or their artificial exclusion from normal contact with unmarried men, causes the virile youth to turn anywhere for satisfaction. In primitive countries where homosexuality at a certain age is rife, the average man is generally, at worst, heterosexual. In the East, or at sea, homosexuality may be the rough and ready satisfaction of a need; in the great cities it has become a fashionable cult, propagated by a blatant exhibitionism. This cult has certain psychological origins in the "despair complex," which is the basis of all the sterilities of the "intelligent woman," and the womanish man—like the man-woman—is the creation and the victim of the city, but "the relaxed mind" that acclaims this phenomenon is a danger to youth which must be confronted and overcome. All phenomena can be explained by the intellectual meanderings which emerge from the theory of Causality, but evils cannot be cured by a mere understanding of their origins.

The horror of the Megapolis and the realization of its menace to the whole life of a culture is, of course, nothing new. In the history of the present European culture, the dangers were already appreciated as early as the eighteenth century. A mass-consciousness of the nature of the city, and a mass-aversion from it, was spreading in the years before the last war. The movement of the countrymen into the cities—in England a very pronounced phenomenon of the Industrial Revolution—was producing a

Fascism and the Crisis of the West | 133

parallel, although numerically lesser, movement away from the cities. While Scots crofters, Irish peasants and English agricultural labourers were forced—and attracted—into the cities their fellows were taking ship to the ends of the earth, only to find and to build there, miniatures of the industrial warrens which had already grown to grotesque proportions in "The Old Country." Such movements had been a flight away from the city. In the middle classes, a similar migration developed among a minority, while the majority showed an inherent dislike of the conditions in which they were compelled to live in order to obtain a livelihood, by developing the practise either of "residing" in the country, or of the "week-end" away from the cities. The Boy Scout movement and the German Youth movements before the last war, were other manifestations of the flight away from the city.

Politically, after the war, the movements of Sinn Fein in Ireland and of Swaraj in India, directed in large part against the domination of "foreign capital," were subconsciously movements *away* from the horrors and the dangers of "megalopolitan" control through the great capitalist centres of Western Europe. In Britain, the Scottish and Welsh nationalist movements, and in France the Breton and Basque movements—emphasizing the national languages and the old national ways—were minor but parallel phenomena. But all these movements were movements of flight. In the mists of the past, Breton and Irish, Basque and Welsh, sought to hide from the glaring horror of the future. It was only with the development of Fascist movements in Italy and Germany that certain European nations began to show that they were prepared to master—and not only anxious to fly from—the formidable problems that had accumulated in the modern world. Mussolini seeks to master the Machine rather than to destroy it, and, by rousing the corporate consciousness of the Italian nation, to organize a stable, balanced people to replace the struggling city mobs and the debilitated proletariat of the country-side. Mussolini, confronted with the conservative reality of the Roman Catholic Church, has emphasized the fundamental and traditional humanities to which the peasant-farmers and the middle-class folk of the small Italian towns can respond from the inner fibres of their being. Hitler, operating in a larger field, where other traditional forces have their weight, can proceed to organize the German people almost as embattled tribes to confront the destiny of the passing century. Assured in the iron discipline of an older Germany, he can undertake policies which might affront the more varied and more independent communities of a united—but infinitely diversified—Italy. The power of the Roman Catholic Church in Germany is not strong enough to inhibit the most modern experiments of a truly German leader, and the sterilization of the unfit and "racial selection" are adventures into the future which are as welcome in Germany as they would be inacceptable in Italy. But fundamentally the two Fascist movements represent a dynamic and consciously controlled effort to master the Machine in economic and the City in cultural life. The emphasis of both Fascists and Nazis is on the country, the peasant family, on manhood and true womanliness—on all the old values which have become subjects for the epileptic giggling and the idiot witticisms of the decadent intellectuals of the Megapolis. Mussolini devotes all the power of modern industry to converting the Pontine marshes into thriving fields for thousands of peasant families, and the mountain glens of the Alps and the Apennines ring each summer with the shouts of hundreds of thousands of the children and the youth of Italy, released from the slums of the old cities. And Hitler, while he cleans out the human sewers of the Kurfurstendamm, and hunts out with the sterilizer's needle the erotic scum of the rich apartment-buildings, is applying all his creative energies to strengthening and enlarging the *bauer* class in Germany—the sturdy peasant families from whom have come all that is worthy in Teutonic life.

Fascism, then, not only seeks to find a solution to the economic problems of the modern European world. It challenges, actually, the inevitability of decline, and seeks to renew the strength and to perpetuate the cultural health of the peoples of Europe.

The philosophy of the inevitability of decline is not new; it was as familiar to Cato and to Seneca as it is to the no less doleful moderns. It has been left to the genius of Oswald Spengler to define and compare all the conditions of world-history, and to produce a composite picture which is a masterpiece of the tragic epic.

Spengler sets within the Faustian world-civilization, not only the European peoples, but also those wide regions of the world whose state of civilization represents an extension of the Faustian will-to-infinity. The crude and boisterous civilization of North America, the exotic and tenuous graftings in the South, the shallow British culture-extensions in Africa and Australia—the great cities set in the almost virgin bush—all these are not new cultures but extravagant and fantastic additions to a civilization which is already expanding to the maximum geographical

Fascism and the Crisis of the West | 135

limits of the planet. Even the Japanese renascence—with its feverish borrowings from an alien world—represents a mere extension of the Faustian-European civilization, as the Hellenistic monarchies were strange unhealthy outgrowths of the Graeco-Roman Apollinian.

The Faustian-European culture-world has yet a great capacity for self-extension and for a continued life, but it can only repeat itself in caricatures, whether European forms are copied in America, or American forms are reproduced on the opposite shores of the Pacific. The European culture-world is not physically threatened. It may be transformed into something more distorted by an American or even a Japanese hegemony, as the old Apollinian culture-world was influenced in one direction by Rome, and might have been in another by the military victory of Carthage. It may be restored and renovated, or it may be destroyed from within, but it can scarcely be overthrown from without. Up against it are the already dead—and partially absorbed—culture-worlds of India, of China and of the Islamic world. Russia, indeed, may have within herself the germs of a new culture, and the bucolic millions of the steppes may become the heirs of European civilization as the North Europeans themselves were of the ruins of the Graeco-Roman world. The only alternative are the not yet culturally conscious negro races of Africa, who already have become subject to the superficial influences of European civilization.

But whether the Europeans, or the European Americans, or the Americanized Japanese secure the ultimate political and economic dominance within the framework of the Faustian world-culture is not an issue of pure historico-philosophic importance. The real issue which faces the peoples of the modern world—both those who have fathered the existing world-civilization and those who have borrowed its accoutrements, is not the issue of which nation shall dominate this civilization, but whether the peoples who are parties to this civilization, *which is the first factual world-civilizalion*, can overcome the organic causes of decay which are manifesting themselves now, as they have at the equivalent life-stage of each preceding civilization. Can Faust renew his youth? Can Faust perpetuate himself? Spengler with the weighty pessimism of the greatest student of his age says that Faust cannot. Meanwhile the children of Faust are thronging the streets of Milan and Genoa, of Munich and of Nuremberg, and all the great cities that saw the birth-pangs of the Gothic culture, and they are proclaiming the rebirth of Faustian Europe. Spengler maintains that if the soul dies the body cannot live, and Faustian youth announces that it has found a new soul which will renew the body.

Spengler, contemplating the new "Caesarism" of his reasoning, which is destined to dominate the last phase of the Faustian world, looks round in vain for the legions. Perhaps the Caesar of his historical determinism is already campaigning in Manchuria, for in a pacifist world the professor finds that "a resolute leader who collects ten thousand adventurers round him can do as he pleases." A Caesar might even emerge out of the gang wars of the American cities. Spengler prefers to see the "Caesarist" form of power, perhaps, in the Press-lords:

> Now, whereas the Classical, and supremely the Forum of Rome, drew the mass of the people together as a visible body in order to compel it to make that use of its rights which was desired of it, the 'contemporary' English-American politics have created *through the Press* a force-field of world-wide intellectual and financial tensions in which every individual unconsciously takes up the place allotted to him, so that he must think, will, and act as a ruling personality somewhere or other in the distance thinks fit... Man does not speak to man; the Press and its associate, the electrical news-service, keep the waking-consciousness of whole peoples and continents under a deafening drum-fire of theses, catchwords, standpoints, scenes, feelings, day by day and year by year, so that every Ego becomes a mere function of a monstrous intellectual Something. (*Decline of the West*, II, p. 460.)

"This is the end of democracy," comments Spengler. But even before the English edition of *Decline of the West* had appeared the Caesars had arrived—out of the streets, and without and against the Press. Indeed, the professor's translator is forced to add the post script: "Radio broadcasting has now emerged to enable the leader to make personal conquests of the million, and no one can foretell the changes in political tactic that may ensue therefrom." So that when Mussolini speaks in Turin to a million Italians another twenty million hear his message, and all Germany attends Hitler in the Tempelhöfer field. The Press, in fact, is not Caesarism, but a projection of the money-power, and as such it shall "be rendered unto Caesar."

What then is this new Caesarism, and whence have come the new legions?

The "Caesar-men" have arrived, and they affront the wincing world of intellect. Unreasonably, and unreasoning, they have emerged to power in the brief space of a decade. "The powers of the blood, unbroken bodily forces, resume their ancient lordship." The airman, type of the modern warrior of the Faustian world, stalks with cynical laughter over the ruins of the Reichstag. Without "programmes" and without theories these Caesar-men have raised their legions from the street, and they stride as the leaders of men into the courts of the money-changers. Have these leaders only the significance of the Caesar-men of the "late" period of a civilization, or have they a new meaning in history? Has the modern man of the Faustian world begun to move against destiny? Can he possess himself of the user of the technical power which no former culture had developed so that he may now frame his own destiny?

These new Caesar-men are neither upstart dynasts nor the aristocratic leaders of great factions. They are out of the earth—Mussolini, the stonemason from the Romagna; Hitler, the obstinate foot-soldier—"the typical German man." Rather they represent great movements of living, sentient men in insurrection against the circumstances of a destiny that seems to threaten to overwhelm them. They are the representatives of a conscious revolt against the machine—the type-object of their civilization. It is not without omen that the dictator of modern Italy stands above all for the old Italian hearth, for the eternal peasant of the Italian land.[4] And Hitler proclaims to the laughter and the dismay of the sophisticated cities—the high worth of the Teutonic *race*.

But these are no individual "men of destiny," who maneuver dumb armies to the conquest of a dying world. These men are rather the expression of some new potent consciousness—the needle-points of a vast corporate surge of great millions of Caesar-men, who emerge to make out of the formless life of the modern world the massive structure of a modern Caesarism which is the Fascist revolution.

Fascism is to the cosmopolitan intellect the most incomprehensible of movements. The mind that can understand the dull slave-revolt of Bolshevism—a *jacquerie* of ox-like primitives roused by gangsters from the ghettoes—falters before the radiant passion of this insurrection of the

---

[4] "From the moral viewpoint, the men of the fields must be honoured, and peasants must be considered as elements of the first class in the national community." (Mussolini.)

élite of the manhood of modern Europe. The Russians pursue the economics of materialism with the religious ecstasy of moonstruck peasants, and they infuse their steel tractors with the same aura of divinity which formerly enveloped their wooden "wonder-working" icons. The Liberal-bourgeois can comprehend the practical adoration of the mere symbols of that thought which he himself evolved, and to which—in his spiritual sterility—he still adheres, although not with the bovine devotion of Slavonic converts. What the God of the Nonconformists is to the negro, the "wonder-working" machine is to the Russian, and the slick cosmopolitan intellectual who has invented both during different periods of his own evolution can still understand the minds that function in terms of his own older mental processes. But the same cosmopolitan man can only explain the new phenomenon of Fascism in the light of his own fears—fears which turn his thin blood into the acid of shrill hatred. He can only explain Fascism as a "bandit movement," as a "violence" which threatens to violate the state of organized immunity in which he himself is free to saunter along the corridors of decadence. He chooses to interpret the terrible passion of Fascism as the reckless bravado of a mere mercenary army which has been provided to intervene in favour of one or other of the contestant political groups of the disrupting bourgeois society. Something vivid, something desperate and dynamic, the greatest insurrection of man, a mutiny against destiny, is quite beyond the ken of the spiritual troglodytes of the cosmopolis.

Fascism is Faustian Caesarism in terms of world historical philosophy, but it has within it the germs of a movement of modern humanity of a far more profound significance. It may prove to be a movement in Nature-history—both primal and timeless. Fascism is not only revolutionary in the political sense; it is revolutionary in the biological sense. Fascism may not be a mere phase of destiny; it may itself make new destiny. The soul of the Faustian world-culture has been manifested in the passion of the Faustian man for infinity—this passion for infinity, in mathematics, in music, in philosophy, has been peculiar only to this latest present culture. And the ultimate expression of this passion, in the crisis of the Faustian world, is the urge to attain the infinity in time of the culture itself. There is a blood-urge, a spiritual passion, a mighty mystical import, in the movement of the modern Faustian man which seeks—with an infinitude of proud ambition—to master the material bases of a destiny which has hitherto brought all civilizations and the men of all time to the doom of an inevitable end. The Fascist insurrection within the modern world is, in certain essentials, a materialist insurrection to the extent that all movements are conditioned by the realities of time and space, but it is, in its wider scope, a profound spiritual insurrection—a rising up of men in a period of moral and material decline, and a revolt of *man* against the destiny of decadence.

In a recent book, *Civilization as Divine Superman*, a young English philosopher, Alexander Raven, has unconsciously defined the philosophical potentialities of the Fascist revolution. While his thought, in many ways, runs parallel to that of Oswald Spengler, and while he does not altogether depart from the pessimistic tendencies of the German, he indicates, in his theory of "Superorganic Integration," certain philosophic bases to which Fascism, as the twentieth-century expression of the Faustian will-to-infinitude, appears to give historical interpretation.

Raven sees all the processes of Nature as a series of biological integrations, and with each new integration old natural laws cease to have their application, and new laws emerge:

> The failure of evolution to supply a satisfactory philosophic basis for world history is most readily explained by the suggestion that mankind has with the advent of civilization attained a higher plane of existence upon which the laws of the lower biological plane no longer hold good. Throughout the metaphysical series with each step of integration on to a higher plane the primitive laws are superseded by more complicated ones...
>
> The failure of the evolutionary principles of biology to supply an explanation of the historical development of civilized man is to be accounted for by the assumption that in a state of civilization a new super-being comes into existence, as real and as distinct as the 'communal' spirit that directs the actions and reactions of the insect communities of hive and ant-heap, and that on the plane of existence of this super-being new laws come into effect.

Developing his theme of civilization as a new super-organism, Raven professes to see in this superorganism the true superman. He continues:

The abrupt break with evolutionary premises evident upon the dawn of civilization is an indication of the advent of a new superorganism, which is formed of many individual human beings, as is the human body of many individual cells... Civilization itself is the superhuman force that expresses and realizes the ideal of the 'superman.' It is futile to seek a superman in personal individual human development at some distant future date when the real superman civilization is already engaged in building towering skyscrapers, driving great tunnels, constructing huge liners and vast airships, linking the lands with radio, and investing mankind with the collective attributes of supermen. We might just as well expect to find a 'super-microbe' as large as a horse, when it is obvious that the multi-cellular organism has long since superseded any such monstrosity. The Nietzschean 'supermen' and the Shavian 'Methuselahs' are no less monstrous individual perversions in the superorganic world of civilization in being. Civilization is not a biological process in the upward progress of mankind; it is a 'super-biological' force governed by 'super-biological' laws, directing the actions of mere men to the realization of its higher aims, the very realization of the 'superman.'

Raven's conclusions in his book are no less pessimistic than those of Oswald Spengler, as Raven writes:

Certain bounds of attainment restrict even the vast possibilities of a superorganism. It may reach a certain height of achievement, even an extraordinary peak of endeavour, but it must inevitably decline and collapse, as much as any other organism when it has passed its prime...
    Civilization is not the servant of man. It is his master and tyrant; the superman that directs and enforces his actions to the greater glorification of himself, and grants him the immense advantages of co-operation and specialization only as a reward for abandoning his freedom of action to the higher aims of the communal spirit. (*Civilization as Divine Superman*, pp. 32-40.)

Thus Raven hesitated on the edge of the soul-despair of bourgeois thought before he donned the black shirt of the Fascist Defence Force. It

Fascism and the Crisis of the West | 141

is symbolic of this modern movement that the intellectual takes his proud place among the rank and file of the street fighters, while the fighting man begins to think. Civilization is the superorganism of the natural world, and as Nature has its spiritual mystery which we call a soul, so the corporate soul of material civilization now emerges in the ardent, seeking will-to-mastery of a modern manhood. Civilization is not superman, but rather super-material, and out of the stone desert of civilization the corporate manhood which is super-man breaks forth to claim and to assert full lordship over matter.

Benito Mussolini and Oswald Mosley at the Fascist Triumph in Rome

Chapter VIII

—The Nature of Fascism—

"Experience shows that the middle classes allow themselves to be plundered quite easily, provided that a little pressure is brought to bear, and that they are intimidated by the fear of revolution; *that party will possess the future which can most skilfully manipulate the spectre of revolution.*" So wrote Georges Sorel, with all his irritable, sardonic penetration, nearly a quarter of a century ago. "I could choose," he continued, "other examples to show that the most decisive factor in social politics is the cowardice of the Government." And he quotes the words of Clemenceau: "Every man or every power whose action consists solely in surrender can only finish by self-annihilation. Everything that lives resists; that which does not resist allows itself to be cut up piecemeal."

In post-war Europe the "manipulation of the spectre of revolution" had become the recognized practice of contemporary politics, and the cowardice of the political class was everywhere clothing that spectre with the significance of reality. All the elaborate technique of threat and surrender had been developed within the framework of the political world, and the democratic groups, always shifting for position, alternated the one method with the other. The basis of the spectre game was the *threat of violence*, but all the political groups were profoundly shocked when any section of the community forced the leaders who had attached themselves to that particular section to implement the threat with action. Lenin had been the first to move from threats to action, and we learn from Trotsky how even the most extreme intellectual Communists—men like Stalin and Bukharin—were hesitant and uneasy at the outcome. The success of Lenin's direct action against the political class in Russia of

144 | Chapter VIII

course confirmed all the worst fears of the democrats in other countries, and the whole methodology of surrender appeared to have been entirely justified by events. The "proletariat" became a standing nightmare of the bourgeois night, and at any hour the democratic politicians felt that they might awake from their uneasy dreams to find the real horny hands of revolution toying with their bronchial tubes. The methods of surrender were feverishly pursued, and it appeared that it was only a matter of a few short years before all power in the State would pass to those who were best able to organize the manual workers and profess to represent them.

But on the other side, so acute an observer as Trotsky had already recognized that the success of the revolution in Russia had been the result of the physical weakness and numerical paucity of the Russian middle class. In the European countries the reaction of the non-political body of the middle classes to the threats which terrified the small political groups of their respective countries had never been seriously considered. Political theorists had come to regard the middle class as a sort of inferior racial group or depressed class within the nation—like the Jews of the Middle Ages. They were not only ignored, but also insulted and pillaged by those middle-class politicians who were anxious to make any future that might remain to them—by permission of the "proletariat."[5]

Yet it does not require much knowledge of the everyday life of any typical West European democracy to realize that the middle classes are not only numerically formidable, but superbly capable of drastic and effective action. It is a truism that they are, in fact, recruited from the most vigorous and intelligent elements from among the manual workers of each generation. It is qualities of enterprise, initiative and dogged, undemonstrative courage which have enabled them to secure the moderate economic alleviations to which they have already attained. Neither their numbers nor their class-psychology really entitled the political class to consider that the middle classes could be ignored and trampled down in the process of adjustments which was taking place throughout post-war Europe.

---

[5] "What Marxist foresaw the power of Fascism—until it overwhelmed the oldest and solidest party in our movement? Which of us predicted that at the phase of history through which we are passing, the lower middle class, and not the proletariat, would become the revolutionary force?" (H. N. Brailsford in *Problems of a Socialist Government*.)

The Nature of Fascism | 145

The reactions of the middle class to the threat of revolution were likely to be three. First, they were destined to resent and to resist the assumption that they were an inferior pariah element, who were to be regarded as entirely subordinate to the new and insurgent interests of the proletariat. Secondly, they were likely to turn upon that political class which had insulted and betrayed them. Thirdly, they were likely to have the intelligence to appraise the character of the real revolution which economic circumstances made inevitable, and they were likely, eventually, to take the implementing of this revolution into their own competent hands. If in Russia, with its great masses of peasants dominated by the remnants of a medieval feudal system, with its concentrated blocks of violent and untended industrial workers, and its small and ineffectual bourgeois class, there existed all the classic elements necessary to a clear-cut struggle of the classes, these textbook conditions did not exist in the vivid and active and changing life of the countries of Western Europe. Here social conditions were far more complicated and far less clear-cut. The class-war, as a means of applying revolutionary method to the reconstruction of European life—given tremendous impetus by the experience of the Russian Revolution—was tried first, but it was bound to fail. The Spartacist movement in Germany had failed by 1920, and the Communist movement in Italy was destined to be liquidated by the end of 1922. Even in comparatively backward countries like Poland and Hungary—whose conditions were not altogether dissimilar from those of pre-revolutionary Russia—the Communist "drives" ended in disaster. But the failure of the attempts at proletarian revolution did not mean either that these attempts would not be renewed, or that real social and economic revolution was not necessary. The difference between Russian and European conditions implied, however, that revolution must take a different form. In Russia, as we have already shown, a fundamental national revolution has always underlain the more superficial class revolution. In Europe, the complicated structure of modern society conditioned a situation where revolution was necessary, but where "proletarian" class-consciousness could not be defined and consolidated, and where the proletarian elements lacked the numerical strength necessary to enable them to overcome by force all the other elements in the community. The result has been a series of "classless" or national revolutions, in which elements from all classes have combined in order to achieve power with the object of carrying through the revolutionary reconstruction necessary in the

146 | Chapter VIII

social and economic life of modern industrial states.

The phenomenon was entirely new. It had not been anticipated by all the social theorists who have written commentaries on the nature of a real life from which they have themselves always been as alien as pure *intellect* must be from *life*. It had not been contemplated, and it could never be understood by those representatives of the old bourgeois mind and of the old political "ideal," who could think in terms of surrender to revolution, but never themselves in terms of *creative* revolution. The mere conception of the integrity of violence as a method whereby to combat disintegrative anarchy was something horrible to them.

Professor Gilbert Murray, a typical specimen of the Liberal-bourgeois mind, writes in his preface to *Italy and Fascismo:*

> To an educated Englishman, especially to one who has been concerned either with politics or with history, it seems amazing that a great nation should allow all its free institutions to be destroyed and itself to be dominated by gangs of young roughs armed with bludgeons and castor-oil bottles, belonging to a private society whose members are above the law... The Fascist Society is only a Camorra on a grand scale... The Italian people, so gifted in all regions of art and intellect, somehow lost grip of the steady and humdrum duties which constitute citizenship, and political power fell a prey to the group that was most violent *and most ready to face risks and to take trouble*... Outside Italy Mussolini is largely regarded as a theatrical performer, and Fascism, with its hysteria and its frizzed hair, as a subject for jests.

This passage has been deemed worthy of quotation in the present context because it illustrates not only the nerveless incapacity of the Liberal mind to appraise any movement which is strange to its own ideology, but it underlines also the peculiarly illogical point of view in regard to violence of a generation and a political philosophy which had been responsible for the greatest outbreak of organized violence in the history of the world. Liberal democracy had thrown the manhood of Europe into the shambles of 1914-18, and they had attained a "democratic" settlement which had been won and held by violence. The streets of all the great cities of Europe were littered with a generation of young men who had been weaned in slaughter—who had known "liquid fire for mother's milk and bombs for cricket balls." Now, after the war, after they had been used for purposes which they could not comprehend, or had learnt to comprehend in their own way, they were left to rot upon the streets, while once a year the top-hatted leaders of bourgeois society paid two minutes' pompous respect to one "unknown soldier" from among all the millions who were neither unknown nor dead, but forgotten, despised, slandered and neglected. Professor Gilbert Murray, and his like, might find some intellectual justification for the slaughters that had "made the world safe for democracy," but they had nothing but horror and abuse for the "young roughs" who might lay their hands upon the sacred hides of democrats.

So there arose no class war, but a fundamental war of types was suddenly exposed to view in all the hiving cities of the West. Those who had suffered violence, those who had *felt* violence, had in its excess lost all their horror of it, and they had learnt the effectiveness of the use of force. They had been taught violence for the ends of others, and now they were prepared to use it for their own. The democratic theorists who could accept the mass-violence of war for the ends of State reacted in terror and despair when that violence spread into the streets as the day-to-day technique of politics, an actual menace to their own soft bodies for which the practice of democracy had hitherto maintained an enviable immunity. Fascism arose, then, out of the din of unrecorded street-fights and the mess of factory brawls and the quick butchery of country-side ambushes, and emerged as a direct and violent will-to-power. The democrats met the movement with the laughable legend that these grim and wild young men were nothing more than the hired hooligan bands of "the capitalists." The explanation was characteristic of the democratic mind, but it hardly accounts for the dynamic surge of armed manhood in no time out of nowhere. In three years the Fascists became the masters of the Italian peninsula.

Shrewd owners of capital may choose to support a movement which they think may win power, or they are often not unwilling to pay blackmail to a movement that they fear. The present author recalls the lament of a Russian statesman that, while the industrialists of Petrograd and Moscow, during the early stages of the Russian Revolution, were failing to assist his own "democratic" organization with the necessary funds, they were making anxious contributions to the coffers of the Bolshevik Party. Something more than the unwilling support of harassed capitalists is necessary to the growth out of nothing of a national revolutionary movement. Such support may be an unconsidered incident of later stages, but it affords a very inadequate explanation of the spontaneous inception and rapid growth of a *new* action. Capitalists do not comprehend the character of this new action any more than democrats, and the first derivative of dawning comprehension is generally a very real fear.

The Liberals are also puzzled by the *lack of theory* in Fascism. Here they are coming nearer to the truth, but it is a truth which is quite beyond their ultimate comprehension. Fascism has no long pedigree of theory, like Socialism, Liberalism and Communism and other products of the intellectual laboratory. Fascism is real insurrection—an insurrection of *feeling*—a mutiny of *men* against the conditions of the modern world. It is completely characteristic of this aspect of Fascism in its early stages, both in Italy and in Germany, that the movement should have grown to full strength without either logical theory behind it, nor cut-and-dried programme in front of it. The men who have built Fascism in Italy and Germany—who are the "common men," the "men in the street," leave theories to the intellectuals and programmes to the democrats who have betrayed them with programmes for a century. The Fascist is concerned with the problem of power, and he aims at the achievement of power through action. When he has secured power, he applies further action to the realities of the moment, as they exist in that moment when he has the responsibility of exercising power over the State. Before he has that power he limits his action and his "programme" to the necessities of the phase through which his movement is passing. He acts, in fact, instinctively, and not theoretically. The opposition between Fascism and Social Democracy is the opposition between life and theory, between man and intellect, between blood and paper. "It is faith," said Mussolini, "that moves mountains, not reason. Reason is a tool, but it can never be the motive force of the crowd. To-day less than ever."

In Italy the veterans of the war, who had felt all the ultimate agonies of individual experience, carried Fascism to power, and Mussolini, the youthful revolutionary who had become a sergeant in the trenches, confronted the quaking pack of the politicals. The ablest of the latter, the suave priest, Don Sturzo, has given us a picture of the new leader which epitomizes all the revulsions of the sleek megalopolitan mind from this new phenomenon in almost the same terms which a "late" Roman might have used to describe some barbarian chieftain:

Of mediocre culture and meagre political experience, Mussolini has the brilliant qualities of the extemporizer and none of the scruples of those who, convinced of an idea, fear to be false to it... His mind, given to excessive simplification, is bound by no formula; he can pass from theory to theory, from position to position, rapidly, even inconsistently, with neither remorse nor regret. In this game he has one constant aim—to lay hold of the elements of imagination and sentiment that make for success...

Another quality which he possesses is his constant ability to seize the moment, to profit by circumstances, to hold in check the most experienced and shrewdest men, to come out of a tight corner with ease and elegance. The fact of his having for a long time been free, both as Socialist and Fascist, to wield with impunity every kind of threat and violence, has given him a profound contempt for the politicians of the past, whether Socialists or Liberals, who tolerated or flattered him... For a long time it was believed by many who were benevolently disposed towards Mussolini that once in power he would tame the extremists of Fascism. In fact, it seemed that 'Il Duce'—as his followers call him—for a long time vacillated between law and violence, between normality and reaction. But he chose his own road. The distinction between Mussolini and the Fascisti was repudiated the day he proclaimed to the Chamber, in January, 1925, that he took on himself the responsibility for all that had been done in the name of Fascism.

Was it fear or courage? None can tell. At that hour, which saw the further development of his system, he was sure that none could call him to account.

With the same theatrical pose, and with an assurance derived from possession of power and the presence of the armed Irregulars, he faced the Chamber of Deputies for the first time on 15th November, 1922, in the role of a lion-tamer, declaring that *of that grey, gloomy House he could have made the bivouac of his Blackshirts, and that it remained for it to decide whether it would live two days or two years.*

... In face of this phenomenon, with all its contradictions and audacities, a great part of the capitalistic middle classes, conservative Liberals and landed Clericals, found themselves bound by their own action to assist what was then called 'The

Chapter VIII

> Mussolini Experiment.' It was their own creation, which, grown suddenly larger and stronger than they had imagined, had turned the tables on them, and they, the philo-Fascisti, now followed the triumphal car and, albeit with fear in their hearts for the unknown future, flung flowers and sang hymns of joy. (*Italy and Fascismo*, pp. 121-2.)

It was now a matter of surprise to experienced politicians when the Duce failed to abandon the Fascists for an alliance with the older parties. Such a maneuvre is, of course, a recognized part of the normal Social Democratic technique. But the leader and the founder of the Fascist Revolution had more in common with the wildest and the most disreputable of his followers than he had with the practised sycophants of parliamentary decadence. "If," said Caesar, "I have had the help of footpads and cut-throats in maintaining my position, I shall reward them in the same way as I do other people." Mussolini had no less the sense of loyalty-in-arms, and the same contempt for the "open conspiracy" of the respectable against their cruder fellows. His struggle with the orthodox political parties during the two years following his accession to power was a struggle of life and death which might well have gone against him. It was only gradually that he could advance towards the "integral revolution" of a "totalitarian Fascism." During the period of "the Aventine" all the opposition parties were massed solidly against him, and he had to threaten "either peaceful co-existence within the bounds of the law, or we shall make of them litter for the Blackshirts." But while he was skillfully absorbing sections of the community and isolated political groups into the Fascist Party, he never compromised the totalitarian position of Fascism, nor attempted to adopt a middle position in order to reinforce his personal standing by seeking to conciliate elements strange to his own party. Even in the most dangerous crisis of the Matteotti agitation he stood firm by those of his party who had allowed themselves to be provoked into violent—and sometimes unjust—reprisals, and he treated that agitation with a superb perspective. He said, in defending himself in the Chamber:

> It is said that Fascism is a horde of barbarians encamped in the nation, a movement of bandits and robbers; the moral question is brought on the stage... Well, here, before this assembly, before the whole Italian people, I declare that I take upon

myself, I alone, the political, moral and historical responsibility of all that has befallen.

If Fascism has been nothing more than castor oil and cudgels, not a superb passion of the best Italian youth, the blame is mine. If Fascism has been an association for crime, then I am the head and responsible chief of this association for crime. If all the acts of violence have been the result of the historical, political and moral atmosphere, then mine is the responsibility for this, for this historical, political and moral atmosphere I have created with my propaganda from the moment of intervention in the war until to-day.

This, then, was the man who, according to the President of the League of Nations Union, has "the same instinctive cowardice which titubates at the last moment and does not dare to be definite."

Later, Mussolini, in discussing Don Sturzo, was to give the epitaph of the Italian political class. "He fancied he would be able to play with me the same game he had played with Giolitti, so I bundled him out neck and crop."

In Italy, in the end, Fascism won the political battle, rather by the exercise of the will-to-power than by the use of force. Opposition crumbled before the knowledge that force was behind that will-to-power. The elaborate facade of the bourgeois-democratic State had collapsed, even before the Blackshirt squadrons could march "seven times" round its outer walls. Mussolini was occupied two years in really mastering the internal political situation, and another two years passed before he began to lay the foundations of the new Corporate State. The revolution had been so peaceful and so complete that it was scarcely regarded as a revolution by the superficial observers of other countries who, obsessed by "the revolution myth," had looked for all the protracted drama of mass massacre.

Fascism is the political expression of the sense of organic being in the nation, and as such its idealism must be national, and its economy corporate—of the body. Nationalism is, of course, no new phenomenon in Europe, and its ideology is not specifically Fascist. Nationalism may perhaps be best defined as a physical consciousness of kind, which permeates the individuals of a community having common historical traditions, a common language and literature, and a familiar way of life. In the historical sense, the idea of nationhood is peculiar to the modern

European world, and was scarcely developed in the earlier culture-worlds. Just as the city was the basis of thought and of political action in the Classical world, and the religious community formed the framework of life in the Byzantine-Arabian world, so the nation has come to express the peculiar sense of *being* throughout the modern world. Economically, the nation comes into immediate conflict with money-power, for capital is, of its very nature, international. And the exaggerated development of the nation-sense during the last half-century is in reality a reaction of the body of the nation against the illimitable and all-pervading power of capital. Many nationalist movements among minor peoples have been openly and consciously directed against "foreign capital" in the interests of which alien political dominations have been exercised, while nationalist movements in states which are politically independent have been directed towards the control of the theoretical substance of capital within the State. But while the desire of the bourgeois parties in different countries to control capital has been expressed only "in fantasy"—witness their concurrent efforts to further a political *internationalism* which leaves international capital altogether untrammelled—the Fascist "plan of action" has always been directed towards securing immediate national control of capital to the utmost extent which is attainable at the given moment. Regarded historically, the emphasis on the nation is defensive, and seeks to protect that nation, not so much from the purely geographical revindications of other nations as from the exercise of a money-power which is fundamentally international.

Fascist nationalism is therefore something very different from the "commercial" nationalism of the bourgeois state of the first quarter of the twentieth century. It is a sacred passion—a mass communion—which symbolizes the devoted sense of organic being within the nation. And this new Fascist nationalism—dangerous as it may become when provoked to defensive action—is in essence pacific. For when a nation grows conscious of its own being, and learns how to respect its own superb individuality, it learns also to feel toleration and friendship towards other national communions beyond its own borders. Fascism as the expression of the European will-to-renewal is essentially a Pan-European movement. It draws its strength from the historic seats of European culture, and it would be a movement destructive of its own purposes were it to envisage war among the parent nations of the European world-culture. There are many problems of adjustment to be

The Nature of Fascism | 153

solved within the borders of Europe, but a Fascism which would find in war a solution to these problems would be repudiating the very fundaments of its own origins. Fascism indeed implies an economic revolution in the bases of national production and distribution which will alter the familiar structure of world-trade as this existed during the past century. But the very measures which will tend to make Fascist nations self-supporting and independent of the operation of external forces will also tend to remove those causes of international friction which—in terms of the Marxian dialectic—have in the past been most productive of war. For it is the uncontrolled ambitions and the irresponsible adventuring of the forces of international Capitalism which have in the past impelled the nations into hostilities. The more the nations concentrate on the effective control and development of their own internal markets, the less important will become the international struggle for access to each others' markets, and international trade itself will become more and more "disciplined" and more easy to control, as it becomes a matter of inter-governmental arrangement, rather than the open field of haphazard and contending interests. Therefore Fascist nationalism has to be regarded in the ultimate implications of a Pan-European outlook, and as the leading nations of Europe become successively Fascist, the purely territorial difficulties between neighbouring European states should prove capable of a realist adjustment. But just as the European nations will be impelled to respect the integrity of each other's nationhood, so the leading powers will come to understand that if the younger nations of the continent are not by force of circumstances to be driven in upon their neighbours, it will be necessary to recognize the physical need of some of these less fortunate members of the European state system for geographical "room." Circumstances have already impelled the older imperial powers to the recognition—or acceptance—of this fact in the Far East, and in the realist atmosphere of a Fascist Europe the myth that it is the duty of organized power to protect the immunity of the remaining "plague-spots" of the world will no longer be sustained. The powers of Europe will turn from internecine strife to the organization of peace throughout the world.

The controlled serenity of Italian Fascist nationalism, which has acquired stability with the confidence of its own strength, may well be compared with the harsher manifestations of German Nazi nationalism, which has come to power in a great popular reaction from the defeats and humiliations of the last two decades.

Mussolini, with his usual philosophic poise, can state reality. He said:

> Of course there are no pure races left; not even the Jews have kept their blood unmingled. Successful crossings have often promoted the energy and the beauty of a nation. Race! It is a feeling, not a reality; ninety-five per cent, at least, is a feeling. Nothing will ever make me believe that biologically pure races can be shown to exist to-day... National pride has no need of the delirium of race.

Hitler, on the other hand, maintains the "myth" of race and confuses it with the reality of the nation. He upholds the "Aryan theory" really as a religious ideal, and superimposes it upon the conception of the Germans as a nation. It is perhaps the consciousness of the existence of nations within Germany—of Bavarians, Prussians, Saxons, Suabians and others—and the knowledge of the disunity which has always disrupted the destinies of Germany that has caused Nazi thinkers to lay emphasis on a philological myth where there is the lack of a coherent historical tradition. The English, the French and the Italians are strong enough to ignore—and to absorb—the Jews, but in Germany they remain a constant intellectual provocation to a people always sensitive to the newness of their nationhood. Mussolini has been able to invoke the might of Rome to obliterate the memories of centuries of Italian disunity, but the Nazis can only turn upon the nearest aliens in the streets to find consolation for the past and assurance for the future. Nevertheless such phases must be passing, for the new Fascist nations will justify their pride of nation within themselves and not in extrovert antagonisms. This new feeling of pride and friendship is already being increasingly manifested in the mass visits of Fascist youth which are being interchanged between one European country and another.

As Mussolini writes:

> Nothing leads one to believe, or will cause one to believe, that the young men who have become the ruling class in the Fascist states, that is—unitarian, authoritarian, totalitarian—will perturb the peace. It can, instead, be forecast that they will ensure it in the world.

And even Hitler can write in *Mein Kampf*:

> The frontiers of 1914 mean nothing in respect of Germany's future. They were no protection in the past, nor would they mean strength in the future. Only one thing is certain. Any attempt to restore the frontiers of 1914, even if successful, would merely lead to a further pouring out of our nation's blood until there was none left worth mentioning for the decisions and actions which are to remake the life and future of the nation. On the contrary, the vain glamour of that empty success would cause us to renounce any more distant objective, since 'national honour' would then be satisfied and the door opened once again, anyhow until something else happened, for commercial enterprise.

A strong and really passionate nationalism is the spiritual background of Fascism. This nationalism is something more and something deeper than the old bourgeois patriotism. It is not a patriotism of war, but of everyday life; not a patriotism of antagonisms, but a patriotism of communion. Paul Einzig, an observer who confesses his lack of enthusiasm for Fascism outside Italy, says:

> The psychological aspects of Fascism should not be underestimated. The movement has succeeded in arousing in the members of the ruling party, and in the nation as a whole, an enthusiasm and public spirit that goes a long way towards making the economic system work. This phenomenon is by no means peculiar to Fascism. An enthusiasm of a similar kind has been worked up by Communism in the execution of the Five Years' Plan; we encounter it in times of war and other major national emergencies; it accompanies the establishment of new religions, and also religious or nationalistic revivals. The object of the Fascist political, economic, social and educational system is to direct this spirit into the productive channels of the Corporate State, and to cause it to become a perpetual and integral part of the national character. It endeavours to eradicate the selfishness ingrained in the minds of mankind by nineteenth-century individualism, which, with its slogan of the 'survival of the fittest' and with its economic conception that

'what is beneficial to an individual necessarily works out to the benefit of the community,' has raised to a maximum the egotistic qualities inherent in human nature. The philosophy of *laissez-faire* is nothing but the apologia and glorification of the mentality that disregards public interest...

In Italy, Fascism has succeeded to a remarkable degree in undermining this cult for selfishness... Fascism in Italy has made in ten years a progress towards the transformation of the national character which ordinarily might have required at least a generation. Nevertheless, it may take several generations before the effects of the teaching of Liberal philosophy and *laissez-faire* economics are completely eliminated. (*The Economic Foundations of Fascism*, p. 8 *et seq.*)

In an answer to Emil Ludwig's observation that Fascism was changing the faces of Italians, Mussolini said:

There is a moral reason for the change. Our faces are becoming more tensed. The will-to-action modifies the features; even sports and physical exercises produce changes. That is why a handicraftsman looks so different from a factory worker.

On another occasion, the Duce[6] said:

Tell your English friends how much our race has improved. That is the great work that I shall leave behind me, the transformation of the moral and physical characteristics of the Italian people. I have succeeded and shall succeed still more. All the other things we have been talking about—the improvements in roads, railways, buildings—could have been done by others. But the Italian character is what I am keenest on.

I want every Italian to be calm and disciplined... I want Italians to be brave without singing, with the cold courage that needs no excitement to spur it on. They have it in them, for we have had wonderful examples in the past; but I want to bring everyone to the same standard. (*Sunday Times*, 12th February, 1933.)

---

[6] Mussolini

The conceptions and ideals of Hitler are very similar, although expressed in less classic language. In the ideas of both leaders is evident the utterly revolutionary reaction from the hypocritical Liberalism and sentimental individualism of the nineteenth century. According to Hitler:

> It is the duty of the National State to recover all that is being let drop now on all sides... It must declare childhood to be the most precious possession of the nation. It must see to it that only the healthy beget children—that it is nothing but disgraceful for persons diseased or with personal disabilities to bring children into the world, though an honourable action to refrain from doing so. On the other hand it must be considered a reproach to deprive the nation of healthy children. The State must place the most modern medical aids at the service of these accepted facts. It must also see that the fruitfulness of a healthy woman is not blocked by the damnable finance of a regime which makes the blessing of children into a curse for the parents.
> The whole of education should be designed to occupy a boy's free time in profitable cultivation of his body... he ought to harden his young body so that life may not find him soft when he enters it. To prepare for this and to carry it out is the function of youthful education, and not merely to pump in so-called knowledge. It must rid itself of the notion that management of the body is the business of the individual alone. No one should be free to sin at the expense of posterity—that is, of the race... The fight against the poisoning of the soul must be waged in company with cultivation of the body. The life of the people must be freed from the asphyxiating perfume of our modern eroticism, as it must be from unmanly and prudish refusal to face facts. In all these things the aim and the method must be governed by the thought of preserving our nation's health in both body and soul. The right to personal freedom comes second in importance to the duty of maintaining the race. (*The Times*, 30th July, 1933.)

The national and corporate spirit of Fascism has, in Italy, been vigorously interpreted in terms of social and economic action. In economics Fascism is not an extremism, but compromise, and as such it has been criticized and attacked by the extremists both of Capitalism and

158 | Chapter VIII

of Socialism.

"Fascism," writes Paul Einzig, "is much nearer Socialism than are either Liberalism or Democracy, which are considered, from a political point of view, to be half-way between the extremes of Fascism and Socialism."

The Fascist conception of the nation as a *corporate entity* or *body* implies the subordination of all parts to the unity of the whole. It implies also the care of the *whole* for the individual *parts*. Thus, industries are organized into corporations, in which the interests of the plant-owners (who in Italy correspond very frequently to the technical management) and of the workers have independently elected and selected representation. These corporations concern themselves not only with questions of wages and general industrial conditions, but also with the conflicting interests of different industries composing the corporations— as, for instance, in the matter of tariffs.[7] Mussolini is, above all things, a realist, and his action is always calculated to meet the forces of the moment. Generally, however, it may be said that the class-interests of Italian capital have been subordinated to the larger interests of the nation. The very definite tendency to bring capital into a strict discipline has been particularly manifested in regard to the Italian banks. As Paul Einzig writes:

> The influence of the authorities upon banks in Italy is not confined to the enforcement of technical regulations; it extends to the sphere of fundamental banking policy. Although the banks are not nationalized, in practice the Government has a power over them which could hardly be greater if they were. This does not mean that their attitude towards individual customers and individual transactions is subject to Government interference. In this respect the freedom of the Italian banks is as great as that of the banks in any country... The banks are left to decide themselves whether they will grant or refuse credit to their customers.
>
> Government intervention in Fascist Italy has a different aim.

---

[7] For a detailed description of the functioning of the Italian Corporative State the reader is referred to two recent books: *The Economic Foundations of Fascism*, by Paul Einzig (Macmillan, 1933), and *The Italian Corporative State*, by Fausto Pitigliani (P. S. King, 1933).

Its object is to secure the better utilization of the available banking resources. To that end the authorities use their influence in a truly dictatorial spirit, and banks are sometimes compelled to pursue a policy that may be entirely against the principles in which they have been brought up. (*The Economic Foundations of Fascism*, pp. 88-9.)

The direction in which the banks were compelled to take action of which they did not themselves approve was in the financing of the great schemes of public works which Mussolini undertook, at once as necessary methods of agricultural and industrial reconstruction and as a means of finding work for the unemployed. The assistance of the banks was vitally necessary in the great "wheat battle," which has now gone far to make Italy virtually self-supporting in regard to cereals—a project once stigmatized as "fantastic" by Mussolini's great Liberal antagonist, Don Sturzo—and in the big schemes of electrification which were to make Italy more independent of foreign sources of fuel supply. The success of these undertakings is the best proof of the wisdom of the "Duce" in overriding orthodox financial opinion. In another direction the Duce pursued a financial policy which was in strict accordance with the most orthodox canons of capitalist opinion. He aimed at—and secured— the stabilization of the *lira* at a figure which was relatively high in relation to other currencies, and as a result the country not only suffered many of the effects which follow a deflationary policy, but some of the beneficial effects of his industrial planning and general methods of reconstruction were nullified. But there were certain very definite issues—largely psychological in character—which made a policy of deflation almost unavoidable. First, there was the pressure from the strong financial countries, Britain and France, which made it difficult for Italy—relatively weak in international finance—not to follow a policy which seemed to be being adopted internationally. Secondly, there was a very real fear of catastrophic inflation, which was widespread in Italy as a result of the experiences of neighbouring countries. Thirdly, the necessity had to be considered of continuing to purchase large quantities of primary products from countries with increasingly favourable exchanges. Fourthly, a conservative exchange policy became the more desirable, as the banks were compelled to depart from their orthodoxy in the matter of financing internal work schemes. And lastly, it was vital to maintain the international prestige of Italy during a period of transition,

160 | Chapter VIII

and to secure the satisfaction of the national pride in the question of the payment of war debts. As writes the economist Einzig:

> It is upon its economic side that Fascism stands or falls... The success of the Fascist system can only be measured in terms of its economic advantages, and it is consequently on these that we must focus our attention...
>
> The main object of the Corporate State is the planning of production and the determination of distribution in accordance with changing requirements. Under the system of *laissez-faire* the factors determining production and distribution are, as a rule, allowed to take care of themselves. During periods of economic stability, stagnation, or gradual progress, this system works, on the whole, to the satisfaction of mankind. It is during periods of instability—whether caused by sudden progress or sharp setbacks—that the disadvantages of *laissez-faire* become evident. The so-called automatic adjustment of production and distribution to sudden changes is a slow and painful process. A great advantage of the Fascist economic system is that it facilitates and accelerates the process of readjustment, reducing to a minimum the "transition periods," and allaying to a great extent their inevitable disadvantages. In a Corporate State wages and salaries, wholesale and retail prices and the cost of living can be adjusted more easily than in a country where the process of adjustment is left to take care of itself. This is also true of the regrouping and rationalization of productive forces.
>
> If the Fascist economic system were to do no more than provide a means for mitigating crises, it would amply justify its existence. In reality, its functions are equally important in normal conditions and during prosperous periods. It is able to secure the utilization of technical and other improvements to the best advantage of mankind.
>
> It is a commonplace of newspaper articles that too rapid technical progress, through its effect upon employment and prices, is one of the main causes of the present economic crisis, and one of the main obstacles to a fundamental recovery. This need not necessarily be so. By planning ahead and by facilitating readjustment, a Fascist system can mitigate the unfavourable effects of technical progress and increase its

The Nature of Fascism | 161

beneficial effects. (*Economic Foundations of Fascism*, pp. 12-13.)

The concentrated barrage of hysterical and vindictive abuse which is directed against the Fascist system by Liberal and social democratic critics is, of course, familiar to all students of contemporary politics. It is therefore of some interest to consider the character of the muddled emotionalism which has become the substitute for all thoughtful criticism in relation to this subject. Fascism, as a compromise between extremes, as a transformation of the old into the new, as a factual interpretation of the nebulous ideals and aspirations of a century, is subject to attack both from those who refuse to accept anything new, and from those who wish utterly to destroy the old. The fact that Fascism is *practicable revolution* exasperates the reactionary, and the fact that it implies a disciplined transformation based on continuity disappoints and infuriates the revolutionary. Fascism is, in fact, *so simple*, such an ordinary sensible solution of economic and political problems, that it inspires antagonism by the very directness of its simplicity. As writes Paul Einzig:

> Notwithstanding the highly inadequate knowledge of Fascism outside Italy, there are unmistakable signs that the present trend of evolution is towards an economic system which, in substance, if not in form, is likely to be very near that of Fascism. The need for planning is beginning to be recognized by all but the few remaining die-hard *laissez-faire* economists...
> The fashionable term 'planning' covers, however, a multitude of different ideas. Many of those who advocate planning have Communism in their mind as the goal, even though for the moment the nationalization of certain branches of production, means of transport, banking, etc., would satisfy them. For others, State Socialism or State Capitalism are not mere intermediate stages, but the end itself. Again, a large number of authors claim that it would be possible to achieve the planning of production and consumption through the management of currency. Amongst those who have Fascist planning in mind, many have come to their conclusion independently of any detailed knowledge of the Fascist

experience in Italy. In fact, some of them suggest the introduction of a system that is fundamentally identical to the Corporate State, without even knowing that they advocate Fascism... *Consciously or otherwise, the tendency of our economic literature is drifting towards Fascism. This is in accordance with the trend of evolution in practical life.* (*Economic Foundations*, pp. 4-5.)

Yet recent developments in England have tended to unite all the orthodox political parties—not excluding the Communists—in "a common front" against Fascism. The "Aventine opposition," in England has, in fact, come into existence with the first appearance of Blackshirts at the street corners of our industrial cities. The recent Trade Union Congress at Brighton lashed itself into a fury against Fascism, and covered its lack of any coherent policy of its own by hysterical and frantic tilting against the looming shadow of British Fascism.

Mr. Bromley, speaking at the Congress, is reported by two newspapers to have used the following words:

Every Blackshirt who stands in the street is a menace not only to the honour of women, but to their disfigurement and maltreatment in the brutal dungeons they will create to the absolute exclusion of the slightest respect for sex...

...Every Blackshirt in our streets to-day was a menace to their honour, and stood for their disfigurement, brutal usage, and the exclusion of the slightest respect for sex. (*Daily Herald*, 8th September, 1933.)

The same Congress chose to advocate international limitation of the hours of labour, but ignored the fact that the only practical step taken in that direction had been by the Italian Fascist Government, whose proposals for a compulsory international Forty-Hour Week were defeated at Geneva by the votes of the British and French Governments, in both of which prominent Socialists held office. At the same time Mr. G. D. H. Cole, a well-known Labour intellectual, was advocating "regulations giving the trade unions a statutory right of negotiation, such as Mussolini has given to the Fascist Unions in Italy," and the whole Congress was abandoning itself to sycophantic praise of Mr. Roosevelt's economic Fascism in America. No less enthusiastic for Mr. Roosevelt,

The Nature of Fascism | 163

and no less critical of political Fascism, are such typical representatives of "big business" as Lord Beaverbrook. The interpretation of these peculiar exhibitions of muddled thinking is that both Socialist trade union leaders and intelligent capitalists recognize the inevitability of economic Fascism, but they wish to avoid acceptance of the political implications of the Fascist Revolution. But the fundaments of Fascism are as much political and moral as they are economic. The dangers to a modern nation of political and moral *laissez-faire* are, in fact, greater than the mere dangers of economic *laissez-faire*. Economic evils only constitute the evidence which can be produced to bring home to the consciousness of the nation the urgency of a disciplined revolution in the whole life of that nation.

The campaign of the present Roosevelt administration in America—so much lauded by trade union leaders and by "enlightened" capitalists of the Beaverbrook type—represents a great effort by the controlling forces of American Capitalism to introduce Fascist economics without either a Fascist Party or a Fascist social and political policy. The present policy of the Roosevelt administration is, of course, similar in many respects not only to the economic policy of Italian Fascism, but also to the policy adumbrated—two years before Roosevelt came to power—by Oswald Mosley in Britain.

Mussolini, writing with the caution which his official position demands, defined the limitations of the Roosevelt policy in a recent article in a London newspaper:

> Many in America and Europe have been asking how much 'Fascism' there is in the doctrine and practice of the American President. One does not have to go far nor does one have to generalize. In common with Fascism there is the principle that the State cannot remain alien to the fate of economics, because this would be tantamount to remaining alien to the lot of the people. There is, in Roosevelt's book, an occasional reference to the necessity for the collaboration of all factors in production which reminds us of the fundamentals of the Fascist corporative state.
>
> But while Fascism has made profound innovations through a real revolution, and has created institutions adequate to solve organically the problems which also face the United States, Roosevelt, in his book, does not face any of these problems,

such as the juridical recognition of workers' and industrialists' syndicates, the outlawing of strikes and lock-outs, labour courts, and, finally, the national and trade guilds, which must lead the various categories to self-government under the protection of the State.

Roosevelt is still sticking to the system of indirect intervention by the State through the action of more or less permanent committees of a political or administrative character. The atmosphere in which the whole doctrinal and practical system moves is certainly similar to the atmosphere of Fascism, but it would be an exaggeration to say more. (*Morning Post*, 3rd July, 1933.)

A leading article in the *Blackshirt*—the organ of the British Union of Fascists—was less tactful:

What happens, when the President tries to carry through the policy which, in face of the facts of the problem, he now sees to be right?

At once a pandemonium of protest is let loose by the great interests, which he has not the Fascist power to overcome.

'The National Association of Manufacturers' sent a bulletin to its members recommending them not to sign the voluntary blanket code which fixes hours and wages. General Johnson, head of the National Recovery Administration, threatened them with 'a sock on the nose.' As General Johnson, however, lacks the Fascist punch, the 'sock on the nose' remains undelivered.

What a wonderful example of the working of democracy, and of the futility of reconstruction without the iron grip of Fascism! Just imagine an Association of Manufacturers circulating its members to disobey an order of a Fascist Government. If this occurred in Italy, the little pleasure steamers which ply between the mainland and the Lipari Islands would indeed be overladen! As Mussolini once put it: '*Under Fascism the capitalists do what they are told, and will go on doing what they are told until the end.*'

But poor democratic Roosevelt thought he could do without Fascism, so he has had to fall back upon the ballyhoo of sentimental appeal. He is using the wire-less, and sky-writing, employing three-minute orators in the cinemas, and a nation-wide campaign of expensive advertisements. What a contrast to the methods of Fascism, under which a disciplined nation would pull together like a well-trained team—calm, efficient, orderly—under clear direction! (*Blackshirt*, 5th August, 1932.)

It is a curious phenomenon of contemporary world-politics that in the countries on the continent of Europe who first created the Fascist Revolution the economic principles of the Corporate State were only later, and gradually, evolved. "Even to-day," writes Einzig, "after ten years of Fascist rule, the ultimate aims of the system are far from clear." On the other hand, in the Anglo-Saxon countries, in America, and in Britain, and to a lesser extent in Australia, the economic theses of Fascism have been developed to a certain stage of perfection, without a corresponding development of either the political or moral background necessary to put these theses into practical operation. Mosley, particularly, in England, had formulated the principles of Fascist economics long before he was prepared to face the political implications of his line of thought, and he spent two years in endeavouring to introduce the economics of Fascism through the mechanism of the democratic political system.

The explanation of this phenomenon is probably to be found in differences of deep-laid racial characteristics. The Italian, if he is only considered in relation to modern European culture, as distinct from the Classical culture, has always shown a genius for creative philosophy and for original action. The Teuton, on his side, has invariably interpreted new European ideas in the surge of great emotional movements. The Anglo-Saxons have followed slowly in the wake of intellectual revolutions—their genius has always been to modify and perfect rather than to initiate. And it is characteristic that change comes to the Anglo-Saxon countries with an economic rather than a spiritual emphasis.

While Americans and Englishmen approach revolution with the scepticism of business-men suspicious of new ways and means, and later hallow change as the logical development of their own habit, suffusing it with all the mellowness of English thought or the commonplace ingenuousness of American idealism, the Germans imbue revolution with the passion of a racial orgasm, and the Latins illumine it in the pellucid light of an eternal philosophy. Mussolini can always interpret the modern movement in terms of final values:

166 | Chapter VIII

> Our conception of the nation is synthetic, not analytic. One who marches in step with others is not thereby diminished... he is multiplied by all those who move shoulder to shoulder with him. Here, as in Russia, we are advocates of the collective significance of life, and we wish to develop this at the cost of individualism. That does not mean that we go so far as to think of individuals as mere figures upon a slate, but we think of them chiefly in relation to the part they have to play in the general life of the community. Herein may be recognized a very remarkable advance in national psychology, for it has been made by one of the Mediterranean peoples, who have hitherto been considered unfitted for anything of the kind. A sense of the collectivity of life is the new spell that is working among us... You see, then, what we Fascists want to make out of the masses. We want to organize their collective life; to teach them to live, to work, and to fight in a great fellowship—but in a hierarchy, not in a mere herd. We want the humanity and the beauty of a communal life... Believe me, the individual loses nothing thereby, but is multiplied. (Ludwig: *Talks with Mussolini*, pp. 125-6.)

Again, he said:

> That which can be called Fascist ferment in the political and spiritual restoration of the world by this time is operating in all countries—England included. There is no doubt that France, the last bulwark of the 'immortal principles,' also must in a not-distant day raise the white flag of surrender. America also is abandoning them...
>
> The appeal to the forces of youth resounds everywhere. The nation which has forged ahead of the times, and has anticipated by a decade the actions of others, is Italy.
>
> There is nothing more interesting and dramatic than this sunset of a civilization, which, even though amidst error, waste and slaughter, has left a deep trace. There is no better omen, and nothing more fascinating, than the dawn of a new civilization. (*Morning Post*, 14th October, 1933.)

A Fascist March in London

Chapter IX

—Mosley and British Fascism—

Rapidly, during the whole period of the New Party, Oswald Mosley had been moving towards the acceptance of the Fascist interpretation of modern conditions. Nearly a decade had passed since he had abandoned the Conservative Party to their own futile efforts to think in terms of an era that had passed, and it was inconceivable that his realist reaction from Socialism should have the effect of driving him again into the Tory ranks. But his break with Socialism was complete, and his realization of his own disillusionment was bitter. He well expressed that bitterness in a speech in Trafalgar Square during September, 1931:

> The element of farce in the political tragedy was provided, as usual, by the spokesmen of the late Labour Government, who claimed that the present crisis was that collapse of Capitalism which they had long prophesied with religious fervour.
>
> When the day arrived which they had awaited ever since Karl Marx put pen to paper, Labour had the unique advantage of being in office. When the great moment came they had the whole resources of the State at their command. The day dawned, but Labour resigned! What were they to think of a Salvation Army which took to its heels on the Day of Judgment?

Mosley was already pursuing the economic theory of Fascism. The political methods of Fascism were soon forced upon him. A "Youth Movement" had been developed within the New Party which was an obvious branch of activity, particularly in view of the fact that that young

Chapter IX

party was largely recruited from among the younger generation. Party members expected to be organized for party work, and they appreciated also any organization which provided for their athletic recreation. One of the obvious necessities of any modern movement—whether political or cultural—is to get young people out of the streets and into the fields. With this object such entirely innocuous and non-political movements as the Boy Scouts had been formed and had been found to fill a very real need in the life of the youth of the country. The Conservatives, the Liberals and the Socialists had all busied themselves to cater for the needs of the younger members of their respective parties, and they had set an example which any new political organization could not avoid following—even had there been a desire to do so. Yet it was the Youth Movement of the New Party which had originally sent shudders through the ample frames of Mr. John Strachey and others of the Bloomsbury intellectuals who had at first flocked into the New Party—as something really *new*. As harder times came, the harder elements in the New Party Youth Movement showed their desire to act as a body in other than purely intellectual and recreational directions. A corps of stewards was formed to protect the meetings of New Party speakers, which, everywhere, were being subjected to the full blast of organized Socialist barracking and of organized Communist hooliganism. As writes the Clydesider, Scanlon:

> When the six resigned opposition from the machine, of course, was to be expected, but no professional psychologist could ever hope to explain the actions of the rank and file. In the interval between Sir Oswald's resignation from the Government and his resignation from the party itself he had made an extensive tour of the constituencies, explaining his policy to Labour audiences. Everywhere he went he was received with enthusiasm, but when he went to address meetings after his resignation, although he was preaching precisely the same doctrines, the audiences which had cheered his first campaign broke up the meetings in the second...
>
> In Birmingham and in Glasgow, where his welcome on joining bordered on hysteria, police protection was required at his exit. (*Decline and Fall of the Labour Party*, pp. 217-8.)

The New Party corps of stewards soon found that they had plenty of work to do. Throughout the tense political campaign of the spring and autumn of 1931 Socialists and Communists made every effort to drive Mosley from the field by the sheer force of their organized violence. Particularly shameful was the effort made to break up the meeting at Dundee in the spring which Lady Cynthia Mosley had to hold instead of her husband, who was at that time lying ill with pneumonia. During the same period a similar attempt to break up one of Lady Cynthia's meetings by hooligan methods was made by the Communists in Hammersmith. When her husband took the field, the action of the "Reds" became even more enterprising. Of one meeting on Glasgow Green, the *Daily Record* reports:

> Sir Oswald Mosley... addressed a meeting of over 20,000 people on Glasgow Green, at which there was bitter and constant interruption; (he) had many duels with hecklers and obstructionists; was mobbed by a jeering crowd on his way to his car; was struck by a stone and threatened with a life-preserver; smiled through it all, and eventually drove away, waving his hat to the crowd, and still smiling. (21st September, 1931.)

At another Glasgow meeting, a month later, in reply to the taunt of the Communists that he was receiving police protection, Mosley left the hall, and, practically unattended, addressed a hostile crowd in the street.

"On a stool in Salamanca Street," writes the correspondent of the *Glasgow News*, "he got a very fair hearing. 'My, he's plucky, that yin,' observed a woman, at her window on the first storey, to her neighbour. 'Aye, he's no' feart,' was the agreement." (20th October, 1931.)

At Birmingham, in October, a meeting was held in the famous Rag Market. According to the correspondent of the *Birmingham Gazette*:

> A large section of the crowd of 15,000 charged the platform, brandishing chairs and chair-legs, hurling bottles, and swept all before them out of the section of the market in which the meeting was held... Very few of the bodyguard escaped unscathed. An ex-international Rugby player received a wound on the forehead from a chair hurled into the mêlée, and the North-East London Regional Secretary to the New Party was carried partly unconscious from under the feet of the mob,

172 | Chapter IX

where he had fallen after being struck in the face with a bottle. Dozens of people received minor injuries in the rush... (19th October, 1931.)

But gradually the Mosleyites were gaining in experience and organization, and they soon showed themselves to be formidable customers. By the end of the General Election of 1931 the Communists were beginning to whine that the stewards were the aggressors, and after one Birmingham meeting some Communists who had got themselves injured as the result of creating a disturbance at one of Mosley's meetings actually had the assurance to bring an action for assault against the New Party leader. Mosley, as usual, had himself taken the lead in restoring order at the meeting. One man complained that "Sir Oswald struck him and knocked him over." Another, who gave evidence that he had been "thrown in the crush towards Sir Oswald, who, again without warning, punched his eye and kicked his shins," had to admit in cross-examination that "he did not know that Sir Oswald could hardly move his right leg as the result of an aeroplane accident during the war." The summonses were dismissed.

When Mosley, by the autumn of 1932, had finally developed the political and economic aspects of his Fascist policy, and found still that it was impossible to secure the normal facilities for explaining this policy to the people at public meetings, it was natural that he should turn to the consideration of defensive measures which should assure him those elementary rights of free speech which are reputed to be the basis of the existing political system. Mussolini, in Milan and the industrial cities of the Lombardy Plain, had originally been confronted with the same problem, and in the beginning he had had to wage a desperate struggle to survive the concentration of "Red" terrorism. The remnants of the old New Party corps of stewards, and numbers of the able-bodied recruits who were daily pouring into the ranks of the new Fascist organization, were therefore formed into a Fascist Defence Force. The primary function of this force was defensive, and in no sense aggressive. Its duties were to protect the right of free speech at meetings of the Fascist Party. In a reference to this force, following riotous scenes at a meeting in Stoke in October, 1932, Mosley made himself perfectly clear as to the objects for which the force had been formed. "The Fascists do not want to fight," he declared, "but if violence is organized against us, then we shall organize for violence in reply. We shall have free speech, and we intend to have it."[8]

In the meantime the Fascists had been put into black shirts. Mosley arrived at the decision to allow a distinctive uniform, in spite of the advice of some of his closest adherents, who were obsessed with the idea that the Englishman does not like a uniform. Events have proved that the leader was correct in his own appraisal of his countrymen's psychology, for it is unquestionable that the wearing of a distinctive uniform, if it be disagreeable to the shy "bourgeois," makes a very definite appeal to working people. The black shirt has moreover this supreme advantage within the ranks of Fascism, in that it does away with all those invidious class distinctions which receive emphasis from the wearing of different types of clothing by different sections of the community. In no respect was Mosley's instinct more correct than in the decision to adopt a significant uniform, which is now worn with pride by men and women of all ages in the streets of the great industrial cities of Britain. The Blackshirts have done more to bring the reality of Fascism in Britain home to the man in the street than all the concentrated propaganda which has been put out by Party Headquarters. In a remarkably short space of time the "Reds" began to realize that a new force had entered on the field. They were no longer able to regard certain areas of the industrial quarters of the big towns as their own preserve, and in streets where the speakers of the orthodox political parties had not been heard for a generation Fascists enforced a hearing for themselves. The I.L.P. proceeded to announce that they were going to put their followers into red shirts, but the uniformed warriors of the Moscow tinge have, so far, been conspicuous for their absence. The razor-lads and the bottle-boys prefer to remain as indistinguishable as possible among the crowd in which they always seek to hide. The rapid development of the Fascist Defence Force has had the effect of making the organized Communist terrorists rather chary of openly attacking Fascist meetings. In March of 1933, when the police thought it necessary to intervene to "protect" Communist hooligans at a Fascist meeting in Manchester, Mosley could write in the *Blackshirt* that "at less than 3 per cent of the British Union of Fascist meetings during the past year has any disorder occurred at all."

---

[8] "When we are confronted by Red terror, we are certainly organized to meet force by force, and will always do our utmost to smash it. The bully of the streets has gone too long unchallenged. We shall continue to exercise our right of free speech, and will do our utmost to defend it." (*Greater Britain*, p. 150.)

Chapter IX

(*Blackshirt*, 18th March, 1933.) Nevertheless a recrudescence of Communist violence in the great cities may be expected at any moment, particularly as Fascism gains force, and the "Red" elements, inspired alike by "respectable" trade union leaders of the Bromley calibre and by other less reputable interests, renew their efforts to check the growth of a movement which they well fear will ultimately destroy them. Meantime the battle against "Red" anarchy and organized terrorism is being carried into the very strongholds of Communism. Communist centres, like Battersea and Durham, have some of the strongest Fascist sections established in their midst, and no small proportion of the recruiting to the Fascist Party has been from among former supporters of the Communist Party—who have become thoroughly disillusioned with the activities of that alien-infested organization.

A recent communication, published in the *Blackshirt*, from a Fascist in the Midlands, may be quoted as characteristic of the present activities of members of the Fascist Defence Force:

> We had heard with gathering anger of the disgraceful treatment of our principal speaker in the North-East, Capt. Collier, and had followed his plucky fight against overwhelming odds with the utmost admiration of his Fascist spirit. At last our patience was completely exhausted when at a single-handed meeting at Stockton-on-Tees some ten days ago the Reds spat in Capt. Collier's face and threatened to lynch him.
>
> It was decided to venture to Stockton-on-Tees with a large body of stewards, just to see if the Reds would repeat their insults when they had more than one undefended man to deal with. Picked contingents were gathered from Manchester, Teesside and Tyneside, and paraded in Middlesbrough on Sunday last. They then marched in their well-known column of threes into Stockton, where they found some sort of meeting going on in the Market Square and a large, angry and hostile crowd of Communists, imported into the district for the occasion, assembled. Nothing daunted, however, our men began a rival meeting on the other side of the square. Amid an appalling din of howls and catcalls several of our speakers attempted to give the policy, but it was obvious that the Reds were determined to prevent any resemblance of free speech, and the atmosphere became more and more threatening from

moment to moment. The crisis was reached when one of our members was attacked by a man thrusting his forefingers into his eyes. The man was knocked down immediately and the Blackshirt stewards moved forward like a machine against the Communist section of the crowd. Fighting desperately the Reds were swept back forty yards right across the Market Square, and the platform was left isolated in the centre, surrounded by its small Fascist guard. It was indeed 'a beautiful sight and made one proud to wear a black shirt,' as an eye-witness has said. (*Blackshirt*, 16th September, 1933.)

The fight against "Red" terrorism was long overdue, and it is a fight the benefits of which will be reaped not only by the Fascists. Representatives of other political parties, including, indeed, the Socialists, may well be grateful for the protracted struggle which the Fascists are waging for the restoration of decency in the streets.

The Blackshirts have carried on a long "trench-warfare," the full story of which may one day be told in all the heroism of its unrecorded incidents. It is the unknown Blackshirt—giving his time and his leisure, his brain and his muscle, to the day-to-day struggle—who has in twelve short months succeeded in building up what is already a formidable and independent movement of the manhood of Britain. The Blackshirts are the heart and backbone of the Fascist movement, but when the vital significance of the "activist" side of the movement is borne in mind, it has to be remembered that Fascism in Britain is essentially an orderly, pacific march to power. Loyalty to the Throne is the first tenet of every Blackshirt, and while the Fascist intent is to revolutionize the existing system of government, there is no body of opinion within the movement which contemplates carrying out the necessary transformation through the use of armed force. The muddled hysteria which passes for thinking among social democrats associates Fascist action with the use of force against the State, but this has never been contemplated by British Fascism, and neither Mosley nor any of his responsible supporters have ever publicly stated that they regard the use of force—even if practicable—as a legitimate means of securing power. Mosley has never gone further than to express the intention of using force to meet force, as has already been done wherever Communist violence has been encountered. Should an occasion arise, as a result of the accentuation of the industrial crisis, where the Government of the day proved incapable

Chapter IX

of confronting a growing Communist menace, then only, in Fascist theory, would the use of force—to defeat insurgent anarchy—be justified. If a comparison be made with Fascist movements abroad, it will be found that Fascism emerged in Italy as *the only effective force* after the constitutional power of the Government had completely broken down. And in Germany, the Nazis—after developing for years as the only body which was prepared to offer an active opposition to the growing strength of the Communist Party—were ultimately placed in power as the result of a General Election, after the country had become disillusioned with the weakness and ineptitude of successive "democratic" Governments.

"I could choose," said Georges Sorel, "other examples to show that the most decisive factor in social politics is the cowardice of the Government." Fascists, in the event, have no intention of allowing the British people to become the victims of "the cowardice of the Government," and they have no democratic inhibitions about the use of violence—as they have shown in the protection of their own meetings. They would, if necessary, meet violence against the State by violence on behalf of the nation. But they do not contemplate that such a situation must inevitably arise. Their attitude is merely precautionary, and their "Defence Force" is, as its name implies, solely defensive. They have sufficient confidence in Fascist policy to recognize that that policy will ultimately win through as a result of its acceptance by a majority of the people. Time fights on the side of Fascism, and Fascists have only to wait their time. That time—if they continue to make their present progress and to maintain their present enthusiasm—will not be very long deferred.

The considered policy of the British Union of Fascists was stated by Oswald Mosley in a book, *Greater Britain*, which was published at the time of the inception of the Fascist Party during the autumn of 1932. More recently it has been newly elaborated in a series of four articles, published in the *Blackshirt* during August, 1933, under the title of "Fascist Policy Re-stated."[9]

---

[9] It is not our purpose, in the present work which is written primarily for Fascists and for those interested in Fascism, to summarize the content of Mosley's *Greater Britain*, which all who take a serious interest in the subject will have already read. In general, we shall consider those particular aspects of policy, in which the leader has gone beyond the particular limits which he laid down a year

In his *Greater Britain* Mosley emphasizes throughout the modern Fascist conception of the Corporate State, and he seeks to stimulate that new nationalism through which alone the corporate spirit can be developed:

> Our main policy, quite frankly is a policy of "Britain First," but our very preoccupation with internal reconstruction is some guarantee that at least we shall never pursue the folly of an aggressive Imperialism. It will never be necessary to stimulate the steady temper of Britain in the task of rebuilding our own country by appeals to flamboyant national sentiment in foreign affairs. We shall mind our own business, but we will help in the organization of world-peace as part of that business.

Mosley bases his approach to all problems of national reconstruction on the assumption that the existing world-crisis is a crisis of the capitalist system, and no mere cyclical "slump." He also accepts the fact that the old "export" basis of British trade is gone forever, and that if Britain is to maintain her existing population on a standard of living even equal to that formerly enjoyed, the whole basis of the economic life of the country must be transformed. In addition to the general world-problem of the crisis in Capitalism, Britain is confronted by a very vital special problem—that of transformation from a "free trade" mercantile economy to a new economy, the nature of which will require that the country must become increasingly self-supporting and increasingly self-dependent. The country is therefore faced with the necessity of a gigantic economic revolution, the implications of which must be as profound as the parallel but reverse process of a century ago. As Mosley writes:

> It is now the declared aim of every great nation to have a favourable balance of trade. *Every nation, in fact, seeks to sell more to others than it buys from them—an achievement which, it is clear, all nations cannot simultaneously attain.* So a dog-fight for foreign markets ensues in which the weaker nations go under, and their collapse in turn reacts upon the victors in the struggle by a further shrinkage of world-markets. A

---

ago. A vital policy must be adapted to rapidly changing world-conditions, and this consideration definitely governs Fascist policy.

continuation of the present world-struggle for export markets is clearly the road to world-suicide, as well as a deadly threat to the traditional basis of British trade.

These phenomena appear at first sight to support the Marxian theory. 'In the decline of Capitalism all nations must strive increasingly to dump abroad their production which is surplus to the power of home consumption. A world-scramble for markets ensues, with competitive industrial rivalries which lead inevitably to collapse and to war.' Marxians overlook the fact that certain natural tendencies, and even natural laws, can be and have been circumvented by the will and wit of man. The law of gravity, for example, has been flouted by the aeroplane; the Marxian law that, under Capitalism, all wages would be reduced to a subsistence level has been set aside by a variety of artificial means. In just the same way it is fair to suppose a well-governed nation can avoid the disasters incidental to the world's present industrial over-capacity.

What has been done by accident and by a rough and crude method for a period, can be done permanently under scientific planning. But those tendencies will not be defeated by letting things alone; and it is here that Conservatism falls down. Some of the Marxian laws do actually operate if mankind is not organized to defeat them, and they are operating to-day in the inchoate society which they envisage... If we rely on Conservatism to defeat Marxism, we shall be defeated by Marxism. (*Greater Britain*, pp. 66-7.)

The economic solution—to which Britain is being irresistibly driven by world-tendencies—lies in the "insulation" of the home market, which Mosley had already envisaged as early as his resignation speech in the spring of 1931. But this process of scientific "insulation" is very different from the orthodox Conservative theory of tariffs, which inhibit the rights of the consumer without imposing any sort of control over the capitalist-producer. Mosley:

It is known and proved, that modern industry, properly organized and working at full pressure, can both raise wages and reduce costs. But this cannot happen unless the manufacturer is protected from wage-cutting competitors at home as well as abroad. Hence the necessity for corporate organization, which will regulate wages and prices by permanent machinery. *Protection must protect organization, and not chaos.* Behind the protective barrier the home market must be stabilized and enlarged, and the consumer must be safeguarded. These results can only be achieved within the structure of the organized system which is the Corporate State.

Protection without Corporate organization is no bulwark against unemployment. In countries long protected, such as Germany and the United States, we have witnessed the finest result of a Protective system followed by the inevitable collapse resulting from a lack of corporate organization. In defiance of all Marxian laws wages rose under Capitalism to heights dizzily above the subsistence level. By happy accident, America achieved for a time the fruits of planning. Protective duties afforded comparative immunity from the competition of foreign low-paid labour. At the same time, stringent immigration laws created a shortage of labour in relation to demand, and afforded labour a strong bargaining position on the market. That strong position, even more, perhaps, than the enlightenment of American employers, led to a steady rise in wages and consequently to a steadily increasing demand for goods in a home market rapidly expanding.

The whole expanding system was supported by the policy of the Federal Reserve Board, and yet further extended by the hire-purchase system, which turned every trader into a banker. Even so, it is interesting to note that, even at the height of the boom, competent authorities considered that the market 'was insufficient to absorb the potential production of American industry.' It is a grave mistake to point to the high wage and expansionist system of America as responsible for the evils which it served for a time to stave off. The crash came because that great system was unsupported by national organization and regulation of a corporate character.

The 'philosophy of high wages' succumbed to the first serious test.

It failed chiefly because it was never a philosophy, nor yet a conscious policy. Under the pressure of credit restriction designed to check Wall Street speculation, one manufacturer after another began to curtail his wages, and competitors were compelled to follow suit. There was no industrial planning: the system was unsupported by corporate organization. Its success had been adventitious; it had no resources to withstand a strain. Added to this the credit which should have been used for industrial development and the financing of reasonable consumption was devoted to the uses of Wall Street, where shares were bid up out of all relation to any conceivable real value. The Federal Reserve Board, within the limits of their system, were able only to check credit expansion in a *quantitative rather than a qualitative manner...*

In an effort to check the frenzy of a few irresponsible individuals, the whole great structure of American industry was shaken to foundations which did not rest on the reality of corporate organization. Had private enterprise been acting in accordance with a reasoned national policy, the trouble might well have been avoided... Never was more notable the absence of a coherent national plan designed to check forces inimical to the stability of the State, and to encourage the genuine forces of production and exchange in which national welfare must rest. America made a god of unregulated anarchy in private enterprise. This, she falsely believed, was the only alternative to Socialism. Both in her success and in her failure, in her dizzy prosperity and in her cataclysmic depression, there is an instructive lesson. Throughout the boom she achieved, on a basis purely temporary, what organized planning and corporate institutions can set on a permanent footing. The very energy of American libertarianism is the best argument for Fascist institutions. (*Greater Britain*, pp. 92-5.)

Mosley goes on to quote the words of Sir Arthur Salter as "the finest description yet produced in general terms of the structure of the Fascist State:"

The task is not to find a middle way, but a new way, to fashion a system in which competition and individual enterprise on the one hand, and regulation and general planning on the other, will be so adjusted that the abuses of each will be avoided and the benefits of each retained. We need to construct such a framework of law, custom and institutions and planned guidance and direction that the thrust of individual effort and ambition can only operate to the general advantage. We may find a simile for our task in the arch of a great bridge, so designed that the stresses and strains of the separate blocks which constitute it—each pushing and thrusting against the other—support the whole structure by the interaction of their reciprocal pressure.

The economic policy of British Fascism is, in essence a policy of controlling and subordinating capital to the purposes of the nation. The old individualist-capitalist system, based on the theory of the "Freedom of the Market," has completely broken down, and the capitalist class, through its political organ—the Conservative Party—has for long been maintaining that the State should intervene to modify that "Freedom of the Market" in the interests of private capitalism. But if the nation, through the mechanism of the State, intervenes in the interest of one small section of the community to interfere with the rights and benefits which the entire community have considered themselves as enjoying under the present system, then the very upholders of the existing system have admitted that the State is entitled to intervene over the whole field of national economics.

The extent to which Fascist policy envisages a fundamental modification in the whole system of individualistic capitalism has been underlined in the recent series, "Fascist Policy Re-stated:"

> The trade unions are supposed to maintain wage standards and to unify labour conditions; in practice... the unions have proved quite unable to maintain wages, let alone raise them...
>
> As a result, at the very moment when a larger market is essential to industry, wages and salaries are crashing down, purchasing power is being reduced, and the market is ever diminishing.
>
> *Fascism meets this problem by the machinery of the Corporate State. It is useless to issue vague appeals to employers to maintain wages. This is not a matter for sentiment, hut for organization. The Corporate State of Fascism sets up corporations for the appropriate areas of industry which will be governed by representatives of employers, workers and*

consumers, operating under a ministry of corporations, presided over by a Fascist minister.

These corporations will be charged, not only with the task of preventing class war by forbidding either lockouts or strikes, but the corporations will be charged with the constructive task of raising wages and salaries over the whole area of industry as science, rationalization, etc., increase the power to produce.

Related to the corporations will be the instruments of finance and credit, which will supply fresh credit, not for the purpose of speculation, but for financing increased production and consumption. *Thus for the first time demand will be adjusted to supply.* When more goods can be produced wages and salaries will be raised to provide a purchasing power for the consumer. This process will not result in inflation or price rise, because the higher purchasing power will be balanced by a higher production. Instead of the new credit going to speculators who force up prices, the new credit will go to industry for the legitimate purposes of production and consumption.

It is argued by our opponents that the higher wages paid in industry will result in higher costs, and thus will jeopardize our export trade. This argument is fallacious, because the cost of production in modern mass-producing industry is determined, not by the rate of wage, but by the rate of production. The rate of production will be increased to serve a larger home market, and in spite of the rise in wages, prices can actually be reduced if the rate of production is sufficient...

In fact, by reason of the greater rate of production for a larger home market, industry will be able to lower its cost in the export trade.

Mosley then turns to the problem of the export market, which—although he sees that it can no longer continue to constitute *the basis* of British economy—he is by no means prepared to ignore:

In addition to this advantage to our export trade, the corporate system will provide another advantage. The effect of organization in the corporations will be to unify and to consolidate industry, and to enable the British export trade to speak for the first time with a united voice. Then the power of government can be organized behind our export industries to secure their entry into foreign markets: we can use, for the first time, *our power as a buyer to support our position as a seller*.

After examining the existing system, whereby the chaotic capitalist struggle for markets and the struggle of the private financial houses for foreign loans and their accompanying "influence" leads to international war, Mosley maintains that "our Fascist national organization detaches Great Britain and the Empire from all the follies and dangers of this struggle:"

> The corporate system unifies and consolidates both our buying and selling arrangements abroad. In place of a thousand private interests, struggling for markets and for raw materials, our industries are organized to speak with one voice under the supervision of government.
>
> Our contacts with the rest of the world are no longer chaotic, but are organized. By withdrawing from the struggle for trade outside our own Empire we automatically diminish the prospects of war arising from that struggle.
>
> In cases where we deal with foreign governments, such as other Fascist governments which are similarly organized, the prospects of clash are enormously diminished. Two Fascist nations dealing with each other will deal through organized systems under Fascist government. In place of the haphazard struggle of private interests, we can have peaceful discussion and bargaining between powerful organizations.
>
> *The international school argues, in effect, that organization leads to war: we answer that it is not organization, but chaos, that leads to war.*
>
> To turn for a moment to an illustration in the domestic field, the prospects of industrial peace are always increased when each side is organized. When we have the corporate organization between all the great countries under Fascist government, it will be possible, for the first time, for nations to discuss rationally and peacefully the allocation of raw materials and markets.

184 | Chapter IX

Mosley proceeds then to consider the psychological aspects of Fascist universalism:

> The leaders of those Fascist countries will be men who have struggled through the collapse of their political systems to the achievement of Fascist government. They will all, further, be men who have had the experience of the Great War of 1914. Can anyone seriously believe that these men will plunge the world into war rather than settle international disputes by the peaceful means which the organization of their Corporate States will permit them to employ? Further, they will be aware that world-war will result in world-Communism, which they are sworn to destroy.
> They will have every interest to keep the peace, and through the corporate system, which substitutes organization for chaos, they will have the means to secure peace.
> Those who challenge the national organization of our economic system are in fact arguing that chaos is safer than organization... Let us first set our own house in order, and organize the system of our own nation and Empire. That achievement will lead to other nations following our example, and we can then, for the first time, rationalize the economic system of the world under the guiding hand and inspiring spirit of universal Fascism.

It is to greater economic unity within the Empire that Mosley naturally turns for the solution of the major economic problems, not only of Britain, but also of the Dominions. Independent Fascist movements are already growing up in all the Dominions, and the different bodies have recently been united with the British Union of Fascists within the New Empire Union. The oldest and strongest of these movements is the New Guard in Australia, which under the leadership of Colonel Eric Campbell, D.S.O., has already played an important role in contemporary Australian politics. Other members of the New Empire Union are the New Guard of New Zealand, the New Guard of South Africa and the Ulster Fascists.[10] A Fascist movement has recently developed in

---

[10] "Two or three little societies wearing the label 'Fascist' had previously existed. They did not prosper, because their leaders had not the slightest idea of what

different parts of Canada, and the Blueshirts in the Irish Free State—although not affiliated to the Union—have shown themselves to be deeply influenced by current Fascist thought. The success of Fascism in Britain could hardly fail to give a great impetus to these Dominion movements. While a British Fascist Government could deal on fair and friendly terms with "democratic" governments in the Dominions, and would certainly refrain from all attempts to influence independent opinion in the Dominions, there can be no doubt that collaboration would be greatly facilitated by the arrival in power of Fascist Parties in the Dominion countries.

Mosley's conceptions with regard to Dominion policy are fundamentally revolutionary in the economic sense, but, at the same time, they do not contemplate in any degree interference with the political status and rights within the Empire of the different Dominion countries, who remain equal and independent partners within the Empire. As Mosley writes:

> The Liberal and Socialist Parties have always been frankly against an organized Empire; they embrace the international creed in preference to the idea of developing our own Empire. The Conservatives have always talked a lot about the Empire; but in reality they have always been in the grip of high finance, which has prevented any effective programme for the Empire being carried through. It is easy to see why it is impossible for Conservatives, whether Baldwin or Beaverbrook, to build a self-contained Empire.
>
> To build such an Empire means the exclusion from the Empire of foreign goods which compete with British and Empire products. If those goods are excluded, our international financiers and foreign investors run the risk of losing the interest on the loans they have made to foreign countries. If foreign countries cannot send their goods to this country to pay

---

Fascism really meant. They erroneously believed it to be a White Guard of reaction. All these societies obtained some membership at the time of the General Strike, but subsequently dwindled owing to the lack of policy and leadership. Three out of four of the male members of the Executive of the principal of these organizations resigned and joined the British Union of Fascists on its formation, and were soon followed by the whole active and effective Fascist elements in the country."

the interest on the loans they have received, they may default on that interest, and those who have lent their money abroad will lose their money.

For instance, if Argentine beef is excluded from Great Britain in favour of British beef and Empire beef, it may be impossible for the Argentine to pay interest on the large loans which international financiers have induced a small section of the public to supply to the Argentine. Consequently Conservatives of all brands who are subservient to the financial interests which support the old parties do not propose the exclusion of Argentine beef under the old-fashioned Conservative protection. Consequently the British farmer is still damaged by the competition of foreign products, and the Empire farmer, despite his small preference, is not making much headway in the British market.

Fascism stands for the definite exclusion of foreign products and the division of Empire markets between the British producer and the Empire producer. We also stand quite definitely for the British producer being able to sell his maximum production at an economic price without the undercutting even of Dominion competition. Plenty of opportunity will still exist for Dominion products if the foreigner is excluded, even when we have produced all the food-stuffs we can in this country, at a price which yields a fair return to our farmers...

The Empire to-day imports some £1,420,000,000 worth of goods per annum. £899,000,000 of these come from foreign countries. If those foreign goods are excluded, we can more than make up the loss of our export trade to the rest of the world, because these exports only amount to £240,000,000 per annum.

Here and now it is possible to save the British Empire from the chaos of the backward nations of the world, by building an Empire which is self-contained and holds within its borders the highest civilization the world has ever known.

In his Empire policy Mosley has advanced considerably beyond the position which he adopted a year ago in *Greater Britain*—a position which was in itself a development of the analysis of the economic future which he made at the time when he started to advocate a policy of "scientific insulation." To such a conclusion the logic of the continuing crisis, and particularly the utter failure of the World Economic Conference to achieve any degree of international co-operation, has inevitably driven him.

"I believe," said Mussolini, "that for the benefit of the moral and political prestige of nations it would be advisable to place an embargo on conferences." President Roosevelt has scarcely troubled to veil his contempt for the late Conference, and the Government of Soviet Russia has adopted a very cynical attitude towards all the conferences of the last decade. Great areas of the world's surface, controlled by competent and determined forces, are becoming—or have already become—the scenes of grave new experiments in economic organization, and the peoples of the British Empire—whether they may desire to take the initiative or not—are now finding themselves compelled to organize for corporate life within the boundaries which history has assigned to them.

Mr. Keynes, in a series of articles in *The New Statesman and Nation*, entitled "National Self-sufficiency," has stated the case with all the authority to which his great reputation entitles him:

> It is a long business to shuffle out of the mental habits of the pre-war nineteenth century world, but to-day, at least one-third of the way through the twentieth century, we are most of us escaping from the nineteenth.

Mr. Keynes proceeds to deny that:

> ...a close dependence of our economic life on the fluctuating economic policies of foreign countries is a safeguard and assurance of international peace. It is easier, in the light of experience and foresight, to argue quite the contrary... I sympathize, therefore, with those who would minimize rather than with those who would maximize economic entanglement between nations.
>
> For these strong reasons, therefore, I am inclined to the belief that after the transition is accomplished a greater measure of national self-sufficiency and economic isolation between countries than existed prior to 1914 may tend to serve the cause of peace rather than otherwise.

188 | Chapter IX

The Conservatives, however, still adhere to the internationalist theory with which their share of Whig traditions and their numerous Liberal recruits have imbued them. As Mr. Neville Chamberlain said recently in the House of Commons:

> We, ourselves, still remain of the opinion which we have held all along, and that is that the chief troubles from which the world is suffering to-day are international in their origin, and that they can only be solved by international action and agreement.

Georges Sorel wrote twenty-five years ago:

> Middle-class cowardice very much resembles the cowardice of the English Liberal Party, which constantly proclaims its absolute confidence in arbitration between nations: arbitration nearly always gives disastrous results for England... Sumner Maine observed a long while ago that it was England's fate to have advocates who aroused very little sympathy. Many Englishmen believe that by humiliating their country they will rouse more sympathy towards themselves; but this supposition is not borne out by the facts. (*Reflections on Violence*, p. 72.)

While the gigantic process of national reconstruction is in process, Fascism proposes to relieve the immediate crisis of unemployment by the programme of productive public works which has already been so well justified in Italy. To this purpose the financial resources and existing organization of the country will be directed. Although Fascist policy does not propose that nationalization of the banks which is a prominent part of the declared programme of the Socialist Party, banking resources will be diverted to the service of the national interest, on somewhat the same lines which Mussolini has so successfully secured in Italy. Fascism does not propose bureaucratic meddling with existing institutions where the technical management is capable of efficiently exercising its functions, but all institutions—whether capitalistic or not in character—will be expected to collaborate whole-heartedly in the plans for national reconstruction, and no obstructive opposition will be tolerated. It is not intended to elaborate here the details of the national policy set out in *Greater Britain*, but a summary of the methods proposed to deal with the slum-clearance problem, recently described in "Fascist Policy Restated," may be regarded as characteristic of the practical intentions of Fascism in power. It is stated:

> Fascism would make the slum-clearance problem a national task in the following manner: We would formulate our programme for clearing the slums and rebuilding over a period of, say, three years. For this period, we would give guaranteed employment in the building trade at good rates of wages, which would absorb the labour of the 295,000 now unemployed in that trade. We would divide the slums of each of the great cities into sections to be gutted and rebuilt over the specified period. Outside the city we would erect temporary bungalows to house the inhabitants of Section 1, while the slum was being pulled down and rebuilt. We would also provide a State transport service to carry them to and from their work.
> They would thus live, during the rebuilding of their houses, with the people among whom they were accustomed to live, and the problem of carrying them to their work during the period would be solved by direct State action. When No. 1 section was completed the inhabitants would vacate their bungalows and go back to their new houses.
> The inhabitants of No. 2 section would then vacate their houses and would go to the bungalows and would use the new transport system. When their houses were completed No. 3 section would take over the bungalows and use the transport system, until their houses were complete; and so on, until the gutting and rebuilding of the slums had been completed.
> To do this would amount to a national mobilization of the building trade, and the problem would be treated in much the same way as the problem of providing shells in the war. We know from actual experience that these methods enormously reduce the cost of production. We shall be producing for a demand which is known and can be calculated precisely in advance. A costing system can therefore be developed which will reduce the costs of production to the utmost limit. Once the problem is taken as a national problem, it can be organized on the grand scale and every principle of modern organization and of mass production can be employed.

190 | Chapter IX

By these means we could carry through the destruction and rebuilding of the slums at a far lower cost and at far greater speed than the present political system conceives to be possible. The cost of production would further be lowered by the application of the Fascist principle that no landlord who has not properly maintained his property as a trustee to the State will be permitted to retain that property.

In the clearance of slum property under Fascism, therefore, no question of compensation will arise. As the result of treating the matter as a national problem, and in all these ways reducing the cost of production, the cost of clearing and rebuilding our slums can be reduced to a very low point. In fact, it is almost certain that under such a system the new houses could be re-let to the tenants at an economic rent which was no higher than the rent they had previously paid. If there was any difference between the new economic rent and the rent which they had previously paid, it should fall upon the State as a national contribution to national health. Few things are more foolish under the present system than the method of pouring out millions to cure disease rather than of spending money to prevent disease by such measures as slum clearance.

The State must be prepared to organize and to finance the maintenance of national health. Foremost among these measures to rebuild the physique of the nation will be the rebuilding of the slums.

To implement a national policy of industrial reconstruction, Fascism maintains that the whole system of government requires to be entirely reconditioned. In evidence submitted to the Select Committee on Procedure on Public Business, during the summer of 1931, Mosley outlined his views on the immediate reforms necessary in the mechanism of government:

> It is only necessary here to observe that at most two or three main measures can be passed through Parliament in the course of a session under the present procedure, and that consequently such procedure must be utterly inadequate to the necessities of an emergency situation. No other proposals have yet been advanced by which that situation can be materially altered. In

Mosley and British Fascism | 191

fact, the view is often expressed that the present delay and check upon legislation and the action of the Government is in itself desirable...

We start from the premise that action is desirable; our opponents start from the premise that action is undesirable. There can be no reconciliation between those two opinions. All who believe that rapid and drastic action by Government is necessary must first face the necessity for a fundamental revision of Parliament, whatever their opinions about the nature of the action to be taken.

Only those can reject the principle of profound changes in the Parliamentary structure who believe that no necessity exists for such action in the present situation. The onus rests upon those who reject those proposals of showing either that alternative and preferable plans for securing rapid action by Government can be adduced, or that no necessity for such action exists.

Mosley then proceeded to make the following definite proposals:

1. *General Powers Bill.*

The first act of a government of action should be the presentation of a General Powers Bill to Parliament. That Bill would confer on the Government of the day wide powers of action by order in relation to the economic problem. Orders under the Act would be laid on the table of the House for a period of ten Parliamentary days. If unchallenged during that period by a substantial body of members, they would have the force of law. If challenged, any orders would be discussed in a brief debate, and a "yes" or "no" decision would be given by Parliament. The House would have the power to accept or to reject an order, but not to amend it.

2. *Government.*

The power of government by order would be vested in an Emergency Cabinet of not more than five ministers, without portfolio, who would be charged with the unemployment and general economic problem. The normal Cabinet would be retained for less frequent meetings in order to ensure proper coordination and consultations between the departments of Government...

3. *Budget and Supply.*

The main powers of legislation required by modern Government would be vested in it under the foregoing proposals of a General Powers Bill. The problem of Budget and Supply still remain. It is recognized that the power to refuse supply and to reject taxation is one of the oldest of Parliamentary rights, and constitutes a considerable power of Parliament over the Executive. These rights would be retained by the allocation of supply days as at present, and by the preservation of Parliament's rights to discuss and to vote on the details of a Budget.

The power to abuse the latter right would, however, be removed, and every Budget would be introduced under a strict guillotine procedure.

The general tenor of these proposals subsequently proved to have influenced certain elements in the Socialist Party, and borrowings from them have recently been advocated as part of the official programme of the Socialist Party, but the controversy on "dictatorship" within that party, and the resultant oscillations of Sir Stafford Cripps, make it difficult to comprehend to what extent the Labour Parliamentarians are prepared to venture away from that democratic procedure which suits so well the temper and inclinations of their component units.

The *Blackshirt* comments (14th October, 1933):

> The procedure which the Socialist League has copied from the New Party policy is that of an Emergency Powers Act under which a Government can proceed by Orders, any one of which can be challenged for discussion and decision by a Parliamentary Opposition. The original procedure suggested has been watered down with various obstructive devices at the hands of Lawyer Cripps, but it would, of course, still speed up present Parliamentary procedure...

At present the big bosses of the T.U.C. reject this effort to imitate the first pale shadow of Fascist policy which attempted to make more workable the procedure of a decadent Parliament. Even if it is accepted next year, the effort is entirely destroyed by the provisions which the Conference have adopted this year... These provisions insist on discussion of every big item of Labour Party policy within the Party caucus. On the one hand Sir Stafford Cripps proposes to curtail discussion in Parliament; on the other hand the Conference has decided to increase discussion in the caucus.

If both proposals are adopted, the net effect of Labour Party policy will be to transfer discussion and power from Parliament to the party caucus. Instead of the nation's business being obstructed by men whom the nation has elected, as at present, the nation's business, under Labour, will be obstructed by men selected by a vicious Party caucus. Such a policy will complete the ruin of democratic government.

Sir Stafford Cripps has already stated that his course would lead "to an immediate conflict not only with the Crown..." Cripps further admits that the application of his policy "will lead almost inevitably to revolution and violence, with what results it is impossible to foretell."

We can inform the little lawyer, that the results are not at all 'impossible to foretell.' They are writ large in the recent history of Europe for all to read. These posturing Kerenskis of Socialism precipitate a revolution by a policy drafted in their endless mothers' meetings at the hands of slick little lawyers. They precipitate that situation, but the Communists take advantage of it; that is the historic and inevitable function of social democracy.

Socialists create revolution, but do not create revolutionary instruments. No organization of disciplined manhood is behind them. They have nothing to call upon in the hour of crisis but the frightened yatter of a startled sewing party. For they abhor discipline, leadership, responsibility and every executive instrument of life by which alone crisis can be met and results can be achieved.

194 | Chapter IX

Fascists now intend that a constitutionally elected Fascist majority in the House of Commons would place complete power in the hands of an executive Government selected from among members of the Fascist Party. Following on, or parallel with, the implementing of the Fascist industrial policy, measures would be introduced to adjust the whole system of national representation to the conditions of a modern Fascist State. A similar process has been carried through in Italy without difficulty and without embarrassment, and in Italy it is generally recognized to have proved an unmitigated success. "The political apparatus," says Paul Einzig, of the Italian Corporative State, "has come to work so smoothly that it ceases to present any vital problems. The leaders can afford to forget about it and to devote themselves entirely to their social and economic task."

In Britain the House of Lords would be replaced by a National Corporation which would function as the effectual Parliament of industry.

"Thus," writes Mosley, "we should abolish one form of legislative obstruction, and replace it with a pool of the country's industrial and commercial experience."

So far as direct representation of the people in the House of Commons is concerned, an occupational would be substituted for a regional franchise. While this measure would tend to eliminate the professional political class—so widely recruited from the legal profession—it would ensure that the worker would be represented by men who really understood the problems of the particular section of the community—whether bricklayers or accountants, doctors or fishermen—who had sent them to Parliament. "By such a system as we advocate," writes Mosley, "the technician, who is the architect of our industrial future, is freed for his task. He is given the mandate for that task by the informed franchise of his colleagues in his own industry. A vote so cast will be the result of experience and information."

The *Blackshirt* comments (14th October, 1933):

> The function of M.P.s would not be to remain at Westminster gossiping and intriguing in the lobbies and obstructing in the Chamber, as they do at present and would continue to do under the Cripps proposals. The function of M.P.s would be to act as leaders in their own localities in carrying through the executive work of Fascist government. When Parliament was called

together at intervals to review the work of Fascist government, they could then advance constructive criticism based on practical experience, which would take the place of the uninformed and partisan opposition of the present party system.

The Government would have complete power of action subject to periodic review by an informed and instructed Parliamentary opinion... That technical assembly, by its very nature, would forever abolish party politics and would give stability to a new and revolutionary conception of government. Continuity of government and system would be assured by the fact that a government would no longer be attacked on party grounds, but only on grounds of inefficiency or gross abuse. With the technical assistance available in such a Parliament, Fascist government could complete the transformation of our national life. *Revolution will be stabilized, and when we stabilize revolution we create a new civilization.*

The object of the Fascist state-organization is, of course, to place all power in the hands of the producer, whose interests have been so consistently flouted and ignored under the "democratic" dispensation. As Mosley says:

> The producer, whether by hand or brain or capital, will be the basis of the nation. The forces which assist him in his work of rebuilding the nation will be encouraged; the forces which thwart and destroy productive enterprise will be met with the force of national authority.

The immense advantages which will accrue to farmers, agricultural labourers, merchant marine officers, fishermen, building operatives and other categories of those who do the national work, through direct representation of their interests, instead of through mere scattered representation of their individual members by the puppets of the democratic parties, can easily be envisaged. Parliament will become the living organ which will respond to the movements of all the functional parts of the nation.

The conception that Fascist government constitutes a modern form of personal dictatorship has been widely propagated, and requires examination. Mosley has taken up this challenge and compared the rival merits of Fascist and "democratic" theory in a recent article on "Leadership and Dictatorship" in the *Blackshirt*:

> In fact, in modern conditions the men who are denounced as dictators are not dictators, but leaders. Hitler polled more than seventeen million votes at an election. Is it suggested that all these people voted for him against their will? It is admitted, even by his opponents, that at an election to-day he would poll an overwhelming majority of the German people. In fact, he is not a dictator, but a leader of enthusiastic and determined masses of men and women bound together by a voluntary discipline to secure the regeneration of their country.
>
> Mussolini was long represented as a man governing against the will of the Italian people, with the aid of a few armed hands who had seized power by a mixture of force and cunning. Yet in his recent tour of Italy during the tenth anniversary celebrations of Fascist rule, he was given a popular reception probably exceeding in enthusiasm any reception given to an individual in the history of the world...
>
> ... All this, of course, is anathema to the old men and the old parties. They fear responsibility and they shrink from it. They shelter behind anonymous committees and the indecision of talkative Parliaments. They hate leadership because they are incapable of exercising it, and they fear it because they know it will sweep them and their system away. Every system in its degeneration finally produces its own caricature.
>
> Socialism has reached its final reduction to absurdity in the resolutions on this subject which the National Executive of the Labour Party will submit to their forthcoming Party Conference.
>
> These resolutions are designed to procure but one thing: that no man nor men within the ranks of Labour shall ever shoulder responsibility or come to a decision. The Prime Minister must refer everything to the Cabinet, the Cabinet must refer everything to the Parliamentary Party, the Parliamentary Party must refer everything to the Trade Union Congress and the Labour Party Conference, and so on *ad infinitum* in the happy paths of blether and indecision. (*Blackshirt*, 23rd September, 1933.)

Mosley, writing in the Italian review *Ottobre* on "Modern Dictatorship and British History," said:

> The conception of dictatorship as a popular but disciplined movement, which is the only possibility of dictatorship in the modern world, is rapidly gaining ground. To represent a Fascist leader as a tyrant of the ancient world, governing in defiance of the whole population, was a conception so childish that it could not long endure. It is particularly curious that this superstition should have had any roots in Great Britain, for we can claim that the first emergence of dictatorship in modern form was in Great Britain...
> ...In fact, the forms of modern dictatorship are a familiar and eternally recurrent phenomenon of British history, which invariably coincide with our great periods of dynamic achievement. The forms of dictatorship have recurred beneath many diverse characteristics. They have varied from the bright, gay virility of that highly popular movement, the Tudor dictatorship, to the cold, religious repressions of the Puritans. They emerge again in the inscrutable, romantic and 'so un-English' personality of the yet so English Chatham, who founded the British Empire by overawing a nominal and corrupt Parliament with the power of his popular support...
> ...The forms of dictatorship in Great Britain have varied vastly in the character which they have assumed and in the personalities which they have evoked...
> Fascism has introduced a new phenomenon into history, related like all great events to the past, but independent of its forms, and reaching forward in its revolution to a civilization fundamentally new. Fascism is not only natural to Great Britain, but it is in tune with every great note of British history.

Fascism, in Italy, in Germany and in Britain was conceived in crisis to meet the emergent realities of the immediate situation. In little more than a decade it has been developed into a great revolutionary movement which challenges all the old conceptions. Temporary fluctuations within the capitalist world cannot resist its impetus, nor deflect its course. The present passing boom (1933), largely stimulated by protection and inflation in Britain, and by inflation in America, is significant only of the straits to which the capitalist world is reduced, and emphasizes only more the need for Fascist forms of control within the great capitalist countries. As Mosley wrote during the recent World Economic Conference:

> A rise in prices without a rise in wages and salaries will inflict great hardship on everyone who works for a living, and will cause great injury to industry. Yet every party in the State today advocates a rise in prices without suggesting any system of government for raising wages and salaries. Not only the politicians of this country, but also the politicians of nearly every country represented at the World Economic Conference, whether Conservative, Liberal or Socialist, have at least agreed on this one point—that prices should be raised. Indeed, Mr. MacDonald said at the outset that they could not even 'touch upon hours of labour and rates of wages.

During the Conference, the Italian Fascist Government, through its representative, Professor Alberto Beneduce, opposed Mr. Neville Chamberlain's proposal that the banks should be prevailed upon to raise commodity prices by advancing cheap money. Professor Beneduce's argument was that sales prices were influenced by consumers' incomes. His attitude was a realist sequel to the effort made by the Italian Government during the previous year to secure international agreement on a forty-hour week. Dr. Vocke, the representative of the German National Socialist Government, also objected that an artificial raising of prices would mean new debts and new insolvencies. At the same time a former member of the British Socialist Government, Mr. Lees Smith, was stating that Labour "would make it its policy to raise prices nearer the level of 1929," in which view he was supported by no less authorities than Mr. Ernest Bevin and Sir Stafford Cripps. Mosley continued:

> Let us examine this policy, which Fascism challenges root and branch. Prices are to rise without any rise in wages or salaries. *This means that existing wages and salaries will buy less, because prices are higher.* As a result the purchasing power of the people will be lower, and the market for which industry produces will be less.

> *Consequently fewer goods will be produced, and less labour will be employed to make the goods.*

Mosley wrote on a further occasion:

> In this country prices are now rising while even present money wages are being further reduced in many industries. On the other hand, in America wages are rising as well as prices, but wages have only risen about one-quarter of the extent of the rise in prices. Clearly, therefore, the real purchasing power of the people, even in America, is at present being reduced.
>
> The unreality and danger of the present boom is further proved by figures published by the Government of America, which show that production in that country has increased by 30 per cent (thus reducing unemployment), while wages have only risen by 7 per cent. Industry, in fact, is producing speculatively for a market which cannot exist until wages and salaries have been raised.
>
> *Unless wages and general purchasing power increase, the inevitable result will be a new glut and a new collapse.*
>
> These facts are recognized to some extent by President Roosevelt, who is trying desperately through his National Recovery Bill to raise wages and to shorten hours. Already there are signs that he will fail through the obstruction of the great interests, because he lacks the support of a Fascist movement to carry through the economic revolution which is necessary... For some little time therefore we may expect a speculative boom which will temporarily reduce unemployment by the simple process of reducing real wages. (*Blackshirt*, 15th July, 1933.)

Within a year of its inception the British Union of Fascists has constituted itself into a national force whose growing power is recognized on all sides—not least by its opponents. The fact that the T.U.C. and the Labour Party have seen fit, during the present autumn, to concentrate the full force of their organizations and propaganda against Oswald Mosley and his Fascists is, perhaps, the best evidence of the misgivings which are disturbing the peace of the democratic parties.

Mosley's personal success is only indicative of the latent strength of

Fascist opinion in Britain, and it was his special function to give that opinion the proper channel for its expression. An individual—however gifted—cannot create a national movement, unless the material and the feeling is there which awaits only the necessary stimulus. But where all credit is due to Oswald Mosley himself is in the judgment and the initiative, the courage and the determination, which inspired him to embark, a year ago, upon what appeared to be a desperate—and to many a hopeless—venture, against the heartfelt advice of his closest friends, and in spite of the ridicule and incredulity of the political world. It is ridicule that kills, and it is by ridicule that the upper class in England endeavours always to impose a class discipline upon its members. That self-consciousness which is so characteristic of the nerveless apathy of a class which has lost all confidence in its own ability to confront the changing conditions of modern life is generally effective in inhibiting the Englishman from all initiative and from all originality of thought. The dread of ridicule may yet bring England down, and a sense of humour may grin the Empire into dissolution. A sense of humour—so much valued in this comfortable and easy-going land—is after all the expression of "a sense of proportion," and a "sense of proportion" can sometimes imply merely an abysmal lack of any standards and of any values. The purpose of British Fascism is to recall to British men and women those fundamental standards upon which the British people have built their national life during two thousand years of history, and to proclaim those human values which, for men and women, are eternal.

In a recent address on "The Philosophy of Fascism" Oswald Mosley has thought out the ultimate implications of the Fascist faith:

> I believe that a Fascist philosophy can be expressed in clear terms, and while making an entirely novel contribution to the thought of this age, it can yet be shown to derive both its origin and its historic support from the established thought of the past.
>
> I want to put it to you, in the first instance, that most philosophies of action are derived from a synthesis of cultural conflicts in a previous period. Where, in an age of culture, of thought, of abstract speculation, you find two great cultures in sharp antithesis, you usually find, in the following age of action, some synthesis in practice between those two sharp antitheses which leads to a practical creed of action...
>
> You will think that my suggestion of the marriage of

seemingly antithetical cultures leading in the following age to the production of a philosophic child of the period, which is expressed in action, has some derivative from Spenglerian thought. And it is quite true that to some extent it has. But I think I can show you how in actual practice that thesis works out in the Fascist case. I would suggest to you that in the last century the major intellectual struggle arose from the tremendous impact of Nietzschean thought on the Christian civilization of two thousand years. That impact was only very slowly realized. Its full implications are only to-day working themselves out. But turn where you will in modern thought, you find the results of that colossal struggle for mastery of the mind and of the spirit of man. You had a religion which, so far as the West was concerned, had broadly dominated human thought for many centuries. And suddenly, for the first time, that religion and that thought was effectively challenged, and its foundations, for the moment, at any rate, were shaken. It was denounced with furious energy and with extraordinary genius—fundamentally denounced.

I am not—as you will see later—myself stating the case against Christianity, because I am going to show you how I believe the Nietzschean and the Christian doctrines each synthesize. But at this point it is necessary for me to examine the essential differences in these two creeds, and to see where the differences have accumulated and where the resemblances emerge. Nietzsche challenged, as you are aware, the whole foundations of Christian thought. He said, in effect: "This is the religion of the slave and the weakling. This is the faith of the people who are in flight from life, who will not face reality, who look for salvation in some dreamy hereafter—the salvation which they have not the vitality nor the manhood to seize for themselves here on earth. It is derived from a spirit of weakness and surrender." He denounced it in a great phrase, if I remember rightly, as "the religion which has enchained and enfeebled mankind."

And in place of this faith he created the conception of the superman, the man who faces difficulty, danger, goes forward through material things and through the difficulties of environment, to achieve, to win and to create, here on earth, a world of his own. It was a challenge to the whole basis, not only of thought, but of life. And it rocked to its foundations the thought of the world. It must have appeared to those who were seriously concerned with that controversy at that time that one or other of those creeds must emerge victorious, and one or other must die; that any combination, any synthesis of those conflicting doctrines was entirely out of the question.

Now I believe, as it so often happens in daily life, that creeds which appear to be dissimilar are in fact susceptible of some reconciliation when examined more closely, and indeed of a certain synthesis; and I think I can show you actually that in the Fascist doctrine to-day you find a complete wedding of the great characteristics of both creeds. On the one hand, you find in Fascism, taken from Christianity, taken directly from the Christian conception, the immense vision of service, of self-abnegation, even of self-sacrifice in the cause of others, in the cause of the world, in the cause of your country; not the elimination of the individual so much as the fusion of the individual in something far greater than himself: and you have that basic doctrine of Fascism—service, self-surrender—to what the Fascist must conceive to be the greatest cause and the greatest impulse in the world. On the other hand, you find, taken from Nietzschean thought, the virility, the challenge to all existing things which impede the march of mankind, the absolute abnegation of the doctrine of surrender: the firm ability to grapple with and to overcome all obstructions. You have, in fact, the creation of a doctrine of men of vigour and of self-help which is the other outstanding characteristic of Fascism.

Therefore we find—I think I can claim—some wedding of those two great doctrines expressing itself in the practical creed of Fascism to-day. And that, in fact, works itself out in our whole attitude to life. We can bring it down to the smallest details of general existence. From the widest and most abstract conception we can come down to the most detailed things of daily life. We demand from all our people an overriding conception of public service, but we also concede to them in return, and believe that in the Fascist conception the State should concede, absolute freedom. In his public life a man must behave himself as a fit member of the State; in his every action he must conform to the welfare of the nation. On the other hand, he receives from the State in return a complete liberty to live and to develop as an individual. And in our morality—and I think possibly I can claim that it is the only public morality in which private practice altogether coincides with public protestation—in our morality the one single test of any moral question is whether it impedes or destroys in any way the power of the individual to serve the State. He must answer the questions: "Does this action injure the nation? Does it injure other members of the nation? Does it injure my ability to serve the nation?" And if the answer is clear on all those questions, the individual has absolute liberty to do as he will; and that confers upon the individual by far the greatest measure of freedom under the State which any system under the State, or any religious authority, has ever conferred upon the individual.

The nearest approach to that moral test was probably the approach of the Greek civilization, which in their organization had, of course, a lesser conception of the State than we have today…

The Fascist principle is private freedom and public service.

Turning to the criticism of the historical role of Fascism, Mosley continued:

It is true that Fascism has an historic relationship to Caesarism, but the modern world differs profoundly from the forms and conditions of the ancient world. Modern organization is too vast and too complex to rest on any individual however gifted. Modern Caesarism, like all things modern, is collective. The will and talent of an individual is replaced by the will and ability of the disciplined thousands who comprise a Fascist movement. Every Blackshirt is an individual cell of a collective Caesarism. The organized will of devoted masses, subject to a voluntary discipline, and inspired by the passionate ideal of national survival, replaces the will to power and a higher order of the individual superman. Nevertheless, this collective Caesarism, armed with the weapons of modern science, stands in the same historic relationship as ancient Caesarism to reaction on the one hand and anarchy on the other.

Caesarism stood against Spartacus on the one hand and the Patrician Senate on the other. That position is as old as the history of the last two thousand years. But they lacked, in those days, the opportunities for constructive achievement which are present to-day, and the only lesson that we can derive from the previous evidence of this doctrine is simply this—that whenever the world, under the influence of Spartacus, drifted to complete collapse and chaos, it was always what Spengler called 'the great fact-men' who extracted the world from the resultant chaos and gave mankind very often centuries of peace and order in a new system and a new stability.

…And it has been done by modern Fascist movements, by recognizing certain fundamental facts of politics and of philosophy. Again you have a certain wedding of two seemingly conflicting doctrines. We are often accused of taking something from the Right and something from the Left. It is a very sensible thing to borrow from other faiths; to discard what is bad and keep what is good; directly you get away from the old Parliamentary mind you see the wisdom of any such course. Fascism does, of course, take something from the Right and something from the Left, and it adds new facts to meet the modern age.

In this new synthesis of Fascism, coming rather nearer to our immediate situation, we find that we take the great principle of stability supported by authority, by order, by discipline, which has been the attribute of the Right, and we marry it to the principle of progress, of dynamic change, which we take from the Left. Conservatism—to call it by the name by which it is known in this country—believes in stability and supports it by its belief in order; but where Conservatism has always failed in the modern world is in its inability to perceive that stability can only be achieved through progress; that a stand-pat resistance to change precipitates the revolutionary situation which Conservatism most fears. On the other hand, the Left has always failed to realize, thanks to their Rousseau complex, that the only way to get progress is to adopt the executive instruments by which alone change is made possible.

We have therefore come to this conclusion: that you can only have stability if you are prepared to carry through orderly changes, because to remain stable you must adapt yourselves to the new facts of a new age. On the other hand, you can only have the progress which the Left desire if you adopt the executive instruments of progress, namely, authority, discipline and loyalty, which have always been regarded as belonging always to the Right. By uniting these two principles we achieve the basis of Fascist faith and Fascist organization.

Mosley then proceeds to face the argument that neo-Caesarism carries within itself the seeds of its own decay:

I believe the answer to that case, which is the only really valid case, is that always before the factor of modern science was lacking. You have now got a completely new factor. If you can introduce into your system of government a new efficiency (and everyone admits that such movements, when they come to power, are at least efficient)—if you can bring to government only for a few years an executive power and an efficiency which gets things done, you can release—and you will release—the imprisoned genius of science to perform the task which it has to perform in the modern world. Whatever our divergent views on the structure of the State and economics may be, I think we must all agree that it would be possible, by sane organization of the world, with the power of modern science and of industry to produce, to solve once and for all the poverty problem, and to abolish once and for all poverty and the worst attributes of disease and suffering from the world.

Therefore, if it is possible to have an efficient form of government, you have available for such a system, for the first time in history, an instrument by which the face of the earth might be changed for all time. Once the essential has been done, once modern science and technique have been released and have performed their task, once you have changed your political and philosophic system from a transitory and political to a permanent and technical basis, there will be no more need of the politics and of the controversies which distract the world to-day. The problem of poverty will be solved, the major problems will be banished, as they can be, and as everybody knows they can be, if modern science is properly mobilized. Then mankind will be liberated for the things in life which really matter.

Therefore, while it is perhaps true that certain of these phenomena in the eternal recurrences of history have been seen in the world before, and seen with great benefit to mankind, yet never before have the great executive movements possessed the opportunity to complete their task which modern science and invention now confer upon them.

At a moment of great world-crisis, a crisis which in the end will inevitably deepen, a movement emerges from an historic background which makes such emergence inevitable, carrying certain traditional attributes derived from a glorious past, but facing the facts of to-day armed with the instruments which only this age has ever conferred upon mankind. By this new and wonderful coincidence of instrument and event, the problems of this age can be overcome, and the future can be assured in a progressive stability. Possibly this is the last great world-wave of the immortal, and eternally recurring, Caesarian movement; but with the aid of science and with the inspiration of the modern mind, this wave shall carry humanity to the farther shore.

Then, at long last, Caesarism, the mightiest emanation of the human spirit in high endeavour towards enduring achievement, will have performed its world mission, will have expiated its sacrifice in the struggle of the ages, and will have fulfilled its historic destiny. A humanity released from poverty, and from many of the horrors and afflictions of disease, to the enjoyment of a world re-born through science will still need a Fascist movement transformed to the purpose of a new and nobler order of mankind; but you will need no more the strange and disturbing men who, in days of struggle and of danger, and in nights of darkness and of labour, have forged the instrument of steel by which the world shall pass to higher things.

In little more than a decade Fascism has emerged as the great fighting creed of the twentieth century. However antipathetic its tenets may appear to the older schools of thought, it cannot be denied that Fascism—as the modern movement—represents a great challenge and a great awakening, and its influence, for good or for evil, will be felt everywhere throughout the modern world.

It is idle also to deny that Fascism can find no spontaneous response from the British character, and that its creed is irrelevant to the conditions and needs of the British people. The influence of Whig historians on the political outlook of succeeding generations of Englishmen has lent the stability of fact to the popular delusion that Parliamentary institutions are the peculiar product of the Nordic Protestant mind, and that these institutions are particularly adapted to the English genius. In actual historic fact it can be shown that the origin of representative institutions cannot be located in any one country and that, like feudalism, Parliamentarism had its beginnings in the special social and economic conditions of a certain period of European history. The earliest development of democratic institutions over the field of European culture was in those areas where the "bourgeois" class, as the result of special trading conditions, first attained a weight in politics. Democratic institutions are, in fact, the political expression of the phase of capitalist economics. This is clear enough in the history of the Greek and Italian trading cities of the earlier Classical culture, and parallels can be established further back in phases of the Aegean and Egyptian cultures. In the history of modern European civilization democratic institutions first assumed importance in just those areas where feudalism had given place to a capitalist system of society—in the Italian cities and in Catalonia, and in the Flemish and Hanseatic towns. As the economic importance of the Italian and Catalonian trading areas declined, the power of the "bourgeois"-capitalist class—and with it their political institutions—also fell into decay. These areas passed under the control of neighbouring feudal-imperialist monarchies. At the same time, with the expansion of trans-oceanic trade, a tremendous impetus was given to the capitalist communities in England and Holland, with the result that they ultimately perverted the national development of the feudal-agricultural states in which they were situated, and the political institutions, suitable to the expression of the power of their special economic class, became the dominant and permanent institutions for all classes in their respective countries. It follows that Parliamentary institutions—far from being the expression of the natural political genius of the Englishman—are the expression of the natural political genius of the "bourgeois" class, which has evolved through these organs of virtually fictitious representation a perfect mechanism for the perpetuation of the dominance of the interests of particular sections of the community as against those of the nation as a whole.

208 | Chapter IX

Parliamentary institutions were no more original to Britain than were any of the other movements and institutions which have affected or directed the course of European history. Roman law, on which our legislation is based, had been subject to ancient Oriental influences. Pan-European Catholicism was a strange amalgam of Asiatic dogma, Mediterranean vision and organizing power, Germanic emotion, and Celtic mysticism. Protestantism, which came into England out of Germany and Bohemia, had its many obscure and diverse origins among the odd religious sects of the Byzantine Empire, where the radical sophistication of a dying world-city had mingled with the crude puritanism of untutored barbarian peoples coming from the Balkans and Asia Minor and beyond. The Rationalism of the eighteenth century was essentially the creation of the new city mind of all Europe. Englishmen, Germans, Scotsmen, Frenchmen and Czechs were its prophets, but even here the earlier Rationalists were influenced by the State-Socialism of the Peruvian Incas, and others, such as Voltaire, by the passivistic thought of India and China. It follows, then, that Fascism is a movement no more foreign to the British genius than was Dutch Parliamentarism, French Republicanism or German Socialism, and it is in far greater degree a movement expressive of the European political mind than is the Asiatic Communism of the Russians, which has borrowed from Europe only a Jewish Messiah. Nor have the British failed to make a major contribution to that development of modern thought which is now being interpreted in Fascist theory and Fascist action. The historical origins of Fascist ideology have never yet been scientifically collated, for in the surge of a decade of action the Fascist leaders have had neither the leisure nor the inclination to catalogue their inspirations. The sources of Fascist theory are indeed diverse, for the movement combines the intense and earnest fire of revolution with the cold serenity of historical philosophy and the proud consciousness of the unique destiny of Europe. Macchiavelli and the Cecils, Strafford and Bolingbroke, Burke, Cobbett, Schopenhauer, Disraeli, Nietzsche, Carlyle and Renan may each and all be shown to have contributed to that stream of realist thought and action which has at last found expression in the dynamic flood of the modern Fascist movement. The diversity of the Fascist inspiration is extreme, but everywhere is noticeable the effective contribution of the British mind towards the final formulation of all these searching ideas in contemporary Fascist action. As writes the biographer of Mussolini:

There is no special originality in his ideas, as to the practical realization of Socialism, except perhaps in their detachment from Marxism; he did not accept the Marxian view of materialism nor of anti-capitalist economics, and he recognized the fallacy of Lassalle's 'bronze law.' What interested him as a Latin was the moral and ethical side of the ideal society of the future. He therefore drew nearer to the apostles of Latin Communism, of the Italian Philip Buonarroti, of the French terrorist Babeuf, of Blanqui and the great Proudhon, and the brief experiment of the Paris Commune—nearer, above all, to Georges Sorel. His vision of the future derives much from Wild's *Soul of Man under Socialism*, with echoes of Ruskin and Morris; perhaps their influence on him was more aesthetic than that of real personal conviction. At bottom their particular vision of the future probably had as little appeal for his temperament as a paradise without houris would have for a Mussulman. (Margherita Sarfatti, *Life of Mussolini*, pp. 166-7.)

Of the moderns, both Shaw and Bergson have had their influence on the development of the Fascist conception, and the former—in spite of his long traditional association with Socialism in England—has shown in his more recent writings that he has both sympathy for Fascist action and belief in the Fascist future.

Fascism, far from being alien to the British character, is the modern expression of a very strong and definite tendency in the history of British thought. The authoritarian Bolingbroke and the revolutionary William Cobbett, the emotional Burke and the misanthropic Carlyle, the visionary Disraeli and the chuckling Shaw, have all in their different ways sought after those conceptions which the young Blackshirts of our industrial cities now proclaim from street to street. Nor is Parliamentary democracy so firmly established in the hearts of the British people as its sycophants on Party platforms and in the Press-lords' offices profess to believe. Just before the last war the widespread movement directed against Parliament, in sympathy with the Ulster loyalists, assumed formidable proportions within two years of its inception. That movement, psychologically restricted as it was, and directed only to the safeguarding of certain relatively limited objectives, would have developed—had not the war intervened—into a definite revolt against the whole theory and system of democracy in Britain. The Ulster movement was, in fact, the

210 | Chapter IX

first Fascist movement in Europe—a movement far more threatening to "the King's peace" than is the modern Fascist movement, for while Oswald Mosley and his Fascists seek only to secure power by normal constitutional means, the Tory leaders, during the Ulster crisis, were preparing to oppose an elected Parliamentary majority with armed force. In spite, however, of the difference in scope and character of the two movements—the Tory-Ulster movement openly seditious, the modern Fascist movement entirely peaceful and "legalist"—certain parallel conclusions may be drawn from them. First, the British people are by no means devoted to the Parliamentary system, the alleged advantages of which are so constantly thrust down their throats, and they are by no means inhibited either by their respect for the past or by the massed hypocrisy of propaganda, from rallying to a reasonable and moderate movement which seeks to change the fundamentals of that system. Secondly, the British people have no blind faith in the infallibility of the democratic methodology, and they are never prepared to see the vital interests of the nation—whether those interests happen to be in Ulster, as in the past, or in England and throughout the Empire, as at present—sacrificed to the pretensions of vicious and corrupt theories.

It is against the upholders and the apologists of these vicious and corrupt theories, supported as they are by all the resources of the existing system, that Oswald Mosley and his Blackshirts are summoning the manhood of Britain to a disciplined and peaceful revolution. The Fascists are undertaking a gigantic and portentous task, and the difficulties involved in its achievement might well appear insuperable to men of lesser faith and meaner mettle. But in this moment, when the Fascists face, in confidence and in constancy, the coming battle for the soul of Britain, they can bear in their hearts those words of an ancient writer which Mussolini, in the hour of his great test, recalled:

> In examining the actions and the lives of these men, we see that they had no great assistance from fortune, save opportunity, which enabled them to shape things as they pleased, without which the force of their spirit would have been spent in vain... While their opportunities made these men fortunate, it was their own merit which made them recognize these opportunities and turn them to the glory of their country.

www.ingramcontent.com/pod-product-compliance
Lightning Source LLC
Chambersburg PA
CBHW021424070526
44577CB00001B/47